Radical Visionaries: Feminist Therapy Pioneers, 1970–1975

Radical Visionaries documents and honours those feminist therapy pioneers of the 1970s who moved the mental health establishment, and possibly the world, through radical action, to begin to consider women as fully human. It is remarkable today, even in these difficult times, to realize how far we have come, and to know it was these women who galvanized this move forward toward self-exploration and equality. As we move into the current era of feminism and social justice, it is imperative to pause to consider how these 'second wave' feminist pioneers gave us feminist therapy and all that followed from it. From the earliest stages of the movement, feminists used consciousness raising, which moved into the notion of the egalitarian therapy and ultimately led toward a cultural shift towards female empowerment and the groundswell of women into clinical psychology programs. These founding feminist therapists impacted structures including the criminal justice system, divorce proceedings, domestic violence services, education, medicine, and banking. This book highlights these women's stories, told by the pioneers themselves, as they forged the trail for those of us who follow them.

This book was originally published as a special issue of *Women & Therapy*.

Claudia Pitts is Associate Professor in the College of Professional Studies and Advancement at National Louis University, Chicago, USA, where she is Director of the Master's in Psychology program. She is also a licensed clinical psychologist with a group practice. Her professional interests focus on the intersections between emotional and physical health.

Debra M. Kawahara is Professor and Associate Dean of Academic Affairs at the California School of Professional Psychology, Alliant International University, USA. She also maintains a small private practice. Her primary areas of interest include feminism, multicultural psychology, family systems and processes, cultural competency, and qualitative methodology.

Radical Visionaries: Feminist Therapy Pioneers, 1970–1975

Edited by
Claudia Pitts and Debra M. Kawahara

LONDON AND NEW YORK

First published 2018
by Routledge
2 Park Square, Milton Park, Abingdon, Oxon, OX14 4RN, UK

and by Routledge
711 Third Avenue, New York, NY 10017, USA

Routledge is an imprint of the Taylor & Francis Group, an informa business

© 2018 Taylor & Francis

All rights reserved. No part of this book may be reprinted or reproduced or utilised in any form or by any electronic, mechanical, or other means, now known or hereafter invented, including photocopying and recording, or in any information storage or retrieval system, without permission in writing from the publishers.

Trademark notice: Product or corporate names may be trademarks or registered trademarks, and are used only for identification and explanation without intent to infringe.

British Library Cataloguing in Publication Data
A catalogue record for this book is available from the British Library

ISBN 13: 978-1-138-29565-0

Typeset in Minion Pro
by RefineCatch Limited, Bungay, Suffolk

Publisher's Note
The publisher accepts responsibility for any inconsistencies that may have arisen during the conversion of this book from journal articles to book chapters, namely the possible inclusion of journal terminology.

Disclaimer
Every effort has been made to contact copyright holders for their permission to reprint material in this book. The publishers would be grateful to hear from any copyright holder who is not here acknowledged and will undertake to rectify any errors or omissions in future editions of this book.

Contents

Citation Information		vii
Notes on Contributors		xi
	Preface: A Farewell Letter from the Editor *Ellyn Kaschak*	1
	Introduction: Radical Visionaries – Feminist Psychotherapists: 1970–1975 *Claudia Pitts and Debra M. Kawahara*	5
1.	Jean Baker Miller, MD, Visionary Pragmatist *Judith V. Jordan*	9
2.	Feminist Pioneer: Annette Brodsky Paving the Way *Claudia Porras Pyland and Debra Mollen*	24
3.	Phyllis Chesler – A Life on Behalf of Women *Claudia Pitts*	37
4.	Feminist Therapy Pioneer: E. Kitch Childs *Wytress Richardson*	50
5.	"You Just Know It's the Only Thing You Can Think": A Conversation with Chodorow *Mengchun Chiang*	57
6.	The Amazing Life and Times of Oliva Espín *Debra M. Kawahara*	72
7.	Feminism, Therapy, and Changing the World *Miriam Greenspan*	83
8.	Those Were the Best of Times, and Then . . . *Rachel T. Hare-Mustin*	95
9.	The Proud and Productive Life of a Red-Diaper Baby: Judith Herman *Kayla Weiner*	107
10.	Dis-Illusioning Psychology: Epistemology and the Contextual Psychology of Ellyn Kaschak *Natalie Porter*	115

CONTENTS

11. Hannah Lerman: My Feminist Journey   133
    Hannah Lerman

12. Harriet Lerner: A Feminist Voice From the Wheat Fields   145
    Harriet Lerner

13. Blowing in the Wind: '70s Questions for Millennial Therapists   155
    Jeanne Marecek

14. Sara Sharratt: Global Feminist Pioneer   167
    Ellen Abell and Claudia Pitts

15. Feminist Psychology and Psychotherapy: A Personal Journey   176
    Reiko Homma-True

16. Feminist Pioneer: Lenore E. A. Walker   191
    Giselle Gaviria, Rachel Needle, Rachael Silverman, and Lenore E. A. Walker

Index   207

Citation Information

The chapters in this book were originally published in *Women & Therapy*, volume 40, issues 3–4 (October 2017). When citing this material, please use the original page numbering for each article, as follows:

Preface
A Farewell Letter from the Editor
Ellyn Kaschak
Women & Therapy, volume 40, issues 3–4 (October 2017), pp. 252–255

Introduction
Radical Visionaries – Feminist Psychotherapists: 1970–1975
Claudia Pitts and Debra M. Kawahara
Women & Therapy, volume 40, issues 3–4 (October 2017), pp. 256–259

Chapter 1
Jean Baker Miller, MD, Visionary Pragmatist
Judith V. Jordan
Women & Therapy, volume 40, issues 3–4 (October 2017), pp. 260–274

Chapter 2
Feminist Pioneer: Annette Brodsky Paving the Way
Claudia Porras Pyland and Debra Mollen
Women & Therapy, volume 40, issues 3–4 (October 2017), pp. 275–287

Chapter 3
Phyllis Chesler – A Life on Behalf of Women
Claudia Pitts
Women & Therapy, volume 40, issues 3–4 (October 2017), pp. 288–300

Chapter 4
Feminist Therapy Pioneer: E. Kitch Childs
Wytress Richardson
Women & Therapy, volume 40, issues 3–4 (October 2017), pp. 301–307

CITATION INFORMATION

Chapter 5
"You Just Know It's the Only Thing You Can Think": A Conversation with Chodorow
Mengchun Chiang
Women & Therapy, volume 40, issues 3–4 (October 2017), pp. 308–322

Chapter 6
The Amazing Life and Times of Oliva Espín
Debra M. Kawahara
Women & Therapy, volume 40, issues 3–4 (October 2017), pp. 323–333

Chapter 7
Feminism, Therapy, and Changing the World
Miriam Greenspan
Women & Therapy, volume 40, issues 3–4 (October 2017), pp. 334–345

Chapter 8
Those Were the Best of Times, and Then . . .
Rachel T. Hare-Mustin
Women & Therapy, volume 40, issues 3–4 (October 2017), pp. 346–357

Chapter 9
The Proud and Productive Life of a Red-Diaper Baby: Judith Herman
Kayla Weiner
Women & Therapy, volume 40, issues 3–4 (October 2017), pp. 358–365

Chapter 10
Dis-Illusioning Psychology: Epistemology and the Contextual Psychology of Ellyn Kaschak
Natalie Porter
Women & Therapy, volume 40, issues 3–4 (October 2017), pp. 366–383

Chapter 11
Hannah Lerman: My Feminist Journey
Hannah Lerman
Women & Therapy, volume 40, issues 3–4 (October 2017), pp. 384–395

Chapter 12
Harriet Lerner: A Feminist Voice From the Wheat Fields
Harriet Lerner
Women & Therapy, volume 40, issues 3–4 (October 2017), pp. 396–405

Chapter 13
Blowing in the Wind: '70s Questions for Millennial Therapists
Jeanne Marecek
Women & Therapy, volume 40, issues 3–4 (October 2017), pp. 406–417

Chapter 14
Sara Sharratt: Global Feminist Pioneer
Ellen Abell and Claudia Pitts
Women & Therapy, volume 40, issues 3–4 (October 2017), pp. 418–426

CITATION INFORMATION

Chapter 15
Feminist Psychology and Psychotherapy: A Personal Journey
Reiko Homma-True
Women & Therapy, volume 40, issues 3–4 (October 2017), pp. 427–441

Chapter 16
Feminist Pioneer: Lenore E. A. Walker
Giselle Gaviria, Rachel Needle, Rachael Silverman, and Lenore E. A. Walker
Women & Therapy, volume 40, issues 3–4 (October 2017), pp. 442–456

For any permission-related enquiries please visit:
http://www.tandfonline.com/page/help/permissions

Notes on Contributors

Ellen Abell is Professor of Psychology and Gender Studies at Prescott College, AZ, USA, where she teaches on feminist theory, counselor education, and critical psychology. Her most recent article, "Picking the Bones", was published in *The Fat Pedagogy Reader: Challenging Weight-Based Oppression Through Critical Education* (2016), and is based on an excerpt from her upcoming memoir.

Mengchun Chiang is Assistant Professor at William James College, MA, USA, where her research explores clinical utilities of process and outcome measurement in psychotherapy. Her writing traverses the tension between a phenomenological–existential approach and a post-structural understanding of cultural-crossing and multi-gendered issues. She is also a licensed psychologist, offering both psychotherapy and psychological/therapeutic assessment.

Giselle Gaviria is a doctoral student in Psychology at Carlos Albizu University, Miami, USA. Her interests include human trafficking, gender violence, immigration, and trauma. She is co-editor of *Sex Trafficking: Feminist and Transnational Perspectives* (with Lenore Walker and Kalyani Gopal, 2018). She has presented nationally and internationally on topics such as human trafficking,

Miriam Greenspan is a psychotherapist, consultant, writer, and workshop leader. A pioneer in women's psychology and psychotherapy, her work focuses on a holistic mind/body/spirit model of emotional transformation and healing. She is the author of *A New Approach to Women and Therapy* (1983) and *Healing Through the Dark Emotions: The Wisdom of Grief, Fear, and Despair* (2003), which was a Boston Globe bestseller and won the 2004 Nautilus Award in self-help/psychology for "books that make a contribution to conscious living and positive social change."

Rachel T. Hare-Mustin has published extensively on feminist family therapy, epistemological issues in psychology, and psychotherapy ethics. She is the editor of *Women and Psychotherapy: An Assessment of Research and Practice* (with Annette Brodsky, 1980) and *Making a Difference: Psychology and the Construction of Gender* (with Jeanne Marecek, 1990). Her 1994 article "Discourses in the mirrored room: A postmodern analysis of therapy" has been used in training psychotherapists throughout the world.

Reiko Homma-True has developed culturally responsive services to underserved populations in California and in the United States, actively promoting services to meet the special needs of women and children, particularly those who are victimized and abused. She has also advocated for nurturing and promoting leadership roles for women. She was involved in organizing and providing disaster mental health assistance in California and Japan. Her achievements include directing San Francisco mental health and substance abuse services and training Asian and Japanese clinical psychologists.

Judith V. Jordan is the Director of the Jean Baker Miller Training Institute at the Wellesley Centers for Women, MA, USA, and Assistant Professor at Harvard Medical School. She is a founding scholar of the Relational-Cultural Theory and has written *Women's Growth in Connection* (1991) and *Relational-Cultural Therapy* (2010). She is the editor of *The Power of Connection* (2008), *Women's Growth in Diversity* (1997), *Creating Connection* (2013), and *The Complexity of Connection* (2004).

Ellyn Kaschak is Professor Emerita of Psychology at San Jose State University, CA, USA, and Visiting Professor at the United Nations University for Peace in Costa Rica. She has been widely recognized as one of the founders of the field of Feminist Psychology and Psychotherapy. She has been honored with many awards in the field for her continuing intellectual and epistemological contributions, including her two groundbreaking books, *Engendered Lives: A New Psychology of Women's Experience* (1992) and *Sight Unseen: Gender and Race through Blind Eyes* (2015).

Debra M. Kawahara is Professor and Associate Dean of Academic Affairs at the California School of Professional Psychology, Alliant International University, USA. She also maintains a small private practice. Her primary areas of interest include feminism, multicultural psychology, family systems and processes, cultural competency, and qualitative methodology.

Hannah Lerman is an independent clinical psychology practitioner in Las Vegas, NV, USA. She has taught online at Walden University since 2005. Most of her clinical work involves consulting with residents of nursing homes, and she has worked as a clinician, feminist advocate and scholar focused on preventing sexual abuses by professionals. She is the author of *A Mote in Freud's Eye: From Psychoanalysis to the Psychology of Women* (1986) and *Pigeonholing Women's Misery* (1996).

Harriet Lerner is currently in private practice, and lectures and consults nationally. She previously served as a staff psychologist at the Menninger Clinic in Topeka, KS, USA, where she published on the psychology of women and family relationships, revising traditional psychodynamic concepts to reflect feminist and family systems perspectives. She is the author of books including *The Dance of Anger* (1985) and *Why Won't You Apologize? Healing Big Betrayals and Every Day Hurts* (2017).

Jeanne Marecek is Professor Emerita at Swarthmore College, PA, USA, and an editor of *Feminism & Psychology*. Her work concerns the cultural and social bases of psychological suffering, with a focus on the gender order. Her current research focuses on young women's suicide-like acts in Sri Lanka. She is author of *Gender and Culture in Psychology: Theories and Practices* (with Eva Magnusson, 2012) and *Doing Interview-based Qualitative Research* (2015); and the co-editor of a special issue of *Feminism & Psychology* titled "DSM-5 and Beyond: Feminist Engagements with Psychodiagnosis".

Debra Mollen is Professor and Director of the Counseling Psychology Master's program in the Department of Multicultural Women's and Gender Studies at Texas Woman's University, USA. She is a licensed psychologist and one of six Certified Sexuality Educators in Texas recognized by the American Association of Sexuality Educators, Counselors, and Therapists. She is Co-Chairperson for the APA Revisions for the Guidelines for Psychological Practice with Girls and Women.

NOTES ON CONTRIBUTORS

Rachel Needle is a licensed psychologist and certified sex therapist at the Center for Marital and Sexual Health, and Adjunct Professor of Psychology at Nova Southeastern University, FL, USA. She is also the founder of both the Whole Health Psychological Center, and the Advanced Mental Health Training Institute, a continuing education provider company. Her interests include substance abuse, sexual function and dysfunction, relationship concerns, battered women, and trauma.

Claudia Pitts is Associate Professor in the College of Professional Studies and Advancement at National Louis University, Chicago, USA, where she is Director of the Master's in Psychology program. She is also a licensed clinical psychologist with a group practice. Her professional interests focus on the intersections between emotional and physical health.

Natalie Porter is Professor in the Clinical PhD Psychology program at the California School of Professional Psychology, Alliant International University, USA. She has published widely in the area of feminist therapy and cultural diversity, and her research interests include gender, anti-racist, and social justice issues pertaining to child, adolescent, and women's development, and to therapy, ethics, and leadership. She has served in numerous governance roles such as President and APA Council of Representatives for Division 35, Society for the Psychology of Women.

Claudia Porras Pyland is Assistant Professor in Counseling Psychology at Texas Woman's University, USA. She has served as a state representative for the Southwest Psychological Association and is a member of APA's Division 16, Continuing Education Committee. Her research interests include intimate partner violence, romantic attachment styles, and the academic success and resilience of diverse students.

Wytress Richardson is Associate Professor in the College of Professional Studies and Advancement at National Louis University, Chicago, IL, USA, where she chairs the Applied Behavioral Sciences program. She has held positions as a dually certified counselor in mental health and substance abuse, and is the founder of Girls of Grace Youth Center, a non-profit (501c3) organization dedicated to mentoring and equipping young women with valuable leadership and life skills.

Rachael Silverman is a licensed clinical psychologist in private practice, specializing in providing child, adolescent, adult, couple, and family therapy as well as psycho-educational testing, personality assessments, comprehensive reports, and court appointed psychological evaluations. She is also a qualified, court-appointed expert witness and works with professional athletes as a sports psychologist. She is the Editor-in-Chief of the American Board of Professional Psychology Academy *Couple & Family Psychology* newsletter and the Academy's Early Career Psychologist Board Member.

Lenore E. A. Walker is Professor and Coordinator of the Forensic Psychology Concentration, and Program Director of the Forensic Psychology MS at Nova Southeastern University, FL, USA. After her ground-breaking psychological research on intimate partner violence, she named the "Battered Woman Syndrome", which has been used in psychotherapy offices and courtrooms around the world to help better understand the counter-intuitive behavior of battered women. An early feminist psychotherapist, she has also mentored hundreds of psychologists.

Kayla Weiner recently completed almost 30 years as a psychotherapist in private practice. Though her employment has been primarily in professional fields, her identity is clearly set in her non-paid work as a social justice activist. In retirement she has returned to her first love of teaching by volunteering in an elementary school.

PREFACE

A Farewell Letter from the Editor

To My Colleagues, Students, and all the Readers of *Women & Therapy*,

I have been Editor of the journal *Women & Therapy* for 20 years now. Finally, this is my last issue. This was not an easy decision for me to make, but a necessary one. That is because it is time for me to move on and to work more intensely on the several books I hope to write in the next years. Perhaps even more importantly, it is time to invite another generation of feminists to shape the material in this journal and in the field of feminist therapy, which I helped invent so many lifetimes ago. I am passing the torch. Those of you receiving it, please keep it brightly lit.

I have had the privilege and responsibility of shaping the material published in our field and often of mentoring first time writers and editors, who have gone on to publish many volumes successfully. I could name names, but you all know who you are and the list would just be too long.

I believe that we were the first to devote our journal to single topic issues, giving each topic a sense of cohesiveness and depth. Many journals and edited APA books now use this format. We actually "invented" it because the quality and quantity of submissions that we were receiving voluntarily were not of a quality that I could publish. Innovation was born of necessity.

Like much of my feminist work and a lot of my teaching, I learned without mentors. My generation did not have any. Instead, we made up feminist psychology as we went along, and we are all living with that result today, for better or for worse. While mostly for the better, I do have one regret about the development of feminist therapy, and that is how professionalized it has become. In its own way, it has been swallowed up by capitalism and has provided many therapists with a fine professional income. Had I had my way though, it would have remained free or on a scale that slid down to $2.50, as did mine and many others when we began. Of course, these are 1970 dollars, but still, I shudder every time I hear of a feminist therapist charging $150 or more a session.

At a minimum, I wish we had free drop-in groups for women much like those of the 12-step programs. I will resist the temptation to write out the 12 feminist steps here, but I will not resist the temptation to advocate for the many women who have been abused, trafficked, and hurt in the many other ways that girls and women know so well. Most of them have no easy and accessible place to turn for anonymous feminist support and help. Often, they have no idea that they have the right not to be treated that way and no way to escape without endangering their own lives or the lives of their family members. There are now agencies and NGOs that do some of this work, but that is not the same as what I had in mind. We went from a revolution to a profession, much to my regret.

In the last several years, I have been dismayed to hear the misinformation that our very own group has about the origins of feminist therapy. They have a vague idea of its inception, an even vaguer idea of the original pioneers, and sadly, almost no idea about where our ideas came from, including the very central concept of gender. I do not know why so many Americans are only interested in history that goes as far back as their own lives, but I know this to be the case even among many professionals and intellectuals. It is a virtual stereotype about Americans in other countries where I live. While no stereotype is universally true, there is that grain that continues to chafe, a sort of cultural narcissism.

I cannot tell you how many times I have mentioned President Kennedy or even Reagan in my classes to hear the response, "How can you expect me to know that? It happened before I was born."

I do not want to hear an analogous comment from younger feminists, although it is already too late for that. Thus was born the idea for this issue. In it are described the earliest feminist psychologists, the earliest days of organizing, and the earliest writing about the discrimination women faced in those days. We not only could not get into PhD programs and find work as professors, but we could not even own property or have credit in our own names. We belonged to our husbands and fathers. Rape and violence by one's own husband were just considered part of the normal life of a woman. While this has changed, it has not changed enough or in enough places on the planet.

The then DSM had many diagnoses that specifically discriminated against women, those that pathologized ordinary behavior of women, and, as is more well known, that declared normal sexual preferences abnormal and pathological.

In the first class that I taught in feminist therapy at UC Berkeley in 1973, virtually every student had a story to tell about having been involuntarily hospitalized and often administered ECT for having had an abortion, having complained of domestic violence, or even for having requested a divorce from a cheating or violent husband. All rights to these decisions were held by the husbands of these women.

We were the first generation not to accept this status quo and followed in the footsteps of the suffragists, who had struggled against domestic violence, as well as advocating for the vote for women. They have been largely forgotten or remembered in the worst way that a woman can be as ugly "battleaxes."

That is, the axes that they used to do battle are conflated with the women themselves. As feminists, they had to be ugly, and as women, their appearance is what mattered. While women have the vote in many countries today, our leaders are still judged by their looks, their weight, and the shape of their ankles.

Our work was cut out for us, and we took it on eagerly and righteously. This is one of the aspects of being Americans. We felt that we had the right to fight. As the younger reader is only too aware, some of these issues, such as a woman's right to control her own body, have once again resurfaced. Will there ever be full equality for women in the United States where we have been unable to pass an Equal Rights Amendment or elect a woman president (I hope there will be one by the time this issue is in press)? We are not right back where we started in the early 1970s, but we are not as far as we had hoped.

Those of us who engaged in these struggles do not want to be forgotten or made into "battleaxe" caricatures by younger women. Many of our issues may no longer be relevant, but your respect for the world we created for you should be. It is essential for our generation to support and respect those of younger generations and to offer what we also request from you.

During my 20-year tenure as Editor of this journal, I have tried to broaden and deepen the field and to give access to voices that might not otherwise have been heard. We have published such diverse issues as Assault on the Soul: Women in the Former Yugoslavia, Third Wave Feminisms, Lesbian Violence, A New View of Women's Sexual Problems, Spirituality in Feminist Therapy, Violence in the Lives of Black Women, Invisible Disabilities, Biracial Women, Client Suicide, Women in Prison, Asian-American Women, Stone Center Working Papers, A Minyan of Women, Border Crossings, Immigrant Women, Women and Cancer, and Whiteness and White Privilege, along with many other important contemporary topics generally guest edited by leading scholars in each of those areas.

There are too many important topics and scholars to be able to name them all in this brief article, but the interested reader can find them all online on the Taylor & Francis website. The journal was originally published by the Haworth Press under the supervision of Bill Cohen in New York. He eventually sold all his journals, including us, to a huge corporation, Taylor and Francis, which is an arm of Routledge Press and publishes out of London. Such are the ways of the 21st century, and we have had to adapt to working with interchangeable cogs in a corporate wheel.

As of 2018, the new Editor of this journal will be Debra M. Kawahara. The vision for the next 20 years will be hers and those of her editorial board and cohorts. I wish her 20 productive years of change in the journal as the world changes. Whether she serves for 20 years is her choice now.

It is a pleasure then to end my tenure with this issue remembering the early pioneers of our field and with a look back at the inception of our field. They must not be forgotten or erased from history. I wish to honor those women who sat in those 1970s rooms dreaming of a new world for women and girls and arguing passionately about how to get there. And here we are.

For the last time in this capacity—

Ellyn Kaschak
Editor
Women & Therapy

INTRODUCTION

Radical Visionaries – Feminist Psychotherapists: 1970–1975

Claudia Pitts and Debra M. Kawahara

ABSTRACT

The work of feminist scholars, activists, therapists, and theorists has continuously impacted the United States and international cultural narrative since the radical days of the 1960s and 1970s. This special issue was created to highlight contributors to this remarkable transformation by documenting the narratives of their lives and careers. These profiles, nearly all written by or with the pioneers themselves, highlight their contributions to feminism, feminist psychology, and the vast societal change that followed their work.

As we look into our own recent past, women were widely believed to be psychologically inferior to men, therapists were routinely having sexual contact with clients, incest reports were often viewed as wishful projections, and women around the world were expected to unquestioningly accept the domestic roles into which they were cast. The work of the pioneers in this issue were profoundly important in bringing change to these and many other forms of institutional and cultural sexism. The "second wave" of feminism, occurring in the 1960s and 1970s in the United States and abroad, brought with it deep societal changes, many of which were tied directly or indirectly to the writings, activism, and therapy done by feminist psychotherapists.

This special issue documents and honors these feminist therapy pioneers from the first half of the 1970s, who moved the mental health establishment through radical action from within and outside to consider women as fully human. As we move into the current manifestation of feminism and work for social justice, it is imperative to pause to consider how these "second wave" pioneers gave us the beginnings of feminist therapy. These women, starting from the earliest stages of the movement, gave us consciousness raising, the notion of egalitarian therapy, female empowerment, the grounds-well of women into clinical psychology programs, and many other positive changes. They impacted systems and processes such as the criminal justice systems, divorce proceedings, domestic violence, education, medicine, and law, to name but a few.

The articles in this special issue are designed to illuminate each of the feminist pioneer's life stories/narratives to ensure that their contributions and legacies will be known to current and future feminists. The articles are focused on each pioneer's lived experiences: her early family and academic circumstances, how and why she became a feminist and evolved into a feminist pioneer, her individual contributions to feminism and feminist psychotherapy, as well as her hopes and dreams for the future and future generations. For the most part, the articles have been written by the pioneers themselves. Others were written by feminist therapists, academics, or authors who were interested in documenting these narratives based on interviews of and information by the pioneers. For those pioneers unavailable to be interviewed due to death or illness, someone who knew the pioneer's work and life personally served as the source for the interview. Through these articles, we seek to recall and preserve the legacy of these brave and insightful women who saw failings and inequality in the mental health, legal, governmental, and domestic establishment and beyond and risked clinical, academic, and personal rejection and judgment to address these defects and ultimately, to make lasting and significant changes to discriminatory systems.

These are pioneering women to whom we owe a debt of gratitude and who marked the path for those behind them to follow.

Jean Baker Miller was a significant theorist who created Relational-Cultural Theory (RCT), carried forward by members of the Stone Center's collaborative group. She offered new understandings of women's, and men's, development with a special emphasis on the impact of power and marginalization on personal and collective wellbeing.

Annette Brodsky is a renowned scholar who advocated for and studied, among other topics, the effect of consciousness-raising groups. Her work also engendered critical scholarship that revealed the harm of therapists' sexual abuse and facilitated improved ethics and guidelines for psychologists in their work with clients.

Phyllis Chesler, known as an author and world citizen, made, and continues to make, significant contributions on topics as diverse as pornography, prostitution, motherhood, custody, surrogacy, a woman's right to self-defense, racism, including anti-Semitism, Israel, Islamic gender and religious Apartheid, as well as feminism. Her widely read books and articles were often groundbreaking, being among the first to raise awareness for significant controversial issues.

E. Kitch Childs was a prominent scholar and activist who influenced the establishment toward changes in the legal and educational systems. Her work also impacted the banking industry, the field of medicine, and even understandings of the family structure.

Nancy Chodorow is an influential feminist theorist and author who brought together the academic fields of sociology, anthropology, and psychoanalysis in her work related to feminist theories and psychoanalysis. Her well-known books present a rich interplay among socio-structural influences (i.e., culture) as well as intra- and inter-psychic dynamic processes, emphasizing the importance of individuality and subjectivity.

Oliva Espín is a renowned, prolific, feminist and multicultural psychologist and academic who has meaningfully contributed to a broader understanding of feminist therapy in an international context. Her career greatly impacted global feminism, feminist psychology, and ultimately humankind.

Miriam Greenspan is known as an influential author who created a model of therapy that incorporates the political and spiritual dimensions of experience. She used this model to address the successes and challenges that psychology and psychotherapy faced in an age of global threat.

Rachel T. Hare-Mustin, a significant feminist activist in academia, the professions, and clinical practice, has been a thoughtful advocate of change for women. Her work of applying feminist theory to the study of gender has given voice to women, not only in therapy, but in the wider society as well.

Judith Herman is a noted feminist psychiatrist, political activist, intellectual, and writer whose work in the field of abuse and trauma resulted in a number of important works, including the influential *Trauma and Recovery*. This book and her other scholarly work were influenced by previous generations of thinkers, and in turn, it informs future generations.

Ellyn Kaschak had beginnings as a founder of one of the first feminist counseling services in the country in the early 1970s. She has gone on to substantially influence decades of feminist and family therapists through her teaching, writing, journal editing, as well as her feminist epistemology and theory development.

Hannah Lerman is a groundbreaking therapist who still gets recognized for her early feminist writings and her remarkable book on Freud. Despite these noted works, her annotated bibliography of the literature about sexual abuse by professionals is often seen as her most important and influential work.

Harriet Lerner is a noted author and an astute psychologist whose well-known books bridged the gaps between professional and popular literature. Her writings offered the insights of psychology and feminism to an entire generation of newly forming feminists.

Jeanne Marecek was an advocate for psychotherapy in the 1960s when some declared that feminist therapy was an oxymoron. She was one of the first feminists in the mental health professions who borrowed practices, ethical ideals, principles, and goals from the Women's Movement to create innovative models of therapy, which she continues to advance.

Sara Sharratt is a prominent psychotherapist, scholar, and activist, whose most well-known and salient work was during the years she spent witnessing and giving voice to victims at war crime tribunals in the former Yugoslavia.

She has dedicated her life to insuring that the voices of women throughout the world be heard so that justice and peace might prevail.

Reiko Homma-True is a leader, therapist, and activist who focused on Asian American women struggling under the double oppression of racism and sexism. She was inspired by minority psychologist leaders to develop a feminist treatment approach that addresses the cultural diversity issues unique to Asian American women.

Lenore E. A. Walker is a vital thought leader in feminist therapy whose work deeply influenced scientific and cultural views of domestic violence, the legal representation of both men and women, and the public perception of psychology. She also was instrumental in creating the professional culture of feminist therapy within and beyond its traditional structure.

As we read though these life stories and career trajectories, we can see the development of feminist therapy and more generally U.S. and global feminism from the foundation laid by these thinkers, therapists, activists, and authors. This path was not clear, and it was these women who risked so much, personally and professionally, to reach toward their goals and openly state their conclusions about the culture. Each story and each pioneer is a step toward the movement for full equality for women in the therapy room, the courtroom, and the bedroom. It is nearly unimaginable to see how we could have come this far without them and their profoundly important work. It is further inconceivable to allow their sacrifices and victories to be forgotten so we dedicate this special issue to documenting and celebrating their achievements.

Jean Baker Miller, MD, Visionary Pragmatist

Judith V. Jordan

ABSTRACT

Jean Baker Miller's 1976 book, *Toward a New Psychology of Women*, was an overnight success. It struck a deep chord in many women because it was based on listening to women's stories. Instead of seeing women through the lens of male psychology with its emphasis on separation and autonomy, Jean suggested that relationships are central to women's experience of themselves and the world. Traits that were typically pathologized (needing other people, attending to the messages of emotions, wanting to participate in growth fostering relationships for all involved) were revisited by Jean and her colleagues who discovered strengths where others had seen weakness. The resulting work is known as Relational-Cultural Theory (RCT) and has offered new understandings of women's and men's development with a special emphasis on the impact of power and marginalization on personal and collective wellbeing. Jean's work is carried forward by members of a collaborative group with whom Jean worked for many years. RCT theorists have written and edited over 20 books, 115 works in progress, and numerous chapters and articles that continue to elaborate on Jean's groundbreaking work. RCT is applied to both clinical and social justice settings. Jean was devoted to contributing to the creation of a more just society.

Jean Baker Miller's life story is one of courage and connection. With the help of caring relationships and people who saw something special in her, Jean faced many challenges. She not only met those challenges, but grew through them. From an early age, she lived the values and beliefs that she would come to write about and for which she would be celebrated. She knew no one "made it alone." She knew that growth-fostering relationships were necessary for human survival and wellbeing. And, she came to see that the many theories of "human development" misrepresented and distorted women's experience, presenting images of girls and women that emphasized their immaturity, neediness, weakness, and failure. The work of Jean's lifetime was devoted to finding strength and creativity where others saw weakness and incompetence. She named women as the carriers of relationship and caring in the culture, and she went about listening to women's voices and accurately describing their life experiences. She did not seek to make women into "better men";

she sought to accurately represent women's experiences and to show how vital women's skills and concerns are to the wellbeing of all people. Responses from readers to her best-selling book *Toward a New Psychology of Women* (Miller, 1976) were gratefully offered again and again: "Your book changed my life. Thank you." Jean once noted that the shift from a psychology of separation to a psychology of relationship "changes everything." And so it does. I offer this brief and very incomplete look at Jean Baker Miller's life with enormous gratitude and hope, in honor of a brilliant mentor and dear friend who has changed many lives and provided us all with a sense of renewed possibility.

Early Years

Jean Baker Miller was born on Sept 29, 1927, to a working class, immigrant family in the Bronx, New York. Her mother was of Irish descent, and her father of German heritage. She was the third of three children with an older brother, Henry, and an older sister, Irene. Times were tough; joblessness was rampant during the Great Depression. Jean's father, Henry, managed to keep his job as a clerk for the city, but faced never-ending cutbacks, while her mother, Irene, was a traditional housewife. When she was only 11 months old, Jean was diagnosed with polio. Although the family had a tendency to minimize this illness, Jean noted she spent much time in hospitals, was subject to repeated and painful surgeries, and had ongoing treatments in dreary clinics where she eventually immersed herself in books. Characteristically, Jean did not lament this affliction, but instead she reported having been inspired to pursue a career in medicine while in the care of two devoted nurses, twin sisters named Stone. These nurses took an interest in this shy, bright, and appealing child. Confined to an orthopedic ward for two six month stints, Jean started a ward newspaper, and she reported that "I read and I read ... like Nancy Drew Mysteries." She did not remember her physical disability as being limiting.

Jean described her parents as emotionally reserved "WASP types." Jean felt that underneath her quiet demeanor, her mother was "spunky." Jean's Aunt Hermine and cousin Irene were two women in the family who established some sense of making lives for themselves out in the world, and Jean remembered being impressed by them. Jean also recalled having very supportive and encouraging teachers in the New York public school system. The twin nurses persuaded Jean's mother to let her attend Hunter College High School for gifted young girls. During the war, Jean and her friends worked on war relief activities: knitting, packing bandages and so on. Jean noted this was a "woman's thing."

Education

When an interested teacher asked Jean where she was planning to go to college, she responded she had to go to a public college because she had no money; the teacher urged her to look into scholarships. Jean did, and she also took in the message from this teacher: "You could really do something." Her intellectual interests burgeoned. She applied to and got a scholarship to Sarah Lawrence College. At Sarah Lawrence, she was exposed to wealth and society in a way that made her feel "outside." She saw elitism and privilege up close, and she initially felt lonely and "different." But, she was also exposed to brilliant teachers, mostly women, and they inspired her.

Her first year advisor, Helen Merrill Lynd, was welcoming to Jean and introduced her to psychology. With her husband, Robert, Helen had written an influential sociology book: *Middletown: A Study in Contemporary American Culture* (Lynd & Lynd, 1929). Jean later described Helen as very "devoted" and kind to her. Jean took Lynd's course in Social Philosophy, and in this rich and engaged intellectual atmosphere, Jean flourished. She steadfastly believed she was able to thrive because of the people who took an interest in her. She felt that Helen Lynd "took me into her family." While visiting at Helen's home, she met Margaret Mead and Gregory Bateson. In the presence of these "intellectuals," Jean felt shy, quiet, and sometimes "stupid." Later, Jean dedicated *Toward a New Psychology of Women* (Miller, 1976) to Helen Merrill Lynd (Lynd, 1958).

Jean eventually found her peer niche with the intellectual, liberal set of girls she lived with at Sarah Lawrence. But, Jean was also beginning to gain a sense of direction and purpose. She loved science and had a strong sense of wanting to contribute to the wellbeing of others; she had also developed a desire to work for social justice which grew more intense over the ensuing years.

Around this time, Jean's determination to go to medical school was getting clearer. For each advance she made in life, Jean credited the importance of women who fostered her development: the Stone sisters, Helen Lynd, and Aunt Hermine. She once described her history as made up of a "line of women"; "these people opened up worlds to me" (Cohn, 1997, p. 197).

Pursuing her goal to become a physician, Jean was again encouraged to apply for a scholarship. Of the 110 students in her class at Columbia Medical School, ten were women. Jean reported the climate in medical school was decidedly sexist. There was little of the camaraderie of high school and college. The atmosphere at Columbia was cold, competitive, and unfriendly. Jean found the curriculum uninspiring. It was a "horrible atmosphere" with no awareness of feminism or the special stressors of being a woman in medical school. In one bright spot that had quite an impact on her, Jean attended a symposium on female psychology and was inspired by Bernard Robbins who suggested that women had certain strengths that men lacked. His ideas were laughed at and scorned by the mainstream psychoanalytic community, but Jean was resonant with his message, and it remained with her.

Upon completing her MD in 1952, she pursued residency programs at Montefiore Medical Center, Bellevue Hospital Center, the Albert Einstein

College of Medicine, Upstate Medical Center, and New York Medical College while she completed her psychoanalytic training. Jean went into analysis with Walter Bonime who had trained at the Horney Institute. She saw him four times a week for six years. Jean felt he was "on her side," but not especially empathic about women's concerns.

While pursuing her professional interests, Jean was also meeting interesting and creative people engaged in academia and social activism. At a New Year's Eve party on Dec 31, 1953, Jean met Mike Miller, a sociology professor who was passionately involved in addressing issues of poverty and inequality. Mike was involved with a project with David Riesman which sought to make social science data available for the use of progressive politicians. Jean and Mike were drawn to each other's intellects, political awareness, and social justice activism (And, of course, Jean noted, "I loved him."). Sixteen months after they met a second time (the first time they met, there was little mutual interest), they married.

Mike's career was taking off as his area of interest, poverty and its related consequences, was becoming an important focus in the early Kennedy White House. Jean's own political involvement continued when she joined the Women's International League for Peace and Freedom and the Council on Racial Equality. Mike and Jean together participated in marches and demonstrations. Jean also became involved nationally with an active student association of interns and medical students which promoted progressive health care policies. As a consequence of these activities, Jean was called into the dean's office and told to disengage from this group or be subject to scrutiny of the House's Un-American Activities Committee. Jean refused and lost her scholarship.

In 1956, nine months short of fulfilling her specialty training in psychiatry, Jean was asked to leave her residency training at Albert Einstein when the dean discovered she was pregnant. Her future in psychiatry was in jeopardy, and Jean felt "Now I am out of academic medicine." Not allowed to continue her training at Albert Einstein, Jean set up a private practice, while she also worked hard at mothering an active young baby, her son Jon. Despite Mike's engaged fathering (remarkable for the time), Jean felt stressed by the demands of profession and mothering, and several moves for Mike's career complicated Jean's career development.

Between the ages of 27 and 33, Jean had married, had two sons, and committed to the study and subsequent practice of psychiatry. When Mike was wooed in 1973 by the Sociology department at Boston University, the family of four, now including younger son Ned, relocated to Boston. Jean was appointed as a Clinical Professor of Psychiatry at Boston University School of Medicine and was on the faculty at Harvard Medical School. She practiced psychiatry at Beth Israel Deaconess Medical Center and was a member of the American College of Psychiatrists, the American Psychiatric Association, and the American Academy of Psychoanalysis.

Increasing Feminist Awareness

When she was in her forties, Jean's interest in feminism was sparked by Friedan's (1963) *The Feminine Mystique.* Consciousness-raising groups increased her engagement with feminist ideas. A supervisee urged Jean to join a consciousness-raising group. At first, Jean refused: "Those are for young people." But, colleagues continued to press Jean to join a group, and she did so in 1968, 1 year after the first women's consciousness-raising groups met in New York. Her group was composed of two secretaries, two teachers, a nurse, and a doctor, Jean. In this group, Jean heard many of the same stories and dilemmas that she had heard from her patients; they struggled with a sense of being "supposedly maladapted females." There was a decidedly political cast to these discussions which were occurring in turbulent political times. There was also empowering validation. Women were listening to one another, resonating with each other's stories and reaching out to support one another. Jean saw women being helped by one another, and she was impressed and moved by the power of these groups. After joining such a group, Jean remembers thinking "these groups are doing more [for women] than I am for my patients" (Miller & Welch, 1995, p. 337). What she was hearing and learning from these women was beginning to feel relevant to her practice of therapy. People spoke honestly, and their stories were moving and were not being represented in mainstream developmental and clinical theories.

Later, in Boston, she met with a group of women analysts who were interested in women's issues. But, she was still searching for ways to represent women's voices. Her first publication in 1971, "On women: New political directions for women," was published in the *Journal of Social Policy* (Miller, 1971). In it, she addressed the idea of "unnecessary people who were on the periphery of economic and political power" (Cohn, 1997, p. 248). In her 1973 book *Psychoanalysis and Women,* Jean brought the historical contributions of women like Karen Horney and Clara Thompson to the fore as she sought to make visible the often invisible contributions of women to families, workplaces, and the broader society (Miller, 1973). She revealed how necessary "unnecessary" people are.

Toward a New Psychology of Women

It was a friend of a teacher of her son Jon, Ann Bernays, who pushed Jean to take her thoughts about women and the psychology of women seriously. In February, 1975, Ann, a successful writer, who also was the granddaughter of Sigmund Freud, had been approached by Beacon Press to write a book on women. A novelist and busy with other work at the time, Ann interviewed Jean for the book and came to the conclusion that Jean, not she, was the person to write this book. She urged Jean, "You're the one who should write this book, not me." Jean protested, "I can't do it. I don't want to write a book. I can't do it." Mary Ann Lash, an editor at Beacon Press, provided encouragement. She suggested Jean take some already written papers and think about pulling them together into a book. Mary Ann said simply, "Try until the end of August and see what you can get done." At the end of the summer, Jean had written a book! *Toward a New Psychology of Women* (Miller, 1976) was launched.

The core ideas of the book were: cultural context and power dynamics exert a deep influence on women's lives; relationships are the central organizing feature of women's development; and forces of dominance and subordination shape the lives of those at the margin and those in positions of power in ways that undermine the full development of our human potential. Jean's model showed a deep appreciation of women's relational qualities and activities as strengths, not signs of weakness.

Though Jean's 1976 book was *Toward a New Psychology of Women*, her thinking was always fully infused with an appreciation of social and political forces in people's lives, and she soon came to see that traditional developmental theories did not accurately represent men's or women's life experiences. She explored power relationships at a time when most therapists still ignored issues of dominance or subordination and the impact of "power over" dynamics. Early on, Jean saw the power of connection in people's lives, but also saw the destructive consequences of systems marked by "power over" others. Jean was dedicated to not just a better understanding of women's lives, but she sought to bring about a deeper appreciation of the forces of marginalization for all people. She sought to expose the distorting effects of domination and subordination on individuals and on society.

Jean took what were presented in traditional theories as women's weaknesses and found the strength and life giving forces instead. She listened as her patients and colleagues spoke of the importance of their relationships (all relationships, not just romantic or maternal), of how they came alive in relationships, and grew and discovered their creativity and strength in relationships. She pointed to the ways in which these strengths are trivialized or disparaged. She noted that when we misunderstand and distort people's psychological development, we participate in their disempowerment. We pathologize that which deviates from the norm of the dominant, norm-setting group. Thus, in a society that valorizes independence and individual competitive achievement, those that are more open to their investment in and need of relationships are seen as weak and failing. At a societal level, those who do not "rise to the top" are seen as failures, lacking a work ethic, lazy, defective, and undeveloped.

Jean named the effect of the distribution of power on everyone: individual men and women, people of color, people in same sex relationships, groups of people at the margin of society, and also people who were at the center. Jean vigorously questioned the notion of a level playing field and of a meritocracy where goods are distributed in some equitable way. She knew the ways in which privilege (McIntosh, 1988) infused the feeling of success or failure, happiness or lack thereof. While admonishing all of us to listen to the voices of women (voices, not voice), she also encouraged us to pay attention to the dynamics of power, stratification, and the ways cultural assignations affected all of us. She noted the difference between temporary inequality where the goal is to end the inequality versus inequality that enforces ongoing and continued inequality.

In "power over" systems, one group is defined as inferior. Superiors label it as defective or substandard. Dominant groups define acceptable roles for the subordinate groups, and the subordinates are said to be unable to perform the preferred roles (Robb, 2007). Their supposed incapacity is ascribed to innate defect, and the stratification is seen as necessary.

Jean described a relational model of human development (which as later elaborated came to be known as Relational-Cultural Theory). She proposed that growth-fostering relationships are a central human necessity and that chronic disconnections are the source of psychological problems. Relational-Cultural Theory proposes that isolation is one of the most damaging human experiences which is best treated by reconnecting with other people. Therapists, therefore, should foster an atmosphere of empathy and acceptance for the patient, even at the cost of the therapist's neutrality.

The theory is based on clinical observations and sought to prove that there was nothing wrong with women, but rather that the way modern culture treated them was disempowering and misrepresented them. Jean saw strengths where others saw weakness. She did not try to "alter" women's weaknesses to resemble men's so called strengths. She asked "What do women bring to the culture?" and responded: they are the carriers of relationship. And, she felt her job was to name and describe the many ways that women participated in building relationships that carried and changed the culture (Robb, 2006, 2007).

Jean's work started with a firm commitment to telling the true stories of women. She felt that existing developmental and clinical theories misrepresented women in a way that pathologized and dismissed the importance of their contributions. As Jean noted in the forward to her revised 1986 edition, "The task, then is, to begin a description of women's strengths and to account for the reasons that they went unrecognized. Out of this can follow a new framework for understanding women ... and men" (Miller, 1986, p. x). Jean also wanted to strongly oppose the notion that women should become men or even become like men. She believed in creating new visions and wanted to show people why we needed new images and visions rather than imitations of old models. As Jean noted, "Our past models of all life have been distorted because they were created by only half the human species ... men" (Miller,

1986, p. xi). Women assumed they were deficient because they didn't fit old models. As Jean noted, also in the introduction to her 1986 edition of *Toward a New Psychology of Women*, advances for women have largely been for more advantaged groups of women. Jean pointed out that the women of the whole world are connected in an economic and political system that continues to force the poorest women of the world into worsening economic conditions (Robb, 2006).

She further noted that members of the dominant group discourage truth saying and confrontation coming from the subordinate group. Subordination by definition discourages open conflict. Any questioning of what is "normal" and how it is defined is threatening to the dominant group. Subordinates are pushed to concentrate on basic survival; self-initiated action is to be avoided. Subordinate groups then typically resort to disguised and indirect ways of acting and reacting as they are supposed to continue to accommodate and please the dominant group. Many women have participated in trying to change political, social, economic, and cultural conditions, but there are pervasive pressures to go along with existing gender ascriptions.

Jean also recognized early on that her voice and the early voices of women drawn to the work were limited by race, ethnicity, class, and sexual orientation. Early on, she listened to the critiques that this was a White, middle class, heterosexual model of women. And, Jean worked hard to open the work to the many voices of women. Early on, she invited more diversity into the theory group, and she specifically sought women of color and lesbians to contribute to the "Works in Progress" being fashioned at the Stone Center. Maureen Walker and Amy Banks joined the core theory group in the 1990s, and others also contributed on issues of race, class, and ethnicity.

Impact

Jean's book was an immediate success, and Jean became a nationally recognized leader in the psychology of women. She was recruited to many boards such as the Massachusetts Psychiatric Society's Committee on Women. She chaired the American Orthopsychiatry Association's first study group on women. She experienced a period of great creative productivity and professional recognition. She also received hundreds of letters from grateful women readers, thanking her for validating them in deep ways with her new theory about women.

At the same time, other's women's groups were coming into being, particularly in the Boston Area: the first published *Our Bodies Our Selves* in Boston Women's Health Collective (1971), Carol Gilligan and her colleagues at Harvard were looking at female adolescence and published *In a Different Voice* in 1982 (Gilligan, 1982); Judith Herman was establishing the field of trauma treatment (Herman, 1992), and Belenky, Clinchy, Goldberger, and

Tarule (1986) wrote *Women's Ways of Knowing*. Boston was a center for women's studies and feminist political activism.

Toward a New Psychology of Women (Miller, 1976) was a book that changed the lives of many women. Its very title captures a wealth of information about Jean. In framing it as "Toward" a new psychology of women, Jean stayed true to her deep and pervasive humility. She was not claiming this is *the* book on the psychology of women, but it was a statement of a developing understanding, open to learning, open to correction, and, most importantly, based on listening carefully to the stories women were telling. It provided a deeply validating and respectful message to women. They no longer had to be put in theory boxes constructed by and for men; these previously inaccurate representations of girls and women inevitably led to pathologizing women and portraying them as deficient men.

Jean's thinking has had a broad impact in the area of women's studies, psychotherapy, and an integration of psychological and sociological/social justice scholarship. Given the power of the ideas, we may ask when and why Jean had to be coaxed and persuaded to collect her thoughts into a book. This process could be presented as a sign of lack of self-confidence, or it could be viewed as demonstrating exactly what Jean believed: that our creativity, intelligence, and clarity emerge in relationship, not in splendid isolation (Robb, 2006).

Collaborative Feminist Theory Building

Jean's thinking was encouraged and supported by colleagues, notably her Stone Center theory group (Judith Jordan, Irene Stiver, and Janet Surrey). The ideas that came to be known as Relational-Cultural Theory (RCT), introduced in *Toward a New Psychology of Women* (Miller, 1976), were deepened and expanded in this collaborative group. In speaking with Chris Robb whose book *This Changes Everything* (Robb, 2006) documents the developmental trajectories of three groups of feminist writers all working in the Boston area in the late 1970s, Jean very deliberately and pointedly said to Chris, "You do know, don't you, Chris, that this changes everything." Jean was humble, but not afraid to name the power of the work of which she was so clearly at the center.

The collaborative group came into being when Jean moved to Boston and was looking for colleagues who were also interested in the psychology of women. Judith Jordan, Janet Surrey, and Sarah Greaves, who had been meeting to talk about women's issues, invited Jean in 1977 to join a study/support group with them. They were delighted and stunned when Jean agreed. The ongoing group was interested in re-thinking psychological theory in feminist ways, but had no clear agenda for developing a new theoretical model. Irene Stiver was also invited to this meeting and agreed to come once (and stayed for 30 years!). Sarah Greaves did not stay with the group as she was looking for something less theoretical. The group remained a collective entity for 35 years, meeting twice a month in Jean's living room in Brookline, MA. Rarely did anyone miss those meetings. They were sustaining, exciting, filled with laughter and serious inquiry. At times, there was tension, but the group always put "the work" first. There was an exceptional dedication to developing ideas and working together in a way that vitalized and honored our effort to better understand women and to help build a model of women's growth that was inclusive, accurate, and empowering.

In 1981, Miller became the first director of the Stone Center for Developmental Services and Studies at Wellesley College. She and her colleagues from the Monday night theory group established a colloquium series (which drew hundreds of people) and a working paper series in 1981; thus, the group had a forum for presenting their ideas. The working paper series was a success, stood outside academic journals, and became a kind of "written consciousness raising group" (Robb, 2006). This group honored Jean's foundational work and extended the thinking in many new and exciting directions. In 1991, Miller was the co-author, along with Judith Jordan, Alexandra Kaplan, Irene Stiver, and Janet Surrey, of another best-selling classic: *Women's Growth in Connection* (Jordan, Miller, Stiver, & Surrey, 1991).

When the working paper series was initiated at the Stone Center at Wellesley College, Jean insisted it be called "works in progress." She did not want to present this as the final word, imposed from above, but as an evolving, democratic, and inclusive model. This model was carried forward by the collaborative group, which was sometimes called the Monday night theory group or the Stone Center theory group. Initial members of the ongoing core theory group were Jean Baker Miller, Irene Stiver, Judith Jordan, and Janet Surrey. Although the body of work was captured as works in progress, the ideas were bold and there was nothing tentative about the papers.

As the Monday night theory group worked together, spinning ideas, and challenging long held and cherished shibboleths in the field of psychotherapy, Jean Baker Miller, the driving force in all of this, began to urge us to take our ideas seriously and to put them into print and present at local and larger national conferences. Starting in 1981, the group wrote and presented papers at the Stone Center Colloquium series. The topics were widespread: empathy and the mother–daughter relationship, power, race, mutuality, marginalization, feeling like a fraud, shame, and authenticity in therapy (see jbmti.org publications; Jordan, 1997, 2008, 2010; Jordan, Miller, Kaplan, Stiver, & Surrey, 1991; Jordan, Waler, & Hartling, 2004; Miller & Stiver, 1997; Walker & Miller, 2000; Walker & Rosen, 2004).

In 1981, after the group had been meeting for about three years, Jean suggested the ideas were big, important, and needed to be presented to an even wider public. Several of us did feel tentative and somewhat shy about claiming a public airing of the ideas, but Jean prevailed. In 1981, the group was signed on to present at the Orthopsychiatry conference in Toronto. This event brought out over 600 people and launched the group into increased public exposure. People sought us out as speakers, and publishers approached us to write books. As Director of the Stone Center, Jean took the opportunity to steer the thinking in the direction of collective as well as individual health and wellbeing. Collaborative conferences with Harvard Medical School (Learning from Women), which attracted groups of 500 to 2000 people, further spread the word of this new understanding of women's development. The Works in Progress, now 115 in number, were first published in 1982, and Jean's focus throughout the early 1980s was the Stone Center and elaboration of the work of the theory group. Jean enjoyed the sense of developing revolutionary theory with colleagues.

Jean's humility and conviction that the world had to change and that she was going to be a part of that change provided a compelling image of strength without arrogance and of speaking the hard truths about power and domination in a way that people could feel understood and validated rather than attacked (Robb, 2006). While there were some who did not embrace her ideas (usually those in the established power positions), they either ignored or misconstrued some of her early work. There were feminists among the detractors who worried that the work was too essentialist, that it was sending women back in to the jobs of taking care of the dominant group, or expending all their energy in trying to make non-mutual relationships "good enough." Nothing was farther from Jean's intentions. Jean was not a part of the movement to empower women to beat the men at their own game nor did she want to suggest that women were "essentially" relational and should dedicate themselves to taking care of the more privileged in the society. As Robb (2006) noted, she wanted to change the game. But, at times, this was misunderstood as surrendering power. With regard to the question of essentialism, all development is based on an intricate weaving of genetic and contextual. We now know that the division of nature and nurture does not even apply. The field of epigenetics has shown us that gene expression and gene development are ultimately subject to change from environmental factors.

Chris Robb, a Pulitzer award-winning reporter at the Boston Globe, was intrigued with the excitement this work was generating and, in 1988, wrote a lead article for the Boston Globe magazine section, which explored and celebrated this work. It was called *A Theory of Empathy: The Quiet Revolution in Psychiatry* (Robb, 1988). The article became an instant underground hit sent to people, mostly women, all over the country. Later, Chris was to write a book about the three women's groups in Boston who were changing the face of the psychology of women: *This Changes Everything: The Relational Revolution in Psychology* (Robb, 2006). And so, the group took on a public voice, raising more questions than they answered, but knowing that for the good of women, they had to persist (Robb, 2006; Jordan, 1997, 2008, 2010; Jordan et al., 1991; Jordan, Walker, & Hartling, 2004; Miller & Stiver, 1997).

Jean continued to work collaboratively with Judith Jordan, Irene Stiver, and Janet Surrey until the end of her life. Over time, these four became not just colleagues, but good friends. Alexandra Kaplan joined the group for several years, but was not one of the founding members, and her wonderful contributions were sadly cut short when she developed early-onset dementia.

Relational-Cultural Theory

The initial response to Relational-Cultural Theory was to ignore it. Next, it was decried as "dangerous," and finally, people at the center suggested, "We knew this all along." One of the clear messages of Jean's work has been the importance of having allies and of building groups of like-minded individuals to support the development of new ways of thinking and being. The message is we grow in relationships throughout the lifespan. Her work challenges the hyper-individualistic messages of the culture. We do not flourish by standing alone. As she pointed out in her "five good things," the outcomes of growth-fostering relationships are zest, clarity, worth, productivity, and seeking more connection. Jean embraced feminism in its broadest scope. She sought to improve the lot of all marginalized peoples: women, people of color, gays, and lesbians.

Relational-Cultural Theory (RCT), based on Jean's core contributions, was expanded in the theory group. It does not pretend to be value-free and is based on a set of values that are not the dominant values of this culture. RCT posits that we grow through and toward relationships from infancy to old age. We believe people need to give to as well as receive from others and we all want to participate in growth fostering relationships. In their daily lives, women developed psychological qualities that were valuable for the larger society, but went unrecognized. The world sorely needs these strengths, but women have not been encouraged to see their skills in relationships and their concern about others' wellbeing as strengths.

Jean was dedicated to uncovering the false ideas about all marginalized groups. Jean challenged the tendency of the dominant group to name normative categories and experiences. She wanted to transform some of the core ideas in western psychology that celebrated separation, competition, and success defined as being more autonomous and self-interested. Her ideas were resisted and denigrated. These ideas are only now being embraced due to the abundant data from the world of neuroscience which supports the assertion that we are relational beings and that individuals and collectives flourish in growth-fostering relationships, not in splendid isolation.

Neuroscience: Supportive Data

In the last decade, modern neuroscience has been validating each and every tenet of Relational-Cultural Theory (developed over 35 years ago when brain science had little to say about relationships). We are hard wired to connect. Mirror neurons ensure interpersonal resonance that is not fully under our conscious control. While the work of mirror neurons may not exactly represent what we call mutual empathy, it provides a basis for resonance and responsiveness (a complicated matter that we are only beginning to map). We know that the pain of social exclusion moves along the exact same pathways to the same place in the brain [Anterior cingulate cortex (ACC)] as the pain from physical injury. Being connected with others is so core to our survival and wellbeing that evolution has selected the identical pathways to carry messages of social exclusion and physical pain to the same place in the brain. Being included and connecting is as important to our survival as oxygen and water (Banks, 2015; Lieberman, 2013). Relationships are not an add-on, a luxury, for human beings. They are central to our lives; they are essential to life.

Recently, some of our most respected thinkers have weighed in on the importance of connection and empathy, not just for personal wellbeing, but for the very survival of the planet. Einstein (1972) talked about the delusion of separateness and pointed to the essential ways in which we are connected. In a recent interview, Stephen Hawking (2014) noted that empathy is perhaps the one force that can save us all ... and save the future of our planet. At a recent Harvard graduation, Rowling (2008) spoke about the transformative force of empathy, and the Dalai Lama (1995) has addressed the reality of our basic connectedness and interdependence in many of his presentations and writings. The power of connection and the importance of empathy is embraced by more and more people. Many recognize the urgent need for more attention to creating increased empathic responsiveness at the individual and collective level.

Jean Baker Miller Training Institute

In 1995, the Jean Baker Miller Training Institute was established in Jean's honor at the Wellesley Centers for Women. It is an organization that seeks to promote social change by expanding definitions and societal norms of personal strength, human health, and cultural wellbeing. Jean served as its Founding Director and used the institute to teach the theory of Relational-Cultural Theory to mental health professionals, educators, parents, social policy makers, nonprofit organizers, and others.

At the dedication of the Jean Baker Miller Training Institute in 1995, Jean was described as a visionary pragmatist, a living legend, a revolutionary, and a singularly powerful force (Miller, 1995). She noted on this occasion, "Our only hope as human beings, but also our marvelous ability, is our capacity to form growth-fostering relationships with each other. We must learn more about how to do this and how to enlarge and strengthen this ability" (Robb,

2007, p.61). She also observed, "Growth requires engagement with difference and with people embodying that difference" (Robb, 2007, p.61).

Jean noted, "While it is obvious that all of living and all of development takes place only within relationships, our theories of development seem to rest at bottom on a notion of development as a process of separation from others. I believe this notion stems from an illusion, a fiction which men, but not women, are encouraged to pursue. In general, women have been assigned to the realms of life concerned with building relationships, especially relationships that foster development" (Miller's remarks at JBMTI dedication, 1995 from Miller, 1986, p. xxi). Jean added, "Humanity has been held to a limited and distorted view of itself—from its interpretation of the most intimate of personal emotions to its grandest vision of human possibilities—precisely by virtue of its subordination of women."

In her latter years, Jean suffered from worsening emphysema and complications of post-polio syndrome. By 1994, her breathing was markedly impaired, curtailing speaking engagements and professional meetings. Jean's interest in women's wellbeing was passionate and deep. She was a proud feminist, and she continued working on these ideas up until the day before she died. On July 29, 2006, Jean died in her home in Brookline, MA. The work, however, still goes forth. *Toward a New Psychology of Women* (Miller, 1976) has been cited in over 7000 articles, has sold over 200,000 copies, is translated into 20 languages, and published in 12 countries. There are 115 "Works in Progress" and over 20 books written by members of the Jean Baker Miller Training Institute faculty (JBMTI.org). Over 30,000 people have participated in Relational-Cultural trainings all over the world. Jean's vision of growth in connection for both women and men has taken hold and has gained support from many different disciplines.

Jean helped create a new vision of womanhood and of mutuality in human relationships. And, she had the perspicacity to see that this new vision does indeed "change everything."

References

Banks, A. (2015). *Four ways to click: Rewire your brain for stronger, more rewarding relationships.* New York: Penguin.

Belenky, M., Clinchy, B., Goldberger, N., & Tarule, J. (1986). *Women's ways of knowing.* New York: Basic Books.

Boston Women's Health Collective. (1971). *Our bodies, ourselves.* Boston: Simon and Schuster.

Cohn, L. M. (1997). The life story of Jean Baker Miller: Toward an understanding of women's lifespan development. A dissertation submitted to the Wright Institute Graduate School of Psychology.

Dalai Lama. (1995). *The power of compassion.* New York: Harper Collins.

Einstein, A. (1972, November 28). Letter to Robert Marcus, written February 12, 1950. *The New York Times.*

Friedan, B. (1963). *The feminine mystique*. New York: Dell Publishing.

Gilligan, C. (1982). *In a different voice*. Cambridge, MA: Harvard University Press.

Hawking, S. (2014). Remarks at the United Kingdom Premiere of 'The Theory of Everything. Dec. 9, 2014.

Herman, J. (1992). *Trauma and recovery*. New York: Basic Books.

Jordan, J. V. (Ed.). (1997). *Women's growth in diversity*. New York: Guilford Press.

Jordan, J. V. (Ed.). (2008). *The power of connection*. Philadelphia, PA: Haworth Press.

Jordan, J. V. (2010). *Relational-Cultural Therapy*. Washington, DC: American Psychological Association.

Jordan, J. V., Miller, J. B., Kaplan, A. G., Stiver, I. P., & Surrey, J. L. (1991). *Women's growth in connection: Writings from the Stone Center*. New York: Guilford Press.

Jordan, J. V., Walker, M., & Hartling, L. (Eds.). (2004). *The complexity of connection*. New York: Guilford Press.

Lieberman, M. (2013). *Social: Why our brains are wired to connect*. New York: Crown Publishers.

Lynd, H. (1958). *On shame and the search for identity*. New York: Wiley.

Lynd, H., & Lynd, R. (1929). *Middletown: A study in contemporary American culture*. New York: Harcourt Brace.

McIntosh, M. (1988). *White privilege and male privilege: A personal account of coming to see correspondences through work in women's studies* (Report No 189). Wellesley, MA: Wellesley Center for Women.

Miller, J. B. (1971). On women: New political directions for women. *Journal of Social Policy*, 2, 32–45.

Miller, J. B. (Ed.) (1973). *Psychoanalysis and women: Contributions to new theory and therapy*. New York: Brunner Mazel.

Miller, J. B. (1976). *Toward a new psychology of women*. Boston: Beacon Press.

Miller, J. B. (1986). *Toward a new psychology of women* (2nd ed.). Boston: Beacon Press.

Miller, J. B. (1995). Remarks at the dedication of the Jean Baker Miller Institute. Boston, MA.

Miller, J. B., & Stiver, I. P. (1997). *The healing connection; How women form relationships in therapy and in life*. Boston: Beacon Press.

Miller, J. B., & Welch, A. S. (1995). Learning from women. *Women & Therapy*, *17*(3/4), 335–346.

Robb, C. (1988, October). *A theory of empathy: The quiet revolution in psychiatry* (pp. 19–34). Boston: Globe Magazine, XX.

Robb, C. (2006). *This change everything: The relational revolution in psychology*. New York: Farrar, Strauss, and Giroux. [hardback]

Robb, C. (2007). *This changes everything: The relational revolution in psychology*. New York: Picador.

Rowling, J. K. (2008, June). *Commencement address*. Cambridge, MA: Harvard University Archives.

Walker, M., & Miller, J. (2000). *Racial images and relational possibilities* (Talking Paper No. 2). Wellesley College: Stone Center Working Paper Series.

Walker, M., & Rosen, W. (Eds.) (2004). *How connections heal: Stories from Relational Cultural Therapy*. New York: Guilford Press.

Feminist Pioneer: Annette Brodsky Paving the Way

Claudia Porras Pyland and Debra Mollen

ABSTRACT
Even when the culture imposed stringent limitations on women's roles, Dr. Annette Brodsky refused to succumb to these restrictions. As one of only a few women in her graduate school cohort, she broke new ground during her pre-doctoral internship, her post-internship military placement, and in her faculty position at the University of Alabama. Her renowned work advocating for and studying the effect of consciousness-raising groups engendered critical scholarship that revealed the harm of therapists' sexual abuse and facilitated improved ethics and guidelines for psychologists in their work with clients. Dr. Brodsky has served as a pioneering feminist psychologist for several generations of women.

During a time when the social standard defined women's roles as centering on being good wives and raising children, Dr. Annette Brodsky challenged the status quo. Although she faced challenges along her path, she persevered in her efforts to advance the status of women in the United States. She humbly recounted her story during an interview with us, an early and a mid-career psychologist, respectively, during which it became clear that she faced frequent trials as she became one of few women at her university at the time to pursue a graduate education in psychology, breaking what seemed like impermeable disciplinary boundaries, eventually ascending the ranks of academia (A. Brodsky, personal communication, July 15, 2015). She became a role model for women within psychology and academic circles. She faced obstacles and has made a widespread, meaningful difference for those who followed after her. In the ensuing sections, we highlight Dr. Brodsky's path to becoming a feminist psychologist, her groundbreaking work, and her hopes and dreams for future generations of women. In short, our aim is to offer a glimpse to readers of this special issue of *Women and Therapy* of one of the significant pioneering feminist psychologists to whom we feel a debt of gratitude.

The Start of Her Journey

Annette Brodsky was born in Chicago, Illinois, in 1938 to Sadie Axelrod Ratner and Morris Nathan Ratner. Dr. Brodsky's life and subsequent career started with music, a career similar to the one her mother, a concert pianist, had pursued. The median years of education in the late 1930s and early 1940s was about 8.7 years (U.S. Department of Education, Office of Educational Research and Improvement, 1993), so with a high school diploma and her accomplishments as a musician, Mrs. Ratner was considered a well-educated and successful woman. Aside from her musical talent, Mrs. Ratner was not unlike average women in the 1940s as she spent a significant portion of her time at home caring for her family, Dr. Brodsky and her siblings, an older brother and twin sister. Mr. Ratner dropped out of high school in the 10th grade to become a salesman. In 1948, when Dr. Brodsky was 10 years old, her father survived a major heart attack. During that time, there was limited treatment for patients who had had heart attacks, and most either did not survive or lived with complications. Mr. Ratner was one of the first patients prescribed anticoagulants, a treatment just beginning to gain popularity at that time (Marks, 1997). Dr. Brodsky described her father as a "guinea pig" for his use of anticoagulants, as they were still testing its effectiveness in the treatment of heart attack survivors. Further, it was recommended that they move to a warmer climate because the cold Chicago weather put too much strain on his heart, particularly given that he spent the majority of his time outside as a door-to-door salesman. Dr. Brodsky and her family moved to Coral Gables, Florida, in pursuit of a warmer climate. The move required that Mrs. Ratner quit her career as a concert pianist, and once in Florida, she became a private piano teacher and housewife. Dr. Brodsky recalled that Mrs. Ratner did not drive and had to take the bus to each of her students' homes. Dr. Brodsky's father died 12 years later.

Early Steps in Her Academic Pursuits

Initially, Dr. Brodsky followed in her mother's footsteps by becoming a musician; she earned a college scholarship to play the French horn at the University of Miami (UM) and performed with the Miami Symphony from 1956 to 1960. In our interview with her, she noted that acceptable and available work for women at the time included either being a teacher or a secretary. In order to prepare for her future career in secretarial work, she took courses in typing and shorthand. Her left-handedness compromised her ability to master shorthand, a factor that compelled her to pursue a different vocational path. She recalled being taught to sweep her hand across the paper as she wrote, a technique meant to increase her writing speed. Because she was left-handed, however, the technique proved ineffectual as her arm covered what she wrote. She also rehearsed 3 hours a day with the Miami Symphony, which prevented her from attending a required meeting with her professor. Subsequently, she failed the class.

Disheartened by her failed attempt at shorthand, she realized she could not be a secretary. After researching what her career path would entail as a French horn player, she learned that she would need to tour the country with the orchestra. She learned that becoming a brass instrument player in a symphony would mean spending time around some of her contemporaries who drank alcohol, even in rehearsals. Still influenced by gendered stereotypes, she recalled thinking, "This isn't right for a woman! This is not what we're supposed to be doing!" (A. Brodsky, personal communication, July 15, 2015). She found that she had been excelling in her psychology course and found it interesting. With the encouragement of her female classmates, she applied to two doctoral programs in psychology at UM and the University of Florida (UF). She gained acceptance at both and decided to attend UF. As a first-generation college student, she was unaware that she would be expected to decline the offer at UM so she began her studies without doing so. It was not until an old classmate at UM informed her that they had reserved a spot for her in the program and had been waiting for her that she realized her mistake.

Significant Forces in Her Path to Becoming a Feminist

Dr. Brodsky married while she was a graduate student. When returning to class, she was greeted with surprise from her peers at her perseverance in completing her degree, as it was commonplace that married women left behind their education and employment to stay at home to raise their children. Dr. Brodsky was one of three women in her graduate cohort which she recalled made her wonder, "Where are all the women? Why aren't they here?" (A. Brodsky, personal communication, July 15, 2015). Graduate school was the first of many settings throughout her career in which she was a minority among men. The stark underrepresentation of women, coupled with comments made by other students related to her continued presence at the university after marrying, first sparked her interest in women's issues. Her peers' unquestioned assumptions and the reminder of the sad reality that women at the time often sacrificed their career dreams to fulfill their roles as wives and mothers only served to confirm her need to continue in her academic pursuits. Although there were no permanent female faculty members in her department, she had a female supervisor, a well-respected psychiatrist and adjunct professor in the department, who served as her mentor during the latter portion of her graduate studies. It was partly due to this relationship that she chose to pursue a doctorate in clinical psychology and continue her path in academia.

Given the country's state of affairs in the early 1960s, male psychologists were in high demand at military hospitals, and Dr. Brodsky's husband was among the psychology doctoral candidates recruited for a pre-doctoral internship position at The Walter Reed Army Hospital in Bethesda, Maryland. Although a great opportunity for her husband, Dr. Brodsky also needed to complete her internship. It was, however, unprecedented to have a female psychology intern in the program. After attaining special permission from the Surgeon General, Dr. Brodsky became the first female psychology intern to train at The Walter Reed Army Hospital in 1963. She earned her place among the male army officers.

A mandatory component of the Army Psychology Program was a commitment to a 3-year tour of duty following successful completion of the internship year. Since the Brodsky couple had been promised assignment to the same site for the payback tour of duty, only a few sites needing two psychologists were available. The U.S. Disciplinary Barracks at Fort Leavenworth was available, although it had not had any women employed there in any capacity since 1943, which had been the result of a temporary exception due to a shortage of nurses during World War II. After initially being informed by the commandant at the time that they did not hire women, the Surgeon General informed them that if they did not hire Dr. Brodsky along with her husband, they could not hire either. They changed their minds, and Dr. Brodsky became the first female psychologist employed at the Barracks. Special rules were implemented, presumably to ensure her safety, such as needing to be escorted by a male officer any time she crossed the prison yard. Her tour of duty was terminated prematurely, 5 months after notifying them that she was pregnant. Her uniform consisted of a short skirt and heels, and during the final weeks of her tour of duty, she was compelled to wear an army raincoat over her uniform, which eventually became too small for her growing body. She and her family remained in Fort Leavenworth until Dr. Brodsky's husband completed his tour of duty, and their second child was born.

Mentorship and Involvement in the Community

From 1967 to 1972, Dr. Brodsky worked part-time at the counseling center at the University of Southern Illinois-Carbondale (SIU). There, she and two other women developed one of the first Women's Studies programs. Five female faculty members organized a group called Women for Academic Equality (WAE). WAE offered a space for women to share their concerns regarding their employment. The group quickly established a substantial presence at the university. She recalled that on one occasion, representatives from the Department of Health, Education, and Welfare (HEW) were scheduled to visit a professor who had experienced sex discrimination so WAE invited all female faculty members to attend a meeting to voice their complaints to HEW representatives. The number of women addressing their grievances to HEW was so extensive that she recalled, "the school and everyone in the newspapers thought that we were this huge group and there were five of us!" (A. Brodsky, personal communication, July 15, 2015).

When SIU did not express interest in hiring Dr. Brodsky for a full-time position after she completed her doctoral degree in 1970, she and her husband relocated to the University of Alabama in Tuscaloosa two years later. She recounted,

> In Alabama ... they recruited me; they took me seriously as well as my husband. In Southern Illinois, I was somebody's wife; I had a part-time job at the counseling center, a little bit of this and that. I was an afterthought but in Alabama, they really took me seriously. I was in a tenure-track position. In fact, I was the first woman to get tenure in the Psychology Department. (A. Brodsky, personal communication, July 15, 2015)

In the early 1970s, while a faculty member in Alabama, she attended her first Association for Women in Psychology (AWP) meeting and developed a national roster of feminist therapists that permitted therapists to list themselves accordingly with AWP.

Her Family's Response to Her Work

Although accomplished herself, Dr. Brodsky's mother had concerns about her daughter's career choices, particularly her pre-doctoral internship in the military and subsequent tour of duty at an all-male prison, as well as her evocative scholarship on sensitive topics (e.g., sexual misconduct in therapy). Aside from practical fears for her safety, Mrs. Ratner did not understand Dr. Brodsky's drive to pursue such research topics. Dr. Brodsky recalled, "When I said, I'm going to graduate school, she said, 'No, you can't do that! Nobody will marry you!'" She added,

> Mother was embarrassed by my activism in the women's movement, but did not try to persuade me. When she visited, she wanted to know what I cooked, not what I wrote or did on the job. When I published my books, I would give a copy to my sister, my cousins ... but my mother did not want any book in her house that said 'sex.' (A. Brodsky, personal communication, July 15, 2015)

Although her mother never approved of what she did, she also never tried to stop her. Her research and career pursuits soon became topics that were simply not discussed. Her siblings, who pursued different professions from hers, were not very involved with what she was doing.

Major Contributions: Scholarship

Female Offenders—A Voice for the Silenced

Dr. Brodsky's military prison experience represented the cornerstone of her work with female offenders. The Department of Psychology at the University of Alabama had a corrections program for which she developed a conference for women in prisons, and in Brodsky's (1974a, 1974b), Dr. Brodsky published an edited volume of the conference proceedings regarding the unique needs of female offenders and made recommendations for rehabilitation and reintegration into the community. She advocated for more community involvement, opportunities to incorporate family in the treatment process, and the need to decriminalize non-victim-involved offenses. She also advised that female offenders should receive vocational counseling prior to their release to ease reintegration and decrease recidivism.

Women in Academia

Concerned about women's experiences in pursuing advanced degrees, she surveyed the experiences of 73 female and 77 male PhD students across the southeastern United States. While the mean ages for women (25.3 years) and men (26.4 years) in her sample were similar, significantly more men than women were married, 65% and 42%, respectively. Further, while 9% of female graduate students had children, twice as many male graduate students had children. Dr. Brodsky believed these findings, comparable to the national rate, provided support that women who married and had children were less likely to attend graduate school than those who delayed marriage and children (Brodsky, 1974c). Further, women reported more discrimination perpetrated by faculty than their male peers, were less likely to be in prestigious student positions, and were less likely to have administrative aspirations compared to men (Brodsky, 1974c). Paradoxically, the women she surveyed simultaneously felt secure, but perceived discrimination. Perhaps they did not think to view routine experiences of discrimination as evidence that they were not equally valued at the university. Of note, Dr. Brodsky's (1974c) study parallels much of the current research on microaggressions.

Therapy with Women

Dr. Brodsky (1976) recognized the challenges she faced when providing counseling to women as a graduate student in the early 1960s. She recalled a conversation with a student 15 years prior in which the student, a bright woman, vacillated between two possible career options. On the one hand, the student could continue in biology, a topic she found exciting, or she could be an elementary school teacher, a more viable option given her obligations at home coupled with vocational limitations imposed on women during that time. She ultimately decided on the less appealing career route in education, not wanting to sacrifice her future personal life. Dr. Brodsky expressed regret about the way she handled the conversation then, sadly acknowledging that she understood the implications of the student's ultimate decision (Brodsky, 1976). If given the opportunity to correct the experience, she would have encouraged the student not to be so quick to dismiss her true vocational interests for the sake of convenience. She recognized that although there was much further to go regarding equality for women, there were likewise growing opportunities for women in the 1970s. Dr. Brodsky acknowledged the increasing role options for women who were less dependent on being a wife and mother, and she urged that these considerations be made when providing therapy to women. With the right support and tools, women could pursue multiple meaningful vocational, academic, and personal roles that may or may not include being a mother.

Major Contributions: Empowerment and Advocacy

Seeking the Holy Grail

As a graduate student, Dr. Brodsky faced her own doubts related to choosing her career over the socially-constructed schema of women's roles, which at the time centered on being good wives and raising children. While progressing through her own acculturative process, Dr. Brodsky counseled other women with similar doubts. Given the scarcity of women in academia at the time, Dr. Brodsky had limited guidance by female role models. It is understandable, therefore, that she would not know how to address female students' concerns related to choosing careers. Years later, more confidently situated with her own personal and professional successes, she was able to witness firsthand the possibilities of being successful in her career and having a family. She understood the needs of women and recognized the benefits of broadening society's representations of women's roles (Brodsky, 1976).

She advocated for employing Feminist Therapy when providing vocational counseling to women because such a model would create a space for women to explore a broad range of career options without minimizing the desire to pursue traditional roles (Brodsky, 1976). She added that outcome research of new models of Feminist Therapy with women was necessary. She was hopeful that positive change would continue as so much progress had already been made (Brodsky, 1976, 1980). Keeping in mind the advancement of women set in motion by the women's movement, she advised that it was becoming less imperative for women to sacrifice their career aspirations to raise a family. She urged therapists to consider the changing environment and the increasing opportunities for advancement when offering vocational guidance to women so as not to limit them from attaining realistic goals. For women who chose to have children, diverse identities could serve as a buffer for parenting related stressors and the possible sense of loss when children moved out of the home. Summarily, she advised therapists to consider that women who completed childrearing at a young age without establishing their careers first were at greater risk of experiencing depression as they were often left without a sense of purpose or often mourned the loss of a life they could have had had they pursued their career aspirations.

Conversely, she detailed the dangers of portraying mothers as perfect homemakers with an innate desire for and knowledge about childrearing (Brodsky, 1976, 1980). She wrote,

> Until mothers feel that they have a legitimate right to privacy, their own friends, time off, and the expression of anger, we are going to see a continuation of the current trend of the most productive, intelligent, stereotype-free, professional women not choosing to have children. (p. 58)

Nevertheless, Dr. Brodsky was not naïve to the risks of diverging from stereotyped roles, and she warned therapists that their work could not stop at helping women gain confidence and assertiveness. Therapists needed to take the next step of helping women overcome added stressors generated from challenging social constructs and defining newfound identities. She emphasized that women should be aware of the impact their increased assertiveness and divergence from stereotyped roles would have on their social sphere, including their families and career.

Regarding her own experience, Dr. Brodsky reported few difficulties related to being a full-time tenured faculty in the Psychology Department at the University of Alabama, in part because those in her department were very supportive of her and appreciated her input. She added that it helped that the Psychology Department was open to feminist ideas and chaired by Ray Fowler, who later became APA's Executive Director. However, she recalled instances when people were critical about her not being at home with her children. She detailed an encounter with a couple of women at a cocktail party who asked her husband with incredulity, "Oh, so she's a full-time professor here? Well, what do you do with your children when you're at work?" to which her husband replied in jest, "Oh, we just lock them in the closet" (A. Brodsky, personal communication, July 15, 2015). She described difficulties finding babysitters, adding that one of her babysitters expected her to go home for any minor incident that arose. When Dr. Brodsky did not come home, her babysitter responded with anger, criticizing her for not being home with her children. Dr. Brodsky indicated that managing childcare was one of the harder aspects of her multiple roles. She recalled that creativity was often essential for arranging childcare and described organizing a co-op with other mothers at SIU, which enabled them to sign up when they were in need of childcare, and each took turns babysitting for one another. She added that it helped to have other female colleagues with children. She stated that she did not have an active social life for some time, as academic work and raising her children were consuming. She affirmed that balancing work and a personal life became easier once her children were school-aged.

Consciousness-Raising Groups

One of Dr. Brodsky's major contributions to feminism was her research that advocated for consciousness-raising (C-R) groups as a model for therapy. C-R groups provided women a space to offer one another support, share experiences, and gain courage and skills to deviate from their expected traditional roles. C-R groups created spaces for a rare kind of invaluable sisterhood, reflecting the feminist philosophy that *the personal is political.* Dr. Brodsky's research cited early works from Mischel, Epstein, and Amundsen that discredited the commonly-held beliefs that perpetuated traditional gender roles (Brodsky, 1973). She understood well the dangers of unquestionably maintaining rigid gender roles and knew from first-hand experience the obstacles women faced when they chose to challenge stereotypical roles. Dr. Brodsky wrote poignantly, "The battle is a lonely one for those who can overcome the initial fears of loss of femininity, social disapproval and disdain from men and women alike for daring to compete in the male domain" (1973, p. 25). Dr. Brodsky believed C-R groups provided an opportunity to put into action feminist therapy concepts sparked by the Women's Movement. Her research on C-R groups helped transform therapy with women. She highlighted the implications on the treatment of identity problems of women and based her recommendations to therapists on data gathered from these groups. In her recommendations, she highlighted the need for therapists to consider a wider range of roles and personality traits when determining healthy functioning in women, and she urged therapists to view their female clients within the context of their social structures, keeping in mind the limited control they may have on their environment. She cautioned therapists to avoid imposing gendered beliefs that conceived of and maintained women in inferior positions or threatened their sense of identity, independence, and healthy expressions of anger (Brodsky, 1973).

Dr. Brodsky further advocated for psychologists to be involved in the discussions about theoretical models that contained biased or sexist conceptualizations of women (e.g., Freud's work regarding the development of women and Erikson's [1964] inner space theory) (Brodsky, 1975). She argued that these works were anecdotal and stemmed from sexist views. She also questioned the validity of studies that included only male participants yet generalized findings to women. Unless researchers became aware of their own biases and considered the implications of failing to include women in research, Dr. Brodsky expected the widespread biases towards women would continue. To ensure that such biases were addressed in future research, Dr. Brodsky proposed that psychologists, particularly feminist psychologists, be included in interdisciplinary team discussions regarding women's studies.

Sexual Misconduct in Therapy

A meaningful outcome of her work with C-R groups was Dr. Brodsky's accomplishments related to the sexual exploitation of clients, most often women, in therapy. Women from the C-R groups and clients from the SIU counseling center shared stories detailing sexual interactions with former therapists. Sexual misconduct and sex role bias in therapy were topics rarely discussed prior to the 1970s. However, by the early 1980s, Dr. Brodsky had already become an influential voice on the topic and was a leader in raising awareness regarding unethical practices in therapy with women (Freedman & Weiner, 2003). She published several works on the topic and was later asked to testify as an expert witness in formal legal cases against therapists charged with sexually abusing their clients (Bates & Brodsky, 1989; Bouhoutsos & Brodsky, 1985; Brodsky & Hare-Mustin, 1980; Holroyd & Brodsky, 1977, 1980).

In 1975, the American Psychological Association (APA) created the Task Force on Sex Bias and Sex-Role Stereotyping in Psychotherapeutic Practice, which she co-chaired along with Jean Holroyd. Their work on the task force resulted in the creation of guidelines for the provision of nonsexist therapy (Freedman & Weiner, 2003). During Dr. Brodsky's year as President of Division 35 (Psychology of Women) of the APA, the APA, in conjunction with the National Institutes of Mental Health (NIMH), organized a conference aimed at identifying areas of focus for clinical research with women. Based on that conference, Brodsky and Hare-Mustin (1980) subsequently published *Women and Psychotherapy: An Assessment of Research and Practice*, which was an edited volume grounded in data gathered from participants at the conference. The book was considered "a core text in the area of women and psychotherapy" (Freedman & Weiner, 2003, p. 258), and it propelled events that led to APAs amendment of its ethical codes, which included explicit prohibition of sexual contact between therapist and client (Freedman & Weiner, 2003). Other disciplines would soon follow (Bouhoutsos & Brodsky, 1985).

Shortly after the development of APA's Task Force on Sex Bias and Sex-Role Stereotyping in Psychotherapeutic Practice, Holroyd and Brodsky (1977) conducted a nationwide survey ($n = 666$) and found that a majority of psychologists believed that erotic contact ("that which is primarily intended to arouse or satisfy sexual desire" [p. 843]) between therapists and clients would never be useful for therapeutic purposes and therefore should not be used. However, about 10% of male and 1.9% of female psychologists acknowledged engaging in erotic practices or contact with clients. Additionally, 5.5% of male and .6% of female therapists admitted to engaging in sexual intercourse with their clients. Their findings highlighted the need for clear restrictions related to sexual contact with clients and guidelines for addressing violations. In the ensuing decade, she detailed the dangerous ramifications of sexual contact between a therapist and a client (Bates & Brodsky, 1989) and made a very clear distinction between ethical and non-ethical behaviors, thereby facilitating the identification of clear criteria for ethical violations (Bouhoutsos & Brodsky, 1985). She ameliorated confusion regarding what was considered a therapeutic relationship, where the responsibility rested when sexual contact occurs in the therapeutic relationship, what made a relationship sexual, and how the topic should be addressed if sexual contact occurred.

Recognitions

Dr. Brodsky has been recognized for her efforts toward improving the field of psychology through her activism, therapy, and research. In 1989, she and Gerald P. Koocher were the first recipients of the Jack D. Krasner Memorial Award, now known as APF/Division 29 Early Career Award. The award is given to early career psychologists who demonstrate exceptional promise in the field of psychotherapy (The Society for the Advancement of Psychotherapy, 2015). In 1993, she won the Distinguished Leadership Award for her pioneering work on sexual misconduct in therapy and her training model designed to teach psychologists about gender bias, thereby reducing its prevalence and negative impact on the therapeutic relationship (American Psychological Association [APA], 2015a). A few years later, in 1999, the Association of Psychologists in Academic Centers presented her with a Researcher Award for her exceptional scholarship in the field (Association of Psychologists in Academic Health Centers, 2015). Further, royalties for her co-authored book *Women and Psychotherapy: An Assessment of Research and Practice* now fund the Psychotherapy with Women Award, presented by Division 35 of the American Psychological Association (APA, 2015b).

In 1980, Dr. Brodsky became Chief Psychologist and Director of Training at Harbor-UCLA Medical Center, where she spent the last 23 years of her career training post-doctoral fellows in the Department of Psychiatry. She retired in 2004 and noted that many of her former students are now leading programs in hospitals, mental health settings, and prisons.

Hopes for the Future

As we reached the end of our interview with Dr. Brodsky, we were reminded of one of Dr. Brodsky's earlier works in which she asked students in a Women's Studies group what they thought was going to happen to the Women's Movement by 1980 (Brodsky, 1975). She found that students tended to be optimistic, and we were curious as to how she felt regarding the progress made by the Women's Movement since she wrote the article 40 years ago. She responded:

> I've been thinking about that lately—feminists keep forging ahead and then going back again. Some of the issues are exactly the same—abortion issues, quotas ... I don't think we're ever going to finish. A lot of groups have joined our protests

for related issues ... The Women's Movement stretched out over the years, after we were able to get things going. Issues arise and then they recede. The backlashes are going to keep coming. So it's not a matter of 'we did it.' There's no finished product anywhere ... The vigilance has to be there ... The women's issues will always be there. (A. Brodsky, personal communication, July 15, 2015)

Dr. Brodsky closed by expressing hopefulness that we will continue to raise the glass ceiling. She added that she is excited to see more women in prestigious positions. To end the interview, she left us with a thought to ponder, "As long as women are the primary caretakers of children, I think it will always be an avenue for some men to insist on the dominant role in the nuclear family. Maybe the final frontier is equality of housework" (A. Brodsky, personal communication, July 15, 2015).

References

American Psychological Association. (2015a). *Committee on women in psychology leadership award citations 2014*. Retrieved from http://www.apa.org/pi/women/committee/leadership-award-recipients.aspx

American Psychological Association. (2015b). *Division 35: Society for the psychology of women*. Retrieved from http://www.apadivisions.org/division-35/awards/psychotherapy.aspx

Association of Psychologists in Academic Health Centers. (2015). *APAHC awards*. Retrieved from http://www.div12.org/section8/APAHCAward.html

Bates, C. M., & Brodsky, A. M. (1989). *Sex in the therapy hour: A case of professional incest*. New York: Guilford Press.

Bouhoutsos, J. C., & Brodsky, A. M. (1985). Mediation in therapist-client sex: A model. *Psychotherapy, 22*, 189–193. doi:10.1037/h0085493

Brodsky, A. M. (1973). The consciousness-raising group as a model for therapy with women. *Psychotherapy: Theory, Research, and Practice, 10*, 24–29. doi:10.1037/h0087537

Brodsky, A. M. (1974a). Planning for the female offender? *Criminal Justice and Behavior, 1*, 392–400. doi:10.1177/009385487400100412

Brodsky, A. M. (1974b). *The female offender*. Beverly Hills, CA: Sage Publications.

Brodsky, A. M. (1974c). Women as graduate students. *American Psychologist, 1*, 523–526. doi:10.1037/h0036903

Brodsky, A. M. (1975). The psychologists' role in women's studies. *Teaching of Psychology, 2*, 69–72. doi:10.1207/s15328023top0202_5

Brodsky, A. M. (1976). Seeking the holy grail or the status of women in counseling. *The Counseling Psychologist, 6*, 56–58. doi:10.1177/001100007600600215

Brodsky, A. M. (1980). A decade of feminist influence on psychotherapy. *Psychology of Women Quarterly, 4*, 331–344. doi:10.1111/j.1471-6402.1980.tb01108.x

Brodsky, A. M., & Hare-Mustin, R. T. (1980). *Women and psychotherapy: An assessment of research and practice*. New York: Guilford Press.

Freedman, D. K., & Weiner, I. B. (Eds.). (2003). *Handbook of psychology: History of psychology* (Vol. 1). Hoboken, NJ: Wiley & Sons.

Holroyd, J. C., & Brodsky, A. M. (1977). Psychologists' attitudes and practices regarding erotic and nonerotic physical contact with patients. *American Psychologist, 32*, 843–849. doi:10.1037/0003-066X.32.10.843

Holroyd, J. C., & Brodsky, A. M. (1980). Does touching lead to sexual intercourse? *Professional Psychology, 11*, 807–811. doi:10.1037/0735-7028.11.5.807

Marks, H. M. (1997). *The progress of experiment: Science and therapeutic reform in the United States, 1900–1990*. New York: Cambridge University Press.

The Society for the Advancement of Psychotherapy. (2015). *Early career recipient.* Retrieved from http://societyforpsychotherapy.org/members/awards/early-career-award/.

U.S. Department of Education, Office of Educational Research and Improvement. (1993). *120 years of American education: A statistical portrait. (Publication no. NCES 93442).* Retrieved from http://nces.ed.gov/pubsearch/pubsinfo.asp?pubid−9344

Phyllis Chesler – A Life on Behalf of Women

Claudia Pitts

ABSTRACT

Phyllis Chesler's life and work have made significant contributions on topics as diverse as pornography, prostitution, motherhood, custody, surrogacy, a woman's right to self-defense, racism, including anti-Semitism, Israel, Islamic gender and religious Apartheid, and feminism. Her first major work, *Women and Madness* (Chesler, 1972), was one of the earliest works of the second wave feminist movement to address issues such as the mistreatment of women, particularly in rape and incest; female role models; and spirituality in mental health services. She remains a much sought after speaker, a global activist, and a source of inspiration for many.

Phyllis Chesler was truly a voice in the wilderness. It was Dr. Chesler who was one of the very first to speak the truth about the profoundly damaging role of gender bias in psychiatry and psychology and about sexual interaction between therapist and client. She was one of the first to use the word "patriarchy" in the psychological literature. She founded one of the first Women's Studies programs in the United States. Her first book, *Women and Madness* (Chesler, 1972), has sold over two and a half million copies, and her work in general has been translated into many European languages and into Japanese, Korean, Chinese, and Hebrew. *Women and Madness* (Chesler, 1972) was one of the earliest works of the second wave feminist movement to address issues such as the mistreatment of women, particularly in rape and incest; female role models; and spirituality in mental health services. She has continued to be a voluminous and significant author and expert, influencing the culture on topics as diverse as pornography, prostitution, motherhood, custody, surrogacy, a woman's right to self-defense, racism, including anti-Semitism, Israel, Islamic gender and religious Apartheid, and feminism. She is the author of 16 books, a much sought after speaker, a global activist, and a source of inspiration for many.

Dr. Chesler responded to written questions provided to her by the co-editors. Where the writing is in the first person, it is from her answers to these questions. The remainder of the biography, as noted, is gleaned from published accounts, her website, press reports, book reviews, and various other sources.

Family and Early Life

I was born in 1940 in Borough Park, Brooklyn. My mother, Lillian, worked as a housewife and mother. I was the oldest of three children and the only girl. My father, Leon, was born in Europe, in Ukraine, and my mother was the only child from her immigrant Polish family to have been born in America. We were Orthodox Jews. Although we were working-class and I was the first one in my extended family who graduated from college, I lacked for nothing as a child educationally. I was given Hebrew, drama, elocution, painting, piano, singing, and dancing lessons. (P. Chesler, personal communication, June 22, 2015)

According to *Jewish Women in America* (Hyman & Moore, 1998), Chesler traces her activism back to her experiences as a child when, at age eight, she joined Hashomer Hatzair, a Zionist youth organization, and later Ain Harod, a leftist Zionist youth group advocating Arab–Jewish kibbutzim. In that same interview (Hyman & Moore, 1998), Chesler states that when it became clear to her that, as an Orthodox Jew, she would not be bat mitzvahed, she ate non-Kosher food for the first time. When describing her childhood further, she said,

My father thought that everything I did was wonderful, that I was wonderful. When I would get a 90 on a test, my mother would say: "You could have done better, you could have gotten 100." I was reading Freud on my own by the time I was 13, though I had absolutely no intellectual or professional female role models. I did have at least four extremely kind teachers in high school: two women and two men. At the time, my interests were more literary than psycho-analytic or psychological. (P. Chesler, personal communication, June 22, 2015)

In 1958, Chesler received a full scholarship to Bard College in New York. The completion of her degree was somewhat delayed when, in 1961, she married a fellow student, a Muslim, and they traveled to Afghanistan. Her book, *An American Bride in Kabul* (Chesler, 2013), describes the relationship between herself as a 20-year-old, naïve Jewish girl from New York and her sophisticated and courteous husband who secretly held barbarically misogynistic beliefs about women. The book details the disintegration of this intense relationship into one of abuse, both by her husband and mother-in-law, and how she was kept in captivity in a harem in a polygamous household. On her website (Chesler, 2015b), she says of the captivity: "What I learned there became the basis for my very American feminism. I was already using the word 'patriarchal' in my Kabul diaries in 1961." She goes on to say,

My kind of feminism was forged in the fires of Afghanistan. There I received an education—an expensive, almost deadly one—but a valuable one, too. I understand firsthand how deep-seated the hatred of women is in many cultures. I see barbarism that is indigenous—not caused by colonialism—and unlike many other intellectuals and feminists, I don't try to romanticize or rationalize it. (Chesler, 2013)

After her escape from Afghanistan, she returned and graduated from Bard College with a degree in Comparative Literature and Language. She quickly became quite active in the Civil Rights Movement. Chesler says of the college and graduate school experience,

> I had one very kind female professor in college and I did my dissertation with her; it was about Stendhal. The male professors chased their female students around the room quite a lot, myself included. No one helped place us in graduate school or in internships that would lead to important next steps. However, I discovered and read Karen Horney there in my 20s. She certainly challenged Freud on feminist and psychological grounds and was a significant discovery for me. (P. Chesler, personal communication, June 22, 2015)

Doctoral Education and Faculty Position

Phyllis Chesler obtained her PhD in Psychology from the New School for Social Research in 1969. Chesler, in her interview on June 22, 2015, explains,

> I had a few kind teachers in graduate school, one of whom was a woman: Dr. Ausma Rabe, and I followed her right into brain science and physiological psychology. Thereafter, I began working in a Brain Research Lab, published two articles in *Science* magazine, got a fellowship in Neurophysiology to Medical School, but did not stay. I was too close to completing a Ph.D. in Psychology which I received in 1969. I studied the maternal influence in learning by observation and did formative research on gender preferences involved in choosing a therapist. (P. Chesler, personal communication, June 22, 2015)

Much of Chesler's university faculty career was spent at Richmond College, the College of Staten Island, part of the City University of New York (CUNY), where she was a tenured Professor in Psychology and Women's Studies. In addition to teaching at the college, Chesler was the moving force behind the founding of the College Birth Control and Ob/Gyn Self-Help Clinic, the College Child Care Center, the Rape Counseling Project, and the Counseling for Battered Women Project. She was a founder of the Women's Studies program and was eventually instrumental in the creation of Women's Studies programs throughout the CUNY system (Hyman & Moore, 1998). She also taught a Psychology of Women course at Brandeis and a graduate course in Forensic Psychology at John Jay College (CUNY) (Chesler, 2015b).

Early Feminism

When asked about her early feminism and her place in the roots of the feminist movement, Chesler replied,

> I could not have become a feminist pioneer if I had not been alive at the right moment in history, living in a large city, well educated, and knowing that something—maybe everything—was wrong. I might have written *Women and Madness* in the 19th century, but it would never have had such an enthusiastic readership, one that empowered me so fully as to try and make a difference. In the late 1960s, when I was at a psychoanalytic institute and doing a hospital

internship, I embarked on a study of patients' gender preferences for a therapist. Of course, women and men wanted male, not female therapists, because we believed that God was male, too. I was one of the co-founders of the Association for Women in Psychology and I made a fiery speech on our behalf for "reparations" (one that many of my co-founders feared I would make). I did so in 1969 at the annual meeting of the APA. It made world headlines. None of this would have been possible without the existence of a radical feminist movement alive in the world. I owe a great debt to this opening in history—one through which hundreds of thousands of women walked and began to transform the ruling consciousness of the world. Although I am not a joiner, I joined NOW in 1967. Although I am not an organization type, I co-founded a number of significant feminist organizations, which still exist in the world. These include the Association for Women in Psychology (1969), the National Women's Health Network (1974), the NYC Feminist Passover Seder Group (1975), and the International Committee for the Jerusalem-based Women of the Wall (1989). More recently (2013), I became a co-founder of the Original Women of the Wall. All but one of the founders of Women of the Wall broke with that group and formed a new group that was loyal to their original vision and principles. (P. Chesler, personal communication, June 22, 2015)

Feminist Biography—Early Steps

Dr. Chesler's feminist biography is astounding both for its breadth and its length. There is barely an area of psychology and its impact on women that she has not influenced. As previously mentioned, in 1969, she co-founded the (still very vital) Association for Women in Psychology (AWP) and demanded reparations at the national convention of the American Psychological Association for all the harm done to women in the name of "mental illness."

In 1970, she delivered her first major feminist speech in Great Neck, Long Island, at a distinguished forum, together with Dr. Barbara Joans. Chesler and Joans had already been helping women obtain illegal abortions. Dr. Amy Swerdlow, who would found a Women's History program at Sarah Lawrence College, told her that this lecture is what had converted her to feminism (Chesler, 2014). In that same year, she taught the first course for credit in Women's Studies and pioneered the first Women's Studies program at the City University of New York (CUNY) at Richmond College, now the College of Staten Island, and founded the first feminist salon in New York City together with Vivian Gornick (Chesler, 2014).

Though she was teaching for many years, it took a long time—22 years—for Dr. Chesler to be promoted to Full Professor. She "fought pitched battles to keep [her] job, to obtain tenure, to keep tenure, to be promoted from Assistant to Associate Professor, to obtain a salary increase. Year after year, major feminist leaders had to sign petitions on [her] behalf" (P. Chesler, personal communication, June 22, 2015).

By 1971, working as a faculty member, Dr. Chesler secretly acquired Richmond College data that helped the class action lawsuit (Melani v. Board of Higher Education of the City of New York, 1973) on behalf of women at the City University of New York (CUNY). This class action lawsuit was very extensive and time consuming, and even though they, the class of women at CUNY, eventually triumphed, it took 17 years to win. Says Chesler,

> The lawyer, Judith Vladeck, eventually wanted to open a separate cause of action for only me on the basis of my having been persecuted for my feminist/political beliefs. I advised her not to waste time on this. But I was heavily punished by my university because I researched women; published copiously; was also an activist; and committed the enormous crime of being both female and 'famous.' (Chesler, 2014)

Chesler notably delivered a keynote address at the first feminist conference on rape in New York City, which was organized by New York Radical Feminists in 1971. There were several other keynote speakers, including Florence Rush. It was widely reported on, and it eventually led to a book edited by Noreen Connell and Cassandra Wilson based on the conference proceedings and Susan Brownmiller's (1975) *Against Our Will*. Chesler (2014) writes that this address influenced others who came along later and either wrote about or became activists in this area. Also, during 1971–72, she attended and supported the earliest meetings that led to the founding of both Ms. Magazine and Signs, an academic feminist journal.

Women and Madness (1972)

When she published her first book, *Women and Madness* (Chesler, 1972), it became "an instant sensation" (Chesler, 2014). This book's then-radical thesis is "that double standards of mental health and illness exist and that women are often punitively labeled as a function of gender, race, class, or sexual preference" (Chesler, 2015b). The book received a front page *New York Times* review by Rich (1972), who described it as "intense, rapid, brilliant, controversial ... a pioneer contribution to the feminization of psychiatric thinking and practice" (p. BR1). Chesler remembers it as the first front page *New York Times* book review of any feminist work.

> The book went on to sell more than two and a half to three million copies. I also received thousands of letters from women all over the country who wrote to say that this book changed their lives, they signed themselves out of mental asylums, left terrible marriages, went back to college, sued their rapists, sued their unethical therapists, etc. On and on, the letters came. (P. Chesler, personal communication, June 22, 2015)

Women, Money and Power (1976)

Published in 1976, *Women, Money and Power* (Chesler & Goodman, 1976), co-written by former Judge Emily Jane Goodman, was an in-depth study of gender-based economic disparities in America in the 1970s. It was broadly read and well received within the feminist community and was viewed as a challenge from those outside the movement.

About Men (1978)

About Men (Chesler, 1978) was described by Gail Sheehy (1978) in the New York Times Book Review as "psychologically voluptuous, it plunges through the bloody underbrush of male–male relationships ... insisting that we look at men with fresh and fearless eyes." (p. BR4). This book draws on Chesler's own experiences and uses interviews, myth, history, art, and literature to provocatively explore the male psyche as well as the relationships men have with women and each other. She wrote in the Preface to this book,

> I wrote this book in order to understand men ... In the beginning, I thought that I would create a version of *Women and Madness* for men. But books each have their own way ... I write this book not as a tyrant over men, and not as a sycophant of men. I write without blinding contempt for men, and without any irrational fear— or worship—of men ... I write, always, in the belief that understanding can weaken the worship of death—that has dominated patriarchal consciousness and human action for so long." (Chesler, 1978, p. ii)

Judaism, Israel, and Anti-Semitism (1970s)

In 1973, Chesler co-organized the first press conference, together with Aviva Cantor Zuckoff and Cheryl Moch, about anti-Semitism among feminists in New York City. She had been concerned about these issues which led her to travel to Israel for the first time in 1972. She "tried to interest the major Jewish feminists in NYC in creating a Consciousness Raising group to examine anti-Semitism as racism among feminists. Most turned me down flat. Some later went on to build careers in precisely this area." (Chesler, 2015b)

In the mid-1970s, Chesler gave several major feminist speeches in Israel, which helped spark a robust and thriving feminist movement in that country. She also brought hand-picked journalists to Israel for "Artists for Peace in the Middle East" and co-organized the first Speak Out on Jewish feminism. It addressed sexism within Judaism and anti-Semitism among feminist and left political women. Aviva Cantor Zuckoff was also very involved in these events. Nearly 1,000 women attended the speakout in NYC at the McAlpin Hotel. Chesler was subsequently the first cover interviewee in Lilith magazine in winter 1976 and then again in 1980.

Feminist Passover Seder

In the mid 1970s, Chesler co-organized and co-led a feminist Passover Seder. She remained active in this group for 18 years. The first of these Seders was held in her home in New York City and was co-led by Esther Broner. Feminists such as Letty Cottin Pogrebin, Lily Rivlin, Bella Abzug, Gloria Steinem, Bea Kreloff, and Edith Isaac-Rose attended this event. She also participated in and pioneered feminist Jewish life cycle events and feminist Wiccan events. In fact, when Z Budapest and the women of the Susan B. Anthony Coven #1 in California were under siege in San Jose, California, in 1986, Chesler stood with them and their right to religious practice (Chesler, 2015b).

In 1981, Chesler organized the first panel at the National Women's Studies Association meeting in Storrs, Connecticut, about feminism, racism, and anti-Zionism/anti-Semitism. The tapes of this panel discussion were used by Letty Cottin Pogrebin for her article on the subject in *Ms. Magazine*. When the staff of *Ms. Magazine* approached Chesler to ask if Pogrebin was telling the truth, Chesler supported her. Pogrebin's article became the basis for a part of Pogrebin's book which appeared nearly a decade later.

With Child: A Diary of Motherhood (1979)

Chesler was one of only a small number of second-wave feminists to focus on motherhood. In *With Child: A Diary of Motherhood*, Chesler (1979) explored the experience of pregnancy at age thirty-seven, childbirth, and the first year of "newborn" motherhood in psychological, spiritual, and mythic terms as she attempted to understand just what she was looking for in the child she had brought into the world. The book was endorsed by both men (Alan Alda, Gerold Frank) and women (Judy Collins, Tillie Olsen, Marilyn French). It was also widely reviewed in the mainstream media. In 1998, Chesler's 18-year-old son, Ariel, wrote a new introduction for a new edition of the book.

World Conference of the United Nations Decade for Women

From 1979 to 1980, Chesler was employed as a consultant at the United Nations after proposing an international conference of women leaders; they met in Oslo, Norway, right before the 1980 UN World Conference in Copenhagen. The women whom she and her team gathered together in Oslo "ultimately comprised about 30% of Robin Morgan's *Sisterhood is Global* anthology" (Chesler, 2015b).

Mothers on Trial: The Battle for Children and Custody (1986)

In *Mothers on Trial: The Battle for Children and Custody*, Chesler (1986) argued that the U.S. legal system (and the mental health experts who work within this system) is biased and overworked and continues to fail the needs of mothers and children, especially those whose husbands and fathers are violent and vindictive. She discusses topics such as prolonged litigation, joint custody, court enabled incest, brainwashing, kidnapping, gay and lesbian custody, fathers' rights groups, and international child custody laws. This book was reissued in 2011 as a 25th anniversary edition with eight new chapters and a new introduction.

Women, Children, and Custody

For the next several years, Chesler became very involved in issues surrounding child custody. She co-organized, together with NYS-NOW (New York State's Chapter of the National Organization for Women), a first Speak Out on mothers losing custody of children in New York City. This Speak Out was widely attended and covered by the mainstream press. At this event, twenty custodially challenged mothers and many feminist leaders spoke, including Ti-Grace Atkinson, Dr. Paula Caplan, Toi Derricotte, Andrea Dworkin, and Kate Millett, as well as lawyers and politicians. Father's Rights activists demonstrated outside the conference, which was held at the John Jay College of Criminal Justice, CUNY. She also sponsored a Congressional briefing in Washington D.C. on the subject of women and custody, in which both Chuck Schumer and Barbara Boxer (then members of Congress, now Senators) participated. Chesler began helping mothers whose children were being battered and incestuously abused and became the first and only feminist who faced an FBI-convened Grand Jury for this feminist and pro-motherhood work. At the last moment, one of "her" mothers was captured, and she was spared from having to testify, which she says she would not have done and would have resulted in a jail sentence. She credits The Center for Constitutional Rights and a private criminal attorney for helping her through that ordeal (Chesler, 2015b).

Soon after these events, in 1987, she was the keynote speaker at a Speak Out on custodially embattled mothers in Toronto in which Dr. Paula Caplan was involved and was disrupted by Fathers Rights activists. In that same year, she organized demonstrations outside the courthouse for the very high profile Baby M case which was a combined surrogacy and custody case. Chesler worked with Mary Beth Whitehead's (the defendant) lawyer, Harold Cassidy, and helped coordinate the media campaign on behalf of the issues raised by her case. She spoke at the press conference after the New Jersey Supreme Court rendered its anti-surrogacy verdict (Chesler, 2015b).

Sacred Bond—The Legacy of Baby M (1988)

When she published *Sacred Bond—The Legacy of Baby M* (Chesler, 1988), she received a second front page New York Times Book Review (June 26, 1988). *Sacred Bond* discussed the issues raised by the high-profile Baby M case, in which surrogacy was ultimately declared illegal in the state of New Jersey. Despite liberal feminist opposition, Chesler defended the rights of the birth mother, Mary Beth Whitehead, who wanted to keep her child even though the genetic father and his wife were a more educated and higher income couple (Chesler, 2015b).

Following this, Chesler was part of a Canadian feminist team that argued on behalf of a mother who had kidnapped her children and fled the jurisdiction. She addressed the jury directly in this matter. Although the jury found the mother guilty, the judge chose to impose no sentence (Chesler, 2014). Chesler's team was ultimately deemed victorious.

Judaism, Israel, and Anti-Semitism (1980s to the Present)

In 1988, Chesler prayed with other Jewish women at the Western Wall in Jerusalem and was asked to open the Torah for the women for the first time in the women's section. After this deeply moving and profoundly controversial experience, she subsequently co-founded the International Committee for Women of the Wall. She was one of the named plaintiffs in the lawsuit against the Israeli government and the rabbinate on behalf of women's religious rights. The group raised the money to buy a Torah and donate it to the Women of Jerusalem, and Chesler, Rivka Haut, and others brought the scroll to Israel. Their inability to pray with the new Torah at the Kotel (Western Wall) as they had done the previous year became the grounds for them to join the Israel-based lawsuit. They eventually won their legal rights, but enforcing those rights remains substantially unresolved and is now in its 28th year (Chesler, 2014).

In 2002, together with Rivka Haut, her chavruta (Torah study partner), Chesler published *Women of the Wall: Claiming Sacred Ground at Judaism's Holy Site.* This anthology traces the origin, history, and impact of what is now an international grassroots effort on behalf of Jewish women's religious rights (Chesler & Haut, 2002). Chesler also began to publish Devrai Torah (biblical interpretations), which are archived at her website (Chesler, 2015b).

In 2003, Chesler published *The New Anti-Semitism.* She has written literally hundreds of articles on this subject as well as about gender and religious apartheid in the Islamic world. Her focus was the way in which the western intellectuals, academics, and political progressives were again betraying both the Jews and the truth and engaging in racism without, perhaps, realizing it. Her defense of Israel, her critique of the double standard by which Israel is judged, and her documentation of "the perfect storm" coming towards Jews and towards Israel—an alliance of left-leaning intelligentsia and American progressives and lethal Islamic hatred for Jews—rendered her politically incorrect (Chesler, 2003). This book presaged the Boycott, Divestment and Sanctions Movement (BDS Movement) started in 2005, which is a campaign attempting to increase economic and political pressure on Israel by various forms of boycott by academic, business, and entertainment industries. This book, published fully 2 years before the start of this movement, was her first that was not really reviewed by the mainstream media and the first one that had a hard time gaining interview attention.

Aileen Wuornos

In 1990, Chesler organized a team of high-powered professionals, often referred to as a "dream team," for Aileen Carol Wuornos, the Florida prostituted woman who began killing men, presumably in self-defense. Ms. Wuornos was described in the media as the so-called "first female serial killer." Charlize Theron "essentially impersonated" her in the film *Monster*. Chesler's stated goal was to educate the jury and the country about the lives of women in prostitution and the dangerous conditions they routinely face (Chesler, 1993a). She wanted to extend Dr. Lenore Walker's work on Battered Woman's Syndrome to cover prostituted women. The public defender did not call any of these witnesses, which became one of the grounds of the appeal that Wuornos' lawyers launched in the Florida Supreme Court. Chesler wrote about the legal and psychiatric issues raised by the case in the *New York Times, On The Issues Magazine* (where she served as Editor-at-Large), *St. John's Law Review*, and the *Criminal Practice Law Report* (Chesler, 1993b). She is halfway through a manuscript about this case. Ms. Wuornos has since been executed (Chesler, 2014).

Feminism—Looking Ahead, Looking Back

In 1990, Chesler appeared on the cover of the *New York Times* magazine with Kate Millett, Alix Kates Shulman, Ellen Willis, and Ann Snitow (April 15, 1990). The cover illustrated Vivian Gornick's cover story: "Who Says We Have Not Made a Revolution?" She went on to co-edit a book, with Esther D. Rothblum and Ellen Cole, *Feminist Foremothers in Women's Studies, Psychology, and Mental Health* (Chesler, Rothblum, & Cole, 1995). In 1998, she published *Letters to a Young Feminist*. In this book, she wanted to share the history of her generation of feminists with coming generations and to inspire them (Chesler, 1998). These works were lauded by feminists of her own era and to some degree minimized by next generation feminists who did not want to keep "standing on the shoulders" of a previous generation with whom they disagreed and with whom they were in competition. In the early 1990s, Chesler became very ill with Lyme's Disease and Chronic Fatigue Immune Dysfunction Syndrome. She began writing about disability as soon as she could. Luckily, she has since recovered (Chesler, 2014).

Woman's Inhumanity to Woman (2002)

This pioneering book addressed the subject of female indirect aggression, both in the family and the workplace, in childhood and adulthood, historically and globally, and covered woman's capacity for cruelty, competition, envy, and ostracism; the ways in which women, like men, have internalized sexist beliefs; and the importance of acknowledging the "shadow side" of female–female relationships, especially because such relationships are so important to women (Chesler, 2002). The book was reviewed in many publications, and the author was interviewed widely in South America, North America (including *The New York Times*), Europe, and Asia. It received a front page review in the Washington Post Book World, written by Tannen (2002 March 10). According to Chesler,

> Many feminist leaders warned me away from this topic; over time, many have thanked me for publishing this work. Some feminist leaders were angry and frightened because I had challenged the Gilligan thesis that women are more compassionate and more moral than men. Some were worried that I might 'name names.' (Chesler, 2014)

In 2006, Chesler published *The Death of Feminism: What's Next in the Struggle for Women's Freedom* in which she challenged feminists about their multicultural relativism.

Gone is the single standard for universal human rights for women and men—replaced by the view that all cultures are equal and that Westerners, especially, have lost the moral high ground and cannot criticize cultures of color for their misogyny or tyranny (Chesler, 2014).

Chesler claims that their desire to avoid being labeled "racists" or "Islamophobes" eventually trumped feminist concern with women's and human rights in the Third World (Chesler, 2006).

Honor Related Violence and Honor Killings (2009–2015)

Chesler published four studies about honor killings in the U.S. journal *Middle East Quarterly* in 2009, 2010, 2012, and 2015. In one study (2009), she wrote that 91% of the total worldwide cases of honor killings (as reported in English-language media) were Muslim-on-Muslim crimes, including those committed in North America and Europe. Based on her findings in these four articles, Chesler concluded that there are at least two types of honor killings and two victim populations. She identified the first group as consisting of daughters with an average age of 17 who were killed by their families-of-origin and the second group as consisting of women with an average age of 36. In their most recent study, Chesler and Bloom (2012) assert that Hindus, Sikhs, and Muslims commit honor killings, but that only Muslims do so worldwide. Chesler (2015a) recently published a fourth study titled: "Female Perpetrators and Accomplices in Honor Killings."

Chesler argues that honor killings differ qualitatively from the Western domestic killing of women. She acknowledged that "many honorable feminists" disagree with her position, writing that "understandably, such feminists fear singling out one group for violence against women when violence is pandemic among all groups. However, intimate family femicide (or rather, daughter-cide) is not" (Chesler, 2009, p. 61). Chesler's position is that perpetrators of Western-style domestic murders are regarded as criminal in the West, but the same stigma is not attached to honor killings in other societies. The opposite is true—such killers are valorized (Chesler, 2009).

In a 2011 address before the New York County Supreme Court, Chesler lectured about the affidavits she submitted on behalf of Muslim women and converts from Islam whom believed themselves to be in danger of being the victims of honor killing and who sought asylum and citizenship in the United States (Chesler, 2014).

Burqas

In 2010, Chesler wrote an essay in *Middle East Quarterly* calling for the burqa to be banned in western countries. She argued that the Qur'an commands both men and women to dress "modestly"; but that many Muslim-majority countries have, in the past, banned the full burqa or face veil (niqab), and that historically, many Muslim countries have not required that women wear a face veil. She argues that the burqa functions as a "sensory deprivation isolation chamber," and that physical and psychiatric illnesses are associated with such a "moveable prison" and with lack of sunlight. She was not similarly opposed to the headscarf (hijab) on the grounds that it does not obscure a woman's facial identity (Chesler, 2010).

A Remarkable Contribution

Chesler counts among her most prized accomplishments writing and "giving speeches that saved women's lives or sanity, and contributed to feminist awakening, among women, and men" (P. Chesler, personal communication, June 22, 2015). She gave a voice to many, including psychiatric patients, women being deprived of custody, women losing their rights, religious and spiritual identity, and women in prostitution, to mention but a few populations who have not been seen or heard by the larger society. It was her voice that served as a catalyst to the changing of policies, laws, and eventually the culture in so many areas of women's and human rights that without her, we would not be, today, where we are.

References

Brownmiller, S. (1975). *Against our will: Men, women and rape.* New York: Simon and Schuster.
Chesler, P. (1972). *Women and madness.* New York: Doubleday.
Chesler, P. (1978). *About men.* New York: Simon and Schuster.

Chesler, P. (1979). *With child: A story of motherhood*. Crowell, OH: Springfield.

Chesler, P. (1986). *Mothers on trial*. Chicago: Lawrence Hill Books.

Chesler, P. (1988). *Sacred bond*. New York: First Vintage Books.

Chesler, P. (1993a). A woman's right to self-defense: The case of Aileen Wuornos. *St. John's Law Review, 66*(Fall-Winter), 933–977.

Chesler, P. (1993b). Sexual violence against women and a woman's right to self-defense: The case of Aileen Carol Wuornos. *Criminal Practice Law Report, 1*(9), 933–977.

Chesler, P. (1998). *Letters to a young feminist*. New York: Four Walls Eight Windows.

Chesler, P. (2002). *Women's inhumanity to women*. New York: Nation Books.

Chesler, P. (2003). *The new antisemitism: The current crisis and what we must do about it*. San Francisco: Jossey-Bass.

Chesler, P. (2006). *The death of feminism*. New York: St. Martin's Griffin.

Chesler, P. (2009). Are honor killings simply domestic violence? *Middle East Quarterly, 16*(2), 61–69.

Chesler, P. (2010). Ban the Burqa? The argument in favor. *Middle East Quarterly, 17*(4), 33–45.

Chesler, P. (2013, September 21). My life of hell in an Afghan harem. *New York Post*. Retrieved from http://nypost.com/2013/09/21/my-life-of-hell-in-an-afghan-harem/

Chesler, P. (2014). *Phyllis Chesler: A Jewish and feminist biography*. Retrieved from http://www.phyllischesler.com/feminist_bio.pdf

Chesler, P. (2015a). When women commit honor killings. *Middle East Quarterly, 22*(4), 1–12.

Chesler, P. (2015b). *Website*. Retrieved from http://www.Phyllis-Chesler.com

Chesler, P., & Bloom, N. (2012). Hindu vs. Muslim honor killings. *Middle East Quarterly, 19*(3), 43–52.

Chesler, P., & Goodman, E. J. (1976). *Women, money and power*. New York: William Morrow & Co.

Chesler, P., & Haut, R. (2002). *Women of the wall: Claiming sacred ground at Judaism's holy site*. Woodstock, VT: Jewish Lights Publishing.

Chesler, P., Rothblum, E., & Cole, E. (1995). *Feminist foremothers in women's studies, psychology, and mental health*. Philadelphia: Haworth Press.

Hyman, P., & Moore, D. (Eds.). (1998). *Jewish women in America: An historical encyclopedia*. (Vol. 1). New York: Routledge.

Rich, A. (Dec 1, 1972). Women & madness [Review of the book *Women & Madness* by Phyllis Chesler]. *New York Times Book Review*, p. BR1.

Sheehy, G. (1978, March 19). What do men want? Review of *About Men. New York Times Book Review*, p. BR4.

Tannen, D. (2002, March 10). Dangerous women [Review of the book *Woman's inhumanity to woman*, by Phyllis Chesler]. *The Washington Post Book World*, pp. 1, 3.

Feminist Therapy Pioneer: E. Kitch Childs

Wytress Richardson

ABSTRACT

This article will focus on the life of the late Dr. E. Kitch Childs and her impact on Feminist Therapy. It seeks to celebrate and pay homage to her as one of the pioneers who helped pave the way for women in therapy. Dr. Childs was an African American lesbian woman who stood in the gap for social justice with her intellect, tenacity, and bravery and took the lead as a radical visionary.

The 1960s and 1970s brought about an increased awareness of women as an oppressed group in the United States. Inequality, which had been viewed as inevitable, began to be viewed as a problem that could and would respond to radical action. Throughout these times, White women, Women of Color, women of privilege, middle-class women, and poor women were gathering to push back against the old ways of oppression to create voices as the Women's Movement, organizing and raising awareness of the harm created from a patriarchal and racist society toward women (Evans, Kincade, Marbley, & Seem, 2005, p. 269).

Feminist Therapy has its roots in this feminist movement, growing out of the political and social awareness of gender, race, and sociopolitical factors (Evans et al., 2005). It was informed by both feminist ideals and theories of psychotherapy. The early mothers of Feminist Therapy were all therapists, although not all were formally trained and licensed, and their goal was to create a feminist-informed practice in response to social movements of the 1960s. In the 1960s, it was the Women's Liberation Movement that formed to address oppression based on gender, equality, social status, and the rights for women to control their own lives; however, although the social struggle for women's empowerment stimulated change, it was not equal for all women ("But Some of Us Are Brave," n.d.). As White, financially secure women were closer to becoming liberated and aiming for a better way of living, less privileged women often remained more burdened and felt left out of the movement. The Feminist Therapy Movement used tools from the Women's Movement to empower women of all races, classes, and eventually, orientations.

Second Wave feminism formed out of the frustration with the treatment of "common women" (Evans, Kincade, & Seem, 2011). This wave of the Women's Movement strived to improve sociopolitical conditions and the oppression of women. During the 1960s, there was an economic recession, following the post-war economic boom that created the crises of poverty. Traditionally trained male therapists who looked into women's issues found that women's roles and expectations began to change. This created quandaries, as most of these therapists were still untrained in women's issues because psychology was a field formed and controlled by men. There became a need to construct feminist-informed practices in order to cope with the societal changes for men and women that were occurring in the 1960s (Collins, 2002; Evans et al., 2005).

As we moved into the 1970s, Feminist Therapy became more widely accepted since traditional therapy was becoming increasingly less able to meet women's evolving psychological needs. A central philosophy of Feminist Therapy is the assumption that "ideology, social structure, and behavior are interwoven" (Collins, 2002, p. 1). This implied that emotional problems were consequences of "external as well as internal problems, emphasizing behaviors as symptoms of oppression, rather than of illness" (Collins, 2002, pp. 1–2); thus, recognizing that clients are "enmeshed in their sociopolitical and cultural context, and true and lasting psychological change must address the issues with these contexts as well as the individual" (Evans et al., 2005, p. 269). During this pivotal point in the field of psychology and Feminist Therapy, Dr. (Ellen) Kitch Childs arrived. She was a radical visionary with the fortitude to live her life as a fiercely intelligent, gay, Black woman with purpose that included combating the "isms" of society.

E. Kitch Childs, as she is known, was born Ellen Childs in Pittsburgh, Pennsylvania, in 1937. Those who knew her affectionately called her "Kitch." Not many would ever know that the E. stood for Ellen, and as private as Kitch was, very few would ever find out. No one knew why she used her middle name, but those close to her assumed that she was seeking a hipper, cooler name than Ellen.

Kitch was the youngest child and the only girl in her family. She had three older brothers. She and her brothers moved from her birthplace in Pittsburgh to be raised by her grandmother on the Southside of Chicago. Nothing is written about the reason for the move; indeed, much of her life was very private, and not much is written about her childhood and early years. Notably, she grew up in Chicago, which was known for being an extremely violent and segregated city, and perhaps growing up in a climate of civil unrest and oppression sparked the fire for her path as an activist for the rights of others.

For this article, I was privileged to not only research the life of Dr. E. Kitch Childs, but to have the pleasure of interviewing her dear friend, Dr. Ellyn Kaschak. She and Kitch worked on the front lines of this new and evolving therapy, and they broke down barriers together. Throughout the interview, Dr. Kaschak shared a wide variety of memories she had of Dr. E. Kitch Childs trying to convey the essence of her radical and beloved friend.

Although not much is written about Kitch's childhood, Kitch shared with close friends that she was very fond of her oldest brother, Kenny Clarke, an admired jazz musician (drummer). She and Kenny remained very close throughout the years. Additionally, Childs's life was not immune to the harsh consequences of racism. She experienced firsthand the loss of two of her brothers due to racial violence. It is not clear at what ages her brothers were at the time of their deaths, but her passion for racial justice might have stemmed from such horrible encounters.

As a child, Kitch was exceptionally intelligent and was seen as a gifted student. She received a Bachelor's of Science in Chemistry from the University of Pittsburgh as an adolescent, and then she went on to serve in the United States Navy. Later, she attended the University of Chicago where she earned a Master's degree in Human Development. In 1972, she went on to receive a PhD in Human Development from the University of Chicago as well. She was an outstanding graduate student and became one of the very first Black women to earn a doctoral degree from the Human Development program at the University of Chicago. This says a great deal about her determination as she was often on the front lines daring to make a difference, set a standard, and push through barriers for Blacks. At the time of her matriculation through the prestigious university, she did not fit the standard model for a student as a triple minority. She was extremely intelligent, she was a Black woman, she was gay, and she did not display the "typical female" concern with her appearance and reveled in her ability to standup for fairness. In the time Kitch was working toward her Master's degree, she was fearlessly advocating for the rights of others and for what she believed in, namely lesbian and gay rights. Her voice and actions steered her to connect with others who were dissatisfied with the degradation of bigotry and unfairness. Kitch was waging war for the rights of gays and lesbians and was also a founding member of the University of Chicago's Gay Liberation Movement. Furthermore, while pursuing her degree and making efforts to improving herself, she was a staunch supporter and a founding member of the Association for Women in Psychology (AWP), which was founded in 1969. One main impetus for the founding of AWP was because women were frustrated with sexism in psychology.

It is apparent that Kitch welcomed conflict regarding issues about which she felt passionate, bringing about gender equality and affecting societal change. She demonstrated this by aggressively accepting the challenge as an advocate for change in women's and gay and lesbian rights. This was not an easy achievement. Yet, she persevered. Kitch faced a number of challenges being Black, lesbian, poor, and "super smart," and these were part of the grit that kept her fighting for justice. Dr. Kaschak described her as a "Powerhouse who worked super hard for African Americans, the poor, gays/lesbians and even prostitutes. She was an activist seeking justice" (E. Kaschak, personal communication, July 7, 2015).

Interestingly, Kitch was musically talented and had a lovely singing voice. She sang with the Philadelphia Symphony Orchestra's chorus, touring Europe. In graduate school, she often sang and was recorded as a folk singer for an all-night environmental "Teach-Out" at Northwestern University in 1971. Childs last performed publicly as a vocalist at a commemorative event for Audre Lorde, a Caribbean-American writer, radical feminist, womanist, lesbian, and civil rights activist. Additionally, her commitment to lesbian and gay equality eventually contributed to the creation of the City of Chicago's gay and lesbian rights ordinance in 1973. Furthermore, she worked to amend the American Psychological Association's statements concerning homosexuality which led to her 1993 induction into the Chicago Gay and Lesbian Hall of Fame.

E. Kitch Childs was a warrior on the front lines fighting for those who could not fight for themselves. As with any warrior, she learned to compartmentalize her own frustrations, feelings, and emotions. In this case, it is reported that Kitch resorted to one of the self-medicating methods. Kitch preferred the use of cannabis (marijuana) on a nearly continuous basis to ease her pain and make life more tolerable. According to those close to her, Kitch suffered tremendously from both physical and emotional pain. As stated earlier, there is a great deal unknown about her past that may have contributed to her self-medication and her profound need to affect change for disenfranchised groups. What is evident is that Kitch was faced with the challenges of being a triple minority (female, lesbian, and Black) when she enlisted in the United States Navy and attended a prestigious university during a time of racial turmoil and may have suffered emotionally because of these challenges.

At the time of the Civil Rights Movement, Feminist Therapy was beginning to be developed. Contemporary Feminist Therapy and the Black Liberation Movement were organizing. Kitch understood that she was not resilient enough to work in political movements, but it did not stop her. A variety of difficult situations and circumstances impacted her well-being and may have been a contributing factor in her emotional and physical pain, but it was not enough to drive her away. It simply propelled her further.

Early works in Feminist Therapy mostly involved an ecological model for therapy with women. According to Kaschak (1976), Sociotherapy, an example of an ecological therapy, was an alternative to traditional intrapsychic and personal focus of psychotherapy, which helped women to redefine individual problems with the broader social context. She contends, "therapy has been developed and involved the awareness of oppression as a reality and involvement in action leading to its change" (E. Kaschak, personal communication,

July 7, 2015). Thus, therapy created for women must involve awareness of both individual and societal contingencies. Consciousness-raising groups for women had previously formed to engage in deeply revealing discussion regarding their experiences as women in a patriarchal society emerged. The focus was to create a space for women to listen to each other's struggles and move forward by thinking of alternatives. Feminist groups especially focused on actions to improve the situation socially and politically. As Israeli and Santor (2000) state, the four hallmarks of feminist therapy are conscious raising, social and gender role analysis, resocialization, and social activism. Feminist Therapy later developed different models such as self-help counseling, transition houses, modification of women's experience in therapy, referral services, and the eventual development of Feminist Therapy as a field of its own. The self-help model was the one in which Kitch was more engaged and involved.

In the early 1970s, Kitch relocated to Oakland, California, where she inherited a house, possibly from her brother, Kenny. The home was not in a posh neighborhood, but in a lower-class area of Oakland. She operated a private practice to counsel the marginalized at her home and truly engaged in her clients' lives. Her passion and willingness to support those persons from marginalized communities brought her to a point where she developed a sliding scale fee for counseling to assure the accessibility of those she treated. According to Dr. Kaschak, Kitch worked to develop a new model of treatment that was patient-centered and inclusive. This was a client-therapist model that attempted to eradicate obstacles related to the hierarchical ways of past treatment. When initiated, "the Feminist Therapy model used a sliding scale based on ability to pay, and that's how Kitch wanted to keep it. She was true to her clients, and what they could not pay, they did not pay. She would counsel them for what they could afford" (E. Kaschak, personal communication, July 7, 2015).

Kitch sought to leave no one behind and focused on the grassroots efforts of the various groups that promoted feminist ideals and concerns. She wanted to provide services to all people regardless of their ethnicity or social standing. Kitch often saw clients in her home in order to make them feel more comfortable. She did not want to portray herself and her office clinically, and she felt that offering her home was the best way to break the barriers and get clients to feel at ease. She also treated her clients in their homes. This was a component of her new model to equalize power with her clients. Additionally, Kitch never felt comfortable working in a clinic or facility that would not represent the person she was and those for whom she was advocating. She stayed outside the constructs of organizations and was one of the first to offer purposely home-based psychotherapy.

Through the initial developmental stages of Feminist Therapy, things were often conflictual as the field was male driven and the concerns of women were relegated to dismissive explanations such emotional mood swings and an inability to be understood by men. All through the feminist movement, women addressed issues that were concerning them and the issues that had been ignored by the male establishment. Women's rights were minimized rather than equalized as a voice of concern.

As the Feminist Movement was about the equalizing power, Feminist Therapy was focused on helping women to understand how those power inequities were impacting their lives personally and ultimately politically. Kitch went even further by including even more powerless groups such as Black women, gays, lesbians, and even sex workers. During this period of her professional life, Kitch became involved with a group advocating for prostituted women's rights called COYOTE (Call Off Your Tired Ethics), which was founded by Margot St. James and supported by Florynce Kennedy, a political celebrity who Kitch knew very well. The organization's mission was to decriminalize prostitution. Kitch was a free-spirited, non-judgmental person and believed in working with the marginalized. She was a staunch supporter of those women involved in prostitution. According to Dr. Kaschak, Kitch advocated intently for the services of prostitutes to be legalized and for all women, even those involved in prostitution, to have equal rights and fair treatment (E. Kaschak, personal communication, July 7, 2015).

Kitch ran her clinical practice from 1973 through 1990 and also received disability payments throughout that time. It is not known why she received disability payments, but she saw most (or all) of her clients for deeply discounted rates. Kitch grew up poor and was no stranger to that life as an adult. She struggled and lived modestly well below her possibilities. Dr. Kaschak spoke of how Kitch was both frail and tough, could take care of her comrades and still, like most of us, needed caring for herself.

E. Kitch Childs worked unendingly and fearlessly, tackling issues of inequality for women, prostitutes, the homeless, gays and lesbians, and people of color. However, in 1991, she made a decision to move to Paris because she had grown weary of the treatment for disadvantaged people, and she had fallen in love with a woman who lived there and wanted to explore this new relationship. Upon arriving in Paris, Kitch was faced with another form of racism and bigotry, the mistrust and mistreatment of Americans. In addition to the issues she may have faced in Paris as an American, the relationship in Paris did not work out.

When the relationship ended, Childs moved to Amsterdam with her brother, Kenny. He lived there during the era of the "Appeal to Color Citizen of the World Movement," along with many other African-American entertainers and writers. Dr. Kaschak chuckled as she remembered thoughts of why else her good friend Kitch would move to Amsterdam. She says, "Kitch would have the opportunity to smoke all the pot she'd like." (E. Kaschak, personal communication, July 7, 2015).

E. Kitch Childs died of heart failure on January 10, 1993, in Amsterdam, where she had been living since 1991. She was 55 years of age. The world had lost a prominent clinical psychologist, an advocate of gay and lesbian human rights, a feminist and feminist therapist, and a founding member of the Association for Women in Psychology and the Feminist Therapy Institute. Dr. Childs' tenacity and desire to see equal justice for all aided in the creation of Feminist Therapy. Her passion, determination, and empathy for others put her on the cutting edge of a field that is now 50 years old and still evolving. She was a radical visionary for human rights and a true pioneer of Feminist Therapy.

Dr. E. Kitch Childs Selected Bibliography

Childs, E. K. (1992). Racism in the international Women's Movement. In M. Pellikaan-Engel (Ed.), *Against patriarchal thinking: Proceedings of the VIth Symposium of the International Association of Women Philosophers (IAPh) 1992* (pp. 293–296). Amsterdam: VU University Press.

Childs, E. K. (1990). Therapy, feminist ethics, and the community of color with particular emphasis on the treatment of black women. In H. Lerman & N. Porter (Eds.), *Feminist ethics in psychotherapy* (pp. 195–203). New York: Springer.

Childs, E. K. (1972). *Prediction of outcome in encounter groups: Outcome as a function of selected personality correlates* (Doctoral dissertation). Retrieved from ProQuest Dissertations and Theses database (UMI No. 302709011).

National Opinion Research Center. (1966). *Careers in the military service; a review of the literature. Military Man Power Survey* (Working Paper No. 4). Chicago, IL: Childs, E. K.

References

But Some of Us Are Brave: A History of Black Feminism in the United States. (n.d.). *The Thistle Alternative News Collective, 9*(1). Retrieved from http://www.mit.edu/~thistle/v9/9.01/6blackf.html

Collins, K. A. (2002). An examination of feminist psychotherapy in North America during the 1980s. *Guidance & Counseling, 17*(4), 105.

Evans, K. M., Kincade, E. A., Marbley, A. F., & Seem, S. R. (2005). Feminism and feminist therapy: Lessons from the past and hopes for the future. *Journal of Counseling Development, 83*(3), 269–277. doi:10.1002/j.1556-6678.2005.tb00342.x

Evans, K. M., Kincade, E. A., & Seem, S. R. (2011). *Introduction to feminist therapy: Strategies for social and individual change.* Thousand Oaks, CA: Sage Publications, Inc.

Israeli, A. L., & Santor, D. A. (2000). Reviewing effective components of feminist therapy. *Counseling Psychology Quarterly, 13*(3), 233–247. doi:10.1080/095150700300091820

Kaschak, E. (1976). Sociotherapy: An ecological model for therapy with women. *Psychology: Theory, Research and Practice, 13*(1), 61–63. doi:10.1037/h0086487

"You Just Know It's the Only Thing You Can Think": A Conversation with Chodorow

Mengchun Chiang

ABSTRACT

Nancy Julia Chodorow (1944–) is a pioneer feminist theorist who brought together academic fields of sociology, anthropology, and psychoanalysis in her work related to feminist theories and psychoanalysis. Her first book, *The Reproduction of Mothering: Psychoanalysis and the Sociology of Gender* (1978), gave primacy to a more generalized account of the developmental and familial origins of prevalent psychological differences between femininity and masculinity from a psychoanalytic sociological viewpoint. Her later books, *Femininities, Masculinities, Sexualities: Freud and Beyond* (1994), *The Power of Feelings: Personal Meaning in Psychoanalysis, Gender, and Culture* (1999), and *Individualizing Gender and Sexuality: Theory and Practice* (2012), bring in a rich interplay among socio-structural influences (i.e., culture) as well as intra- and inter-psychic dynamic processes, emphasizing more the importance of individuality and subjectivity. Based on an interview I had with Chodorow on the development of her thought, this paper gives Chodorow's account of her personal history and academic background, current manifestations in feminist social science research and feminist psychoanalysis based on her contribution and legacy, and reflective narratives on the unfolding of feminist and psychoanalytic theories from the 1970s onward. Chodorow's note to the next generation of feminist psychotherapists is also included.

With her first book *The Reproduction of Mothering* (Chodorow, 1978) winning the Jessie Bernard Award in 1979, Nancy Chodorow (1944–) is considered a feminist pioneer who brought together academic fields of sociology, anthropology, and psychoanalysis, offering a unique and comprehensive perspective on the complex interrelationship between feminism and psychoanalytic practices (e.g., Chodorow, 1989a). Chodorow's contribution was particularly significant during the 1970s because articulation and thoughts were scarce in remarking and tracing the division and difference among genders. While her then controversial viewpoint in *The Reproduction of Mothering* (Chodorow, 1978) is no longer controversial 30 years later,

Chodorow has not stopped from further expansion of her thoughts into unmarked territories in sociology, anthropology, feminist studies, and psychoanalysis. She seems to be able to utilize the infinite freedom of various unrestricted/unsettled spaces by drawing connections among different disciplines of social science in her articulation of a deeply individualized and yet decidedly intersubjective understanding of gendered and cultured psyche through sociological, anthropological, and psychoanalytic lenses.

After retiring as Professor of Sociology and supervisor and mentor in the Psychology Department at the University of California, Berkeley, Chodorow moved to Cambridge, Massachusetts, to continue her private practice of psychoanalysis and psychotherapy, while also continuing to serve educative roles at the Cambridge Health Alliance/Harvard Medical School. It is in this context that Chodorow and I work together, both in the capacities of mentor-mentee and as colleagues. As a young scholar, the focus of my training has been within clinical psychology, while my thinking and approach to psychological phenomena and clinical formulation have followed a largely human science tradition that encompasses psychology, philosophy, anthropology, and sociology. With a personal interest in the subject related to "difference," a social scientific understanding of gender and culture has been the starting point of my research and theoretical framework. Clinically, I find myself with added attunement to various axes of difference (e.g., gender and/or culture), following a generalist, integrative approach that is strongly psychodynamically informed.

It is in this context that my interest in learning more about the development of Chodorow's thinking emerges. In many ways, Chodorow and I share similar interdisciplinary thinking, pulling together theories of thoughts from a broad social scientific field. We both align ourselves with a feminist approach to the extent that our attunement to various forms of difference becomes an integral part of our ways of thinking and clinical listening.

Within the variety of similarities between our paths, there are, of course, explicit and implicit differences. While Chodorow is trained as a psychoanalyst, I consider most of my clinical work psychodynamically informed. Chodorow began as a social scientist who has training in anthropology and sociology. In comparison, my learning in the social scientific field has always been oriented around the field of psychology, with sprinkles of theoretical understanding of German philosophy, sociology, and anthropology.

Our personal backgrounds also differ. Chodorow's parents were second generation, born to immigrants, and I have been residing in the United States as a "foreign alien" during the last few years. While Chodorow grew up in a family within an academic community, my family background is modest, with working class parents whose hard work made my life context appear similar to that of the middle class. In briefly addressing similarities and differences between us, my conversation with Chodorow not only contains highlights and contributions she offers as a pioneer feminist psychotherapist, but also expands my understanding of a certain pattern and style of thinking that marks an integrative take on feminism and psychoanalysis (Chodorow, 1974, 1992).

With the aforementioned premises, this paper aims to recount Chodorow's thoughts as she speaks them, drawing from her words during the interview. Expressing a reciprocal principle consistent with feminist methodology, it is important to note that much of what is represented in this write-up reflects as much my reading and interpretation of Chodorow's accounts as the "actual" narratives Chodorow spoke. Given the contextual backgrounds implicit in what is represented here, this paper is an attempt to take up Chodorow's work in relation to feminism and psychoanalysis from the 1970s onward.

Before launching into Chodorow's narratives from the interview, I underline two initial observations. First is a certain natural and spontaneous quality in Chodorow's personal take on the development of her thoughts at various fronts of feminist vis-à-vis psychoanalytic theories. Rather than conceiving of herself as thinking in the "forefront," she said, in a matter-of-fact fashion, "You just know it's the only thing you can think." This type of candid and ingenuous remarks occurred a few times throughout our conversation. For instance, she noted in passing, "I just have to write what I need to write about" and "I say what I have to say because I have to say it."

The second observation about the dialogue between Chodorow and me is her intentional and unintentional inclusion of many other feminist and psychoanalytic thinkers of her contemporary era. While her theoretical formulation remains firm and unyielding (as she noted that it is "the only way [she] can think"), her personhood seems to possess an excellent ability to locate herself in relation to others within and across different disciplines. After the interview, I became even more impressed with how she held the tension emanating from the complexity of different disciplines as well as diverse contextual threads in a seemingly effortless manner.

Frames, Context: Personal History and Background

It was a warm Thursday afternoon in the midst of an unusually busy summer both Chodorow and I had. We started our discussion on the topic of subjectivity and individuality, as Chodorow (1999) has emphasized in recent years. To address the question of subjectivity and individuality, Chodorow's accounts drew attention to her family background in history, her academic training background, and her personal temperament/characteristics.

As she has written elsewhere (Chodorow, 2002), Chodorow was born in New York and grew up in California. As a young child, she considered herself a "Jewish cowboy (or cowgirl)" who had "a lot of friends, and no family nearby." While the status of "Jewish New Yorker" marked a certain difference between her and her peers, she considers herself as someone who "come[s] from privilege." Chodorow's father, from a poor immigrant family, was trained as a theoretical physicist, and he founded the Department of Applied Physics at Stanford University. Thus, Chodorow grew up in an academic community in liberal California. She drew parallels between her way of thinking ("I have a structural mind") and her father's ability to "see how physics principles from widely disparate theories could be brought together in an instrument."

Chodorow's mother and several aunts were social workers. Chodorow spoke about her attraction to the qualitative social sciences—sociology and anthropology and her early knowledge that women could have professions (see also Chodorow, 1989b).

> My mother's generation is a high achieving cohort. If you look at the American 1890–1910 birth cohort, which my mother was just at the top-edge of, the women had a higher education and professional participation rate than women born before or after. In my mother's cohort, middle class and upper-middle class women worked and were often professionals. (N. Chodorow, personal communication, June 25, 2015)

Regarding her own academic training, Chodorow said, "I am originally a social scientist who became an analyst." She remarked that her "first social science interest, as an undergraduate, was psychological anthropology." She has always been interested in "cross-cultural individuality." Whiting (1963), the author of *Six Culture: Studies of Child Rearing*, was one of Chodorow's early mentors. Additionally, Chodorow related her anthropological training to her ability to "always see contradictions." In her words,

> I'm aware of the taken-for-granted structure, and then I got trained to be aware of it. Why did I go into anthropology? Because of the taken-for-granted infrastructure. Anthropology is the first huge challenge to the taken-for-granted infrastructure of Eurocentric culture. It turns out that you go to, say, various remote islands in non-Eurocentric countries, and you find that people have very, very different ways of living and being, and so I think anthropology is the first step of that. (N. Chodorow, personal communication, June 25, 2015)

Chodorow began graduate school in anthropology in the Department of Social Relations at Harvard University and left to study sociology at Brandeis University. She found ethnomethodology (established by Harold Garfinkel, 1917–2011) ("somehow ethnomethodology really met me") and studied at Brandeis with Egon Bittner (1921–2011). Chodorow connected various theories[1] and began to write in the feminist field that was still unmarked territory in social science research in the 1970s. Rather than thinking of herself as doing "feminist" research, she aligned her early writing more with the tradition of research that came naturally to her in the context of her training and background in anthropology and sociology. She noted, "Actually all of us, all of Egon's students were looking at the taken-for-granted, and I happened to do feminist theory and gender."

Chodorow also began learning about psychoanalysis during her years at Brandeis. Bennett Simon and Malkah Notman were teachers at the Boston Psychoanalytic Society and Institute, and she studied object-relations theory with George Goethals at Harvard University. She noted that psychoanalysis also challenges the taken-for-granted: that thinking is conscious.

One great benefit of being at Brandeis was a rich feminist community. Brandeis trained many of the leading second-wave feminist sociologists ("really too many to list individually"), including many feminist sociologists of color. Among these, Chodorow named Karen Fields, who wrote on a variety of subjects—African religion, W. E. B. DuBois, the Black family, and who also translated Durkheim's (1912) The Elementary Forms of Religious Life; Collins (2002) whose first book was *Black Feminist Thought*; Judith Rollins (1987), whose first book was *Between Women: Domestics and Their Employers*; and the Moroccan feminist Mernissi (1994), who wrote, among other works, *Dreams of Trespass: Tales of a Harem Girlhood*.

In addition to the family and academic backgrounds that contextualize the early foundations of Chodorow's thoughts around feminism and psychoanalysis, Chodorow noted the particular style of her mind in relation to her scholarly and clinical approach. She said,

> I have a very structural mind. Doing anthropology, you could think about the structure and organization of societies. In contrast, I don't have a very narrative mind, and that's actually a challenge as a clinician. I don't think intuitively metaphorically; I think intuitively structurally. I was really well-placed for the period of structural anthropology and structural sociology—Levi-Strauss and his model, more than the post-modern, non-literal, associative ways of thinking. (N. Chodorow, personal communication, June 25, 2015)

Addressing her individuality and "independent mind," Chodorow noted that the confident tone in her writing also brought criticism. One group of early feminist colleagues accused her of "writing like a man," because of her straightforward manner (e.g., "I just have to write what I need to write" was not without repercussions). In her words,

> I took some really big risks, maybe not such good risks, like I left Harvard when in graduate school to go to Brandeis, and I'm still not so sure that it was the 'right' thing to do at the time. Brandeis was a radical sociology department, and it had eminent German-Jewish refugee intellectuals in it, but it was not the Harvard Social Relations Department, it was not elite. And then I become a psychoanalyst, initially because I thought I couldn't write more about the mind without seeing actual patients, not just reading about them. I knew I wanted to write more about the psyche. (N. Chodorow, personal communication, June 25, 2015)

Contributions and Legacy

With an initial sense of Chodorow's individuality/subjectivity in her personal history and academic background, let us move on to explore Chodorow's legacy, particularly in relation to her contributions as a pioneering feminist thinker and feminist psychoanalyst. Chodorow's first book *The Reproduction of Mothering* (1978) was extremely influential throughout feminist scholarship—in literary studies, feminist philosophy, history, anthropology, political theory, social psychology, and so forth. Eventually, it fostered a generation of feminists in social science and literature who engage in a field of research broadly defined as "motherhood studies." Along with other pioneer feminists, Chodorow was also one of the early social scientists who articulated a way to imagine a "feminist methodology."

On the clinical front, Chodorow offers a psychoanalytic understanding of the female psyche that grew from object relations theory and preceded self-in-relation theory, even as she maintains a psychoanalytic frame that is consistent with ego psychology. Another significant contribution that weaves together Chodorow's social scientific training and clinical sensitivity may be easily spotted in her superb ability to hold the tension between individuality/subjectivity and cultural variation. In the following, Chodorow's narratives that flew naturally through the interview give substance to her accounting for various fronts of her contribution to feminism as a psychoanalyst and a social scientist (see also Chodorow, 1971).

I interviewed Chodorow right after she returned from the "Motherhood and Culture Conference" at Maynooth University in Ireland. Chodorow was invited as one of two keynote speakers. Discussing the field of motherhood studies inspired by her book, Chodorow reported her delight and surprise to find an entire contemporary field of motherhood studies in the social sciences and the humanities, and she mentioned other feminists who engaged in motherhood studies early on, including the philosopher Ruddick (1982), who wrote the book *Maternal Thinking*, and clinical psychologist Susan Contratto, who co-wrote "The fantasy of the perfect mother" (Chodorow & Contratto, 1982) with Chodorow, as well as many other articles on attitudes to mothers.

Chodorow shared her thoughts on the current evolution of motherhood studies, as she observed this at the conference:

> Writing about mothers, mothering, and motherhood ... it was interesting, why and when motherhood and mothering became something you can think about—the role of the mother, the place of the mother, maternal identity, maternal practices, maternal goals, looking at motherhood and its joys, looking at motherhood in different societies. Looking at expectations, looking at what happens, say, when the Icelandic government puts up a website about attachment, which supports mother-infant bonding and a policy that gives new mothers long periods of paid leave. But then, some people think, 'oh this is great,' and some others think, 'this is going to tie woman to the home.'

> So, there were all these debates about motherhood, and so many different studies—interview studies, observational studies, studies of milk banks, and nursing patterns,

and literature, and philosophy, from all over the world. There's much too much to say, from an extended conference, except to notice, I seem to have been part of the generation that 'discovered' motherhood for feminism. (N. Chodorow, personal communication, June 25, 2015)

In addition to providing a foundation for motherhood studies, Chodorow also was one of a generation of social scientists who helped create feminist methodology, which was also a prevalent focus of the conference. Speaking about this, Chodorow was extremely passionate about these "feminist methodology" foundations, including "reflexive sociology, paying attention to the role of the researcher, and paying attention to the research relationship." She gave examples of papers from the "Motherhood and Culture Conference":

> I heard one paper about a researcher, an associate researcher, and one of their subjects, and how the subject came to have a voice, and what she said when she had a voice. How you write a paper that gives the subject of study a voice. And then there was a woman who studied breast milk banks, another who wrote about pumping, others on literature and maternal ideology, and cross-cultural studies. An amazing doctor from a big hospital in Dublin talked about how different women experience the fetus as a baby or a fetus, depending on gestational time and circumstances, a spontaneous or not-spontaneous abortion, a later miscarriage, what does language allow? … It was just amazing! (N. Chodorow, personal communication, June 25, 2015)

It is worth noting that Chodorow also made links between her thoughts on feminist methodology and a theoretical approach emphasizing a relational dynamic that preceded the development of relational psychoanalysis (in Chodorow's words, "how do you make sure that you're not the outside expert who's interpreting to the patient?"). She pointed to other feminist sociologists who have paid attention to the researcher-researched relationship, including, among others, her Berkeley colleagues Arlie Russell Hochschild [founder of the sociology of emotions and author of *The Managed Heart* (1983) and many other books (e.g., Hochschild, 2003)] and Thorne (1993) [author of *Gender Play*]. In this context, she also noted the work of Carole Joffe, who has done field work at Planned Parenthood, studied pre-Roe v. Wade abortion providers, and written extensively on the politics of abortion (e.g., Joffe, 1995 and many other books).

Chodorow connected her social scientific methodological perspective with her clinical position:

> All of us, we were all concerned about the question of the researcher-researched relationship that is also akin to the therapist-patient relationship in clinical work. It doesn't mean self-disclosure, but it does mean paying attention to countertransference, paying attention to your impact, paying attention to your role, to who you are, to what the person is responding to in you. (N. Chodorow, personal communication, June 25, 2015)

It appears that Chodorow's early interest in both psychoanalysis and psychological anthropology and her attempts to understand "women's psyche" were both essential impetuses to her continuous efforts to combine the position of feminist social scientist and that of psychoanalyst. She recalled how, as a social science researcher, when she wrote *The Reproduction of Mothering* (Chodorow, 1978), she carefully took into account the existing psychoanalytic literature, whether or not it was explicitly on her topic, on gender development or mothering.

> I read the literature; I excavated and put together writings that hadn't been put together before. I didn't have any clinical experience. But I could read, so I did this literature search. I went and found articles that would be about infancy, or clinical articles about mothers with their infants or toddlers. And I said, well, if you look really carefully here, the mother is experiencing her daughter differently from her son, even if the analyst isn't noticing this. If you look at how she talks about her baby, she's talking about her girl baby as more like herself, or an extension of herself, than her son. Here are two cases, of mother-daughter and mother-son, and see how, subtly, they differ.' And that's my whole pre-oedipal chapter [in *The Reproduction of Mothering*], noticing unnoticed contrasts. And I re-read all of the classical literature—Helene Deutch, or Lampl-de Groot, for example—that was focusing on pre-oedipal and oedipal development in girls. My writing was saying, let's notice this, let's bring this up. It was already there, now bring it in. I was also writing in the early 1970s, when you were barely allowed to go beyond the Oedipal, theoretically and developmentally. Even when I started analytic training, in the mid-1980's, you were taught that only post-Oedipal people were analyzable. The patient had to have certain ego-capacities, a superego, that were oedipal products. It was a very different time from now! (N. Chodorow, personal communication, June 25, 2015)

Regarding her incorporation of psychoanalysis into sociological research, Chodorow stated candidly, "I needed [psychoanalysis] because you can't understand the mind without psychoanalysis." Along the same vein, a natural expansion of her thoughts following *The Reproduction of Mothering* evolved into her clinical reflections on people's minds. The mind, she said, and not just the female mind, is formed both relationally and individually. She published two early essays that helped to lay a foundation to articulate what became relational psychoanalysis:[2] "Gender, relation, and difference in psychoanalytic perspective" (Chodorow, 1979) claims that differentiation is a form of relatedness and "Toward a relational individualism" (Chodorow, 1986).

In speaking about her identity as a clinician, Chodorow shared in more detail her ways of listening to gendered themes. She said,

> I identify as a psychoanalyst, and I have multiple theoretical and clinical ears. You can find some case examples in *The Power of Feelings* (2001) and, *Individualizing Gender and Sexuality* (2012). But 'feminist therapist' would not be the word I would use about myself as a clinician. Of course I am a feminist, and I'm certainly attuned

to gender-questions, gender-identity questions, sense of self as male or female, sense of sexuality, unconscious conceptions of sex and gender, etc. I would say there's a feminist lens.

But I think there are two different ways of thinking about feminism, and one of them has to do with more, maybe inequality, stereotypes. I don't think clinically I notice that as a general issue, as opposed to perhaps with a particular patient. Of course I'm an advocate for gender equality, but in the consulting room, I'm sensitive to and I hear, I hope, "gendery" and sexual things that are both conscious and unconscious; I hear mother-daughter especially, and I write about that. But I think when people talk about feminism, they mean something specific about inequality, about power. I have a lot of categories around—mother-daughter, son-and-father, and maternity—all the kinship terms and all the unconscious terms. So I'm very much hearing these." (N. Chodorow, personal communication, June 25, 2015)

Chodorow continued to speak about convergence and divergence in her clinical conceptualizations, juxtaposing her psychoanalytic orientation with careful inclusion of feminist ideas,

I'd say I have what I call a gender "prism"—a theoretical transferential prism that includes gender and sexuality. "Prism" is my favorite way of describing transference, though I sometimes use "lens," when I try to explain transference to patients. I like to say that there's nothing wrong with it, it's not pathological, or finding fault. We all refract what comes from without and what comes from within through our own transferential prism, our own particular personality and individuality ... So, similarly, I think ... I *know* ... that I have a mother-daughter lens, a mother-daughter prism, as I work clinically. I notice patients' relations with their mothers, with daughters, with sons and daughters. Another prism is that I notice various forms of masculinity in male patients. Generally, I'm aware of the "gendery" components of my patients' sense of self, their lives, what they talk about, their place in the kinship system in social terms like mother, father, son, daughter, grandparent, grandchild ... Sisters, brothers, siblings ... I notice these. (N. Chodorow, personal communication, June 25, 2015)

In this context, I asked Chodorow to speak more about the notion of "power" in feminist psychotherapy. With regard to power, Chodorow noted,

It's very complicated because if you include in your therapeutic formulation something like power, you're moving outside of the mind of the patient; you are kind of framing them in an external context. (N. Chodorow, personal communication, June 25, 2015)

In this way, Chodorow continues to hold the psychoanalytic frame while remaining very mindful of feminist themes arising in clinical materials. As she holds the positions of both psychoanalyst and social science theorist, what is particularly important about her contribution to feminist clinical practice includes her acute sensitivity to cultural variation and her attunement to gender as an axis in relation to culture. Our dialogue evolved into a discussion on the tension between her emphasis on individuality/subjectivity and her clear position on the plurality of gendered and cultural variations (as Chodorow noted, "gender is decidedly plural"). I then inquired about how she resolves the seeming contradiction in holding the tension. She said,

> You could call it contradictory, or you could call it different. There's what I called 'objective' and 'subjective' culture, which is one part of this. Subjective culture is the conscious and unconscious ways of our experiencing ourselves as cultured … Subjective culture is different in the minds of different people, just as gender can be more or less salient for different people. Certainly in our society, almost anybody from a non-Anglo-Christian culture is more aware of their culture, consciously and unconsciously, but that doesn't mean that some Anglo-Christians aren't aware of their culture. And there's a huge variety within minority individuals about how pervasive subjective culture is to them. The same with subjective and observed or objective culture.
>
> So, how central is culture to one's identity? And what's the unconscious meaning of it? Once you get into the unconscious meanings, then anyone also has their own particular family that filters that culture. And I think this can also shift in the course of work. You know, some people come in and they'll think, 'I'm the way I am because that's the way it is in my culture.' And then later on, you find out that their culture has very little to do with how they are, and more to do with some compromise formation that came from, say, whatever childhood, or birth order, or what place was available still in the family, etc.… In fact it was '*their* mother,' not any *other* mother in their cultural community, who was like that.
>
> So, I go back to the fact that subjective culture and objective culture, or observed culture, these are really good ways of thinking about the impact of culture. What can be really important about culture isn't necessarily conscious, but preconscious. It's clinically limiting when you think that people can tell you about their culture. So, there's no simple answer here. We are all cultured, but we are all perhaps not as conscious of culture as we are of gender. The culture part is, is very hard to get at, I think. (N. Chodorow, personal communication, June 25, 2015, italics added)

Following this discussion, Chodorow gave a brief but elegant address on her way of holding the tension between individuality/subjectivity and cultural variations. In her words,

> It is culture's *impact* on individuality and subjectivity, but it is also, *how*, or *what*, is the cultural part of the individuality and subjectivity. Or what is the 'cultural identity'—the taken-up, individually meaningful part of the culture? (N. Chodorow, personal communication, June 25, 2015)

Meanwhile, Chodorow is not ignorant of the historically "missing social" in psychoanalysis. From the side of sociology, she mentioned a recent book *The Unhappy Divorce of Sociology and Psychoanalysis* (Chancer & Andrews, 2014). Psychoanalysis has also evolved and became more open to the effects of sociological elements. She hinted that her next writing project aims to make visible "the missing infrastructure of social science in psychoanalysis."

In Retrospect (Retrospective Narratives)

This section includes Chodorow's reflective narratives addressing variations of her thoughts—first in relation to working from the position of "margin" in relation to the "center," second with regard to the growing edges of her thoughts, and third with comments on the shifting fields of feminism, women's studies, and sociology in relation to psychoanalysis.

As mentioned previously, Chodorow remarked at multiple occasions during the interview that she "just knows" that it is the only way she can think. Building on this remark, she also reflected on the effects and contexts that foster this personal style. In her words,

> I thought I was trying to push the center. From the margin I'm always trying to see what the presuppositions are, to see what other people are taking for granted, that they don't even notice … It's also [about] *going up against core thinking*. Originally, I wrote about how sociologists should think about the psychological, and recipro-cally these days, I write about how psychoanalysts should think about the social … What I am is willing to take risks, and I don't think of it to myself as marginaliza-tion: *I just do what I have to do*. Maybe it is from margin to center, you know, but often collectively. The woman's movement, I was not alone … . Brandeis was very supportive of psychoanalytic sociology, and no other sociology department was like that. I had mentors, people who supported independent thinking, and a lot of intel-lectual sisters …. *I don't think of myself as going against the current, but I think of myself as looking for an infrastructure, wherever it is, and it may turn out to be against the current*. Most radical thinking does challenge the taken-for-granted. (N. Chodorow, personal communication, June 25, 2015, italics added)

Drawing upon Erik Erikson's "ego integrity" principle, Chodorow was thoughtful in addressing the projects she has accomplished in her life. "You have to live your life," she said. In Erikson's theory, ego integrity is coming to realize that "'this is the life I've lived.' It's a really important goal for patients, for oneself, for one's children." To add an additional life cycle element, she also noted her appreciation of having the experiences of being a mother and having personal relationships. She said,

> One thing we have not talked about at all, but very important, is that I'm so glad that I'm a mother … It's been one of the great pleasures. I don't want to universalize about it, because lots of women are not mothers, by choice or because they can't be, or what-ever. But having friendships, having motherhood, having close family relationships, those are not part of my professional life, but they are absolutely essential. I feel very fortunate to have that. (N. Chodorow, personal communication, June 25, 2015)

While our conversation focused on reviewing the various offerings she has made, Chodorow took care to mention an area that she missed, given the his-torical context in which foundational work for second wave feminism was built. She said,

> I missed the female body, I've said this elsewhere, but Rosemary Balsam, whose book you really want to read, *Women's Bodies in Psychoanalysis* Balsam (2012), says

it best—she describes the body in the female psyche. In the1970s, you did not want 'anatomy is destiny'—it was important that anatomy *wasn't* destiny, so I made it all about the psyche. (N. Chodorow, personal communication, June 25, 2015, italics added)

With regard to the shifting significance of feminism as a discipline within academia, Chodorow first shared candidly her personal experience to emphasize the initial difficulties for feminist thinkers. "I barely got a job when I finished my degree," she said, and furthermore,

I just want you to know that the *Reproduction of Mothering* was turned down by one of the presses I sent it to, and 'Heterosexuality as a Compromise Formation,' one of my best-known papers, was rejected by two different psychoanalytic journals. Reviewers for a feminist journal of 'Seventies Questions for Thirties Women' [1989b – from an interview study of women psychoanalysts trained in the '20s and '30s] said 'why doesn't she just tell us about the result of the research: why is she telling us about her thoughts and the research relationship?'—and in fact I think it wasn't accepted. (N. Chodorow, personal communication, June 25, 2015)

Following this thread, Chodorow shared how other feminist thinkers faced similar difficulties. For example,

people like Malkah T. Notman and Carol C. Nadelson [two very well-known psychiatrist-psychoanalysts], who collected three landmark volumes called *The Woman Patient* that came out in 1978, '80, and '82, but after that they had trouble getting feminist writing published in mainstream journals. (N. Chodorow, personal communication, June 25, 2015).

It is within this historical context of the 1970s that Chodorow was reminiscing about how *The Reproduction of Mothering* was "controversial." Fortunately, the evolution of feminism did not stop in the 1970's. As Chodorow put it,

Feminism went from margin to front and center in the academy. As part of that, I somehow provided a window for people in many different fields to understand something about the psychology of woman. It was not necessarily just about mothering, but it was about the female psyche and the female self. (N. Chodorow, personal communication, June 25, 2015)

While feminism started to claim a more mainstream position within academia, psychoanalysis remained unevenly accepted, both in academia and in feminism. Chodorow noted some initial hurdles she encountered by being a feminist social scientist and a psychoanalyst. She said,

When I first started, feminists—all the first 'big books' except mine and Mitchell's—were so hostile toward psychoanalysis. They thought that it was biologically determinist and [that it] stereotyped women. And the sociologists thought it was too psychological. (N. Chodorow, personal communication, June 25, 2015)

It is in this context that Chodorow noted the evolution of various foci within psychoanalytic feminism. She said,

> At first, after gender and the psychology of women, sexuality and sexual orientation became very prominent. And then, as more transgender and gender crossing issues become more important, you get less focus on what you might call feminist issues, you might call woman's issues … today, [we are] not paying a lot of attention to pregnancy, or breasts, or female sexuality, etc., except Balsam. Psychoanalytic feminism originally had more focus on noticing how invidious psychology and psychoanalysis were vis-à-vis [in relation to] women, and also there were more global categorizations – girl versus boy, women versus men. Now, I think in terms of what I call patterns, or a gender lens. I don't expect to see something that's fixed and universal, but I expect to see patterns; I expect to see mother-daughter, where many other clinicians don't. Are these 'feminist'? I don't know. (N. Chodorow, personal communication, June 25, 2015)

Along with addressing the evolution of feminism, Chodorow also shared her observations on the changing field of sociology. She noted that "many of us who did qualitative work, in-depth interviewing, hanging-out ethnography, we are all retired now." In contrast, "today's sociology is more quantitative, hypothesis-testing, macro, and it's mainly about big data, except our students and their students."

Concluding Remarks: Words for Future Feminist Therapists

In ending, Chodorow shared her hopes and encouragement for the next generation of feminist therapists:

> I hope that anybody who becomes a therapist would understand how central and important it is for themselves to be in therapy, to really get to know themselves…. I think that's true for any therapist: it's both a privilege and a necessity. I think it's important to understand that all cultural categories and identity categories are filtered by the individual, and to always hold that tension in mind, between, you know, there's gender, female-ness, male-ness, being-a-woman, being-a-man, but each person is their own individual man or woman or boy or girl. It's not a free for all and anything goes, because sometimes this gender and sexuality involve harming others, and that's not alright. But, for therapists to understand, both for themselves and for their patients, that there are infinities of identities and choices, and the criteria of clinical evaluation have more to do with affect, with an individual's contentment or discontent, how narrow and driven a category feels, versus whether it's flexible, when you're talking about gender (or really any part of the psyche). I mean it's fine, if you're a 4-year-old girl, if you only want to wear a pink tutu and ballet slippers, or only want to wear shorts, boy-shorts, plus a t-shirt or no t-shirt. Whatever, when you're 4 to 6, you can be as absolutist as you want about gender, but later, I think, it's better to be able to be, if not flexible in one's own identity, at least understand that flexibility and identity are a clinical goal, whether it be in gender and anything else.

> So, I guess, what we started with: I would just say remember the individual; remember individuality. And for me, particularly, if I were to say what have I

learned, it's to remember that people in their gender are embodied, and that's really important ... I've learned that from my feminist medical-psychiatric colleagues, that being aware of one's body and bodily sexuality does not mean that anatomy is destiny, as Freud put it. Feminism means to be attentive to women and women's possibilities and lives, but *women here is decidedly plural.* (N. Chodorow, personal communication, June 25, 2015, italics added)

Acknowledgments

Special thanks to Dr. Nancy Chodorow for her gracious acceptance of this interview as well as her support in reviewing the initial drafts of this article.

Notes

1. In the interview, Chodorow gave examples of how she used theories as tools in her early feminist writings. *The Reproduction of Mothering* (Chodorow, 1978), for example, draws from psychoanalysis, Marxism, functionalism, anthropology, attachment theory, and other theories. Later (e.g., as seen in Chodorow, 2002), for instance, she used generation theory, drawing from Mannheim (1928). Always, she integrated a critical stance against the taken-for-granted that she learned from anthropology and ethnomethodology.
2. See, for example, Mitchell (1974, 1988).

References

Balsam, R. M. (2012). *Women's bodies in psychoanalysis.* New York: Routledge.

Chancer, L., & Andrews, J. (Eds.). (2014). *The unhappy divorce of Sociology and Psychoanalysis: Diverse perspectives on the psychosocial.* New York: Palgrave Macmillan.

Chodorow, N. J. (1971). Being and doing: A cross-cultural examination of the socialization of males and females. In V. Gornick & B. K. Moran (Eds.), *Woman in sexist society: Studies in power and powerlessness* (pp. 259–291). New York: New American Library.

Chodorow, N. J. (1974). Family structure and feminine perspective. In M. Z. Rosaldo & L. Lamphere (Eds.), *Woman, culture and society* (pp. 43–66). Stanford, CA: Stanford University Press.

Chodorow, N. J. (1978; second ed. 1999). *The reproduction of mothering: Psychoanalysis and the sociology of gender.* Berkeley: University of California Press.

Chodorow, N. J. (1979). Gender, relation and difference in psychoanalytic perspective. In H. Eisenstein & A. Jardine (Eds.), *The future of difference* (pp. 54–75). Boston: G. K. Hall.

Chodorow, N. J. (1986). Toward a relational individualism: The mediation of self through psycho-analysis. In T. C. Heller, M. Sosna, and D. E. Wellbery (Eds.), *Reconstructing individualism* (pp. 197–207). Stanford: Stanford University Press. Reprinted in Feminism and Psychoanalytic theory (1989). New Haven, CT: Yale University Press.

Chodorow, N. J. (1989a). *Feminism and psychoanalytic theory.* New Haven, CT: Yale University Press.

Chodorow, N. J. (1989b). Seventies questions for thirties women. In N. J. Chodorow (Ed.), *Feminism and psychoanalytic theory* (pp. 199–218). New Haven, CT: Yale University Press.

Chodorow, N. J. (1992). Heterosexuality as a compromise formation: Reflections on the psychoanalytic theory of sexual development. *Psychoanalysis and Contemporary Thought, 15*(3), 267–304.

Chodorow, N. J. (1994). *Femininities, masculinities, sexualities: Freud and beyond*. Lexington, KY: University Press of Kentucky.

Chodorow, N. J. (1999). *The power of feelings: Personal meaning in psychoanalysis, gender, and culture*. New Haven, CT: Yale University Press.

Chodorow, N. J. (2002). Born into a world at war: Listening for affect and personal meaning. *American Imago, 59*(3), 297–315. doi:10.1353/aim.2002.0015

Chodorow, N. J. (2012). *Individualizing gender and sexuality: Theory and practice*. New York and London: Routledge.

Chodorow, N. J., & Contratto, S. (1982). The fantasy of the perfect mother. In B. Thorne & M. Yalom (Eds.), *Rethinking the family: Some feminist questions* (pp. 54–75). New York: Longman.

Collins, P. H. (2002). *Black feminist thought: Knowledge, consciousness, and the politics of empowerment*. New York and London: Routledge.

Durkheim, E. (1912). *The elementary forms of Religious Life (K. Fields, Trans.)*. New York: Free Press.

Hochschild, A. R. (2003). *The managed heart: Commercialization of human feeling, with a new afterword*. Berkeley: University of California Press.

Joffe, C. (1995). *Doctors of conscience: The struggle to provide abortion before Roe v. Wade*. Boston: Beacon Press.

Mannheim, K. (1928). The problem of generations. In P. Kecskemeti (Ed.), *Essays on the sociology of knowledge* (pp. 276–322). New York: Oxford University Press.

Mernissi, F. (1994). *Dreams of trespass: Tales of a harem girlhood*. New York: Basic Books.

Mitchell, J. (1974). *Psychoanalysis and feminism*. New York: Pantheon.

Mitchell, S. A. (1988). *Relational concepts in psychoanalysis: An integration*. Cambridge, MA: Harvard University Press.

Rollins, J. (1987). *Between women: Domestics and their employers*. Philadelphia: Temple University Press.

Ruddick, S. (1982). *Maternal thinking*. In A. Cafagna, R. Peterson, & C. Staudenbaur (Eds.), *Philosophy, children, and the family* (Vol. 1, pp. 101–126). East Lansing, MI: Springer US. Retrieved from http://dx.doi.org/10.1007/978-1-4613-3473-6_11

Thorne, B. (1993). *Gender play: Girls and boys in school*. Piscataway, NJ: Rutgers University Press.

Whiting, B. B. (1963). *Six cultures: Studies of child rearing*. Oxford, UK: Wiley.

The Amazing Life and Times of Oliva Espín

Debra M. Kawahara

ABSTRACT

Oliva Espín is a prolific feminist and multicultural writer and psychologist who has significantly contributed to feminist therapy throughout her career. This biographical article highlights her many contributions to feminism, feminist psychology, and humankind.

On a cloudy, grey morning in the early summer of 2015, I met with my long-time mentor, role model, and dear friend, Oliva Espín, at her home. A diminutive woman, she would be described as a strong, fierce, independent, wise, cultured, and vibrant person who draws the attention of others she is near, and a force to be reckon with if she is challenged. Although I knew her well in many ways, there were many ways that I did not. This project allowed me to get to know her in new ways and to take you, the reader, through the interesting twists and turns that have been part of her amazing journey as a woman, woman of color, feminist, lesbian, immigrant, Latina, spiritual Catholic, scholar, writer, and counseling psychologist—a few of the interweaving, multidimensional identities that make her who she is.

Background

To begin, much of this background information on Oliva was provided by Oliva's keynote address at the National Multicultural Conference and Summit in 2005 and Lewis' (2011) profile from the Psychology's Feminist Voices project. I added pieces from my interview with her (including verbatim quotes) and my own relationship with her.

Oliva was born on December 12, 1938, in Cuba. Her maternal grandfather was an illiterate immigrant from Spain. As a result, Oliva's mother was particularly interested in portraying herself as middle class and in educating her children. Her father was a lawyer in the Cuban Navy. He was completely unprepared when the Cuban government changed, and he was fired by Batista in 1940 for being unsympathetic to the new government. It was the end of the Depression, and with a teaching credential, he decided to start his own elementary school and commercial academy. This is where Oliva learned to read. She read voraciously. She also began to fantasize about different worlds, and this, she believes, along with her spirituality and her desire to learn, saved her from her family's circumstances. At age 7, she began writing poetry, which her uncle began to publish. This uncle would be very influential in her life: both her father and uncle encouraged her intellectual and scholarly pursuits, counter to the pervasive attitudes of other men and Cuban society that surrounded her.

Her father's school, however, failed miserably, and the family suffered as a result. The saving grace was that Oliva and her three siblings were able to attend private schools for middle class families. This was made possible through church connections. Her diminished social class and resulting childhood of poverty impacted her immensely. It was a constant source of pain, and like her mother, she wanted to hide the fact that her family was poor from her classmates.

In high school, she became interested in psychology when she took her first psychology class and the instructor (who was a psychologist) became her favorite teacher. She knew then that she wanted to become a psychologist. Later, she began to have anxiety and panic attacks, and this allowed her to gain empathy for psychological suffering.

One of her most powerful memories involves winning $4,000 on a television game show in 1958. She remembers that society did not accept women or girls as being smart, intellectual, or equals at the time. Socially appropriate behavior for women and girls was to be quiet and not to contradict men in public. This is her reflection of this life moment:

> Some of the young boys at that time were intimidated and unhappy because I did not say, "Oh ... really, you're so great." It was like, "Just what are you talking about?" I mean, this woman who wins prizes on television is scary. You know, so that was very much there. My father and my uncle were always supportive of my intellectual development. So, in that sense, I had some men who had approved of me, but for young men, it was threatening that I would even win a prize on television. (Oliva Espín, personal communication, June 12, 2015)

With the winnings, she traveled to Europe for the first time. Europe would become a frequent destination throughout her life.

In 1961, Oliva left Cuba and went to Spain, the United States, and Costa Rica. In Costa Rica, she taught psychology and religion at St. Clare College in San Jose, Costa Rica, from 1964–1969. She also attained a BA at the Universidad de Costa Rica in 1969. She then traveled to Belgium with a fellowship from Costa Rica. She also married at that time. When the marriage ended, she returned to the United States to pursue a doctorate in Counseling Psychology at the University of Florida, which she completed in 1974. From 1974 to 1975, she became an interim Assistant Professor in the Department of Counseling Psychology at McGill University in Montreal. Following this, she held an academic position in the Counseling Psychology Program at Boston University for 11 years. She then became a Professor in the Department of Women's Studies at San Diego State University and later was also a Professor in the Clinical Psychology PsyD Program at the California School of Professional Psychology.

Oliva has retired from both positions and attained Professor Emerita status at both institutions. She continues to have an active professional and personal life through writing, presenting, publishing, and mentoring.

Her Circumstantial Feminist Journey

As Oliva recalls, a counseling psychology course awakened her feminist self. It changed her life. She stated,

> I went to school with only girls and I taught in schools where I was mostly teaching girls. So, I was very aware that women are capable of things and so in my first semester, my first quarter actually, of my doctoral program, I needed one more course to be full-time, I needed to be full time to get a fellowship, scholarship, whatever, financial aid. I did that. There was a Psychology of Women course and … I thought I'll take this without really knowing what I was getting myself into, in a way … I was just doing the counseling psych. It was to get another thing and it completely changed my life because it was like this is what I want. And from there my dissertation. I came in thinking that I wanted to do work in therapy, group psychotherapy, which I taught a while after. It was something that always interested me, um, the group therapy. That course sort of redirected me so my dissertation ended up being on feminist issues, women from Latin America in the U.S. comparing … Well, it was like, "Ah ha! This makes sense, you know, I have known this all my life because I have experienced it being surrounded by women, knowing my women students." All those things I sort of knew all along, but this sort of shaped in an organized way the things I knew or the things I had experienced. (Oliva Espín, personal communication, June 12, 2015)

Her emerging interests in feminism and women's issues as well as her developing feminist identity were further supported by a male professor who was interested in women's issues. This allowed her to combine her various interests into her professional scholarship and writing.

> It was a mixture of this course and then David Lane wanting to be supportive of issues of women so my specialization … at that time, I graduated in 1974, was on counseling women. That's why the dissertation was on women. I also did Latin American studies, I did Latin American women in the U.S. That's what the dissertation was. So it opened, it started giving theoretical, or I don't even know if it is even theoretical … I think they would say evidence based, although I hate that term, but information about issues about women. (Oliva Espín, personal communication, June 12, 2015)

She explains the realization that feminism was a part of her and her identity like this,

> I think that is what happened to me. Finding feminism and a better understanding of what happens to women made me realize that it wasn't me for being a smart girl

or whatever. Or the other girls I knew. Whenever I taught in other contexts that there is a social thing about women that is present and that you have to deal with it in one way or another. But it's not … there is nothing wrong with being a smart girl. It's not your fault. (Oliva Espín, personal communication, June 12, 2015)

The Coming Out Process as a Lesbian Psychologist

Although she identified as a lesbian, Oliva struggled with her combined identity as both a psychologist and as a lesbian. At the beginning of her career, she believed that being a lesbian was connected with being psychologically sick. This conflicted with her desire to be a psychologist: could she heal others when she was "sick" because she was a lesbian? As a result, she was very careful not to disclose this part of herself to others professionally to avoid being labeled "sick;" she feared that her dream of being a psychologist would be taken away from her. She remembers,

> I started [to identify as a lesbian] at the beginning of my career, but I didn't tell anybody. The beginning of my Ph.D … It was a big, big secret … It was 1972, it was a sickness. I'm sick. I cannot be a good psychologist. I have to keep it quiet … Initially, in the beginning, it was "I can't talk about this" because it was an illness. I cannot be sick when I am being a psychologist … So there is a different perspective at that time. If you have any of those things, you cannot be a psychologist. (Oliva Espín, personal communication, June 12, 2015)

However, societal attitudes about lesbians and gays slowly changed. As lesbians and gays became more accepted and were no longer labeled as being sick or having a mental disorder, Oliva began to publically identify as a lesbian as well as to advocate, present, and publish on these issues. She also began to be the voice of the voiceless, breaking a deafening silence.

> I think even now, there is much more understanding … so there is, in general, there is a better understanding of mental illness and that wasn't there … then it started becoming more acceptable. There was an association of lesbian and gay psychologists that has pretty much died, but it was part of that push in that direction. There was AWP also very soon. I became a member of AWP in 1973. They had barely started. Then the organization that would help me feel a sense of identity as a woman and as a lesbian. It is possible to be a psychologist and all those things, so then that is the silence I could break. In my council position within the APA was Division 44. Something very funny happened, actually. During a council meeting, someone said something that was racist and I stood up and said something, but of course, I can picture myself: I was dressed in a white suit with a dark blue blouse, high heels, etc. I said, "That's racist, that's inappropriate," and the guy assumed that I was a council representative for Division 45 because I was saying that was racist. When I said, "No, it's 44, " he was very shocked. There were a few things we did in council at that time, prevent APA publications to advertise positions in the military while the military was discriminating against lesbians and gays. (Oliva Espín, personal communication, June 12, 2015)

Breaking the silence and being the voice of the voiceless are hallmarks of Oliva's career.

The Boston Feminist Therapy Collective: Being a Feminist Therapist

An influential impact on Oliva's work as a feminist therapist was the Boston Feminist Therapy Collective. She moved to Boston in 1975 and quickly found a community of feminists that would continue to help her develop as a feminist and a feminist therapist. She recalls,

> And then with feminist therapies especially. When I moved to Boston, of course, I had a full-time academic position, but I read something about this feminist therapy collective and I contacted them ... and I became part of that. I was the only [Latina] of the therapists who worked there ... It was a feminist therapy collective, of which there was many in the early 70s in different places in the country. There was this one in Boston. I was very much part of that. I was not sort of the core people that started it, but I was part of it and I did therapy there for several years in their space because I didn't have a license yet. The collective was like the umbrella of that time. (Oliva Espín, personal communication, June 12, 2015)

The Confusing and Conflicted Road

The road, however, was not always clear, smooth, or direct. Oliva often found that different parts of her identity were not easily merged. She began to question the separation and fragmentation of her multiple identities, particularly race/ethnicity, gender, and sexual orientation, in her own teaching as well as in larger societal dynamics. She remembered,

> A marking event for me occurred at a professional conference in the late 1970s where women of color talked about racial loyalties as being in opposition to women's issues. I remember feeling puzzled and conflicted. Weren't we women? Why see this as oppositional issues? They were both of equal interest to us, I thought. The attitude of these women, of course, I understood later, was partly a manifestation of gender power hierarchies in action. Your husband's career was always more important than yours. And women meant White women in the racial power hierarchy. Therefore, women of color had to choose for or against the interest of others, never for themselves. (Espín, 2005)

However, she was seeing the power differentials and dynamics being manifested right in front of her eyes. Interestingly, her challenge in making sense of the conflicts and contradictions in her professional world and society were parallel to the internal process that she was undergoing, struggling with different aspects of herself and the loyalties that pushed and pulled her.

> Time and again, I felt that that a particular identity or part of me needed to be given precedence over other parts. If I identified as a woman or a feminist, not even mention a lesbian, I was openly challenged as a traitor to my Latino-Hispanic roots.

Because the majority of my clients were women of color and/or immigrants from different parts of the world, grasping what was most important to each one of them was not an easy task. Yes, their ethnicity was an important factor in their life experience, as it was for me, but they lived that ethnoracial experience as women. And that gave it a unique flavor. Yes, some issues took precedence at one point or another, but these different identities were present all the time in me and in my clients, influencing and modifying each other, and creating a unique personal experience. While some of these happened at a professional level, I was also struggling with my own identity and my own understanding of who I was in this U.S. society. Here, I was an immigrant, the ways in which I was seen and I saw myself were sometimes in active opposition to each other, and that may be still be true ... The temptation to peg people to certain categories to the exclusion of others is a powerful force in human interactions. But it is impossible to pick apart and separate these identities in an individual without destroying the person. (Espín, 2005)

The Intersections of Feminism, Multiculturalism, Latinas, Sexuality, and Migration

Multiple interests in Oliva's work started to intersect in her scholarship and presentations. As she interacted with other feminists and psychologists, saw therapy cases, and presented at and attended conferences, her conceptualization of these interweaving issues emerged and she began writing about them.

I always represented myself as a feminist therapist, meaning we know that social factors are part of what affect women's lives. It is not just that women are crazy individually. It is that the external world can make you crazy or contribute to whatever is happening to you. And then frequently, there was then the thing of this is a white women's thing. In the therapy collective, it was interesting because Latino women called in and I ended up being the person who worked with them ... So I started doing that more and more ... ."Don't tell me this is for only white women because Latino women have the same things. They have the same kinds of complications in that ... ." That is why I was looking at a conference in New York. Barnard College did a conference on sexuality every so often. I think it was 1983, 82, around there. They invited me to come talk about Latino sexuality, again from [a] feminist perspective or whatever. And that article was published in a book called "Pleasure and Danger," female sexuality ... It was 1984, so it is from back there and then. So again, it was sexuality, Latinas, and a feminist perspective of what is happening to women in therapy. So I started then writing some about that, and it was difficult for me to write in English. (Oliva Espín, personal communication, June 12, 2015)

Three specific articles signal the start of the intentional integration of her critical thinking and analysis of feminism, multiculturalism, sexuality, migration, Latina women, and identity. The articles were: (a) "Cultural and historical influences on sexuality in Hispanic/Latin women" in 1984; (b) "Psychological impact of migration on Latinas" in 1987; and (c) "Issues of identity in the psychology of Latina lesbian women" in 1987 in *Pleasure and Danger* (please see "Selected Publications of Oliva Espín" at the end of the article).

Those were the beginning of integrating the feminist and the multicultural [psychology] and sexual identity and Latina, all that in there. So those three articles I think were … In the three cases, someone said, "Could you write something about this?" I don't think I would have initiated it because I did not feel confident enough … And when somebody says, "Would you write about sexuality?" "Okay, let me think about sexuality of Latinas and let me see what I think about Latina lesbians." It was, it sort of, those three articles were the first times that I put out my thoughts in writing and they are still cited, so obviously, they did something. (Oliva Espín, personal communication, June 12, 2015)

Oliva spoke about the challenges and risks in writing about these issues: there was not validation or widespread support in traditional academia or the mainstream psychological field. Nonetheless, she did see some early interest from other academics in her writing about these issues. Not one to back down or go away gently, she continued to push her own and others' boundaries into critically thinking and writing more deeply and seriously about the real lives of real people in a scholarly manner. It was not until the 1990s that she began to get more widespread recognition for her work.

They're [the three articles] from the 80s … then the APA award was in 1991, so I put those things out and people started noticing, which is interesting because the capacity to write and not write and who has access to writing and all that makes a difference on how ideas get out there. It is not like I didn't have ideas until 1984, but I never wrote about them until 1984. (Oliva Espín, personal communication, June 12, 2015)

She further discussed the challenge of finding the tools and psychological concepts to explore, discover, and learn about others who had not been previously visible in the psychological literature. The absence of available appropriate methods in mainstream psychology ultimately led her to the use of qualitative research methods.

When you start working on things like that, you also don't have the tools that are established. That is what brought me to qualitative research … really because I tried using a couple of instruments and translating a couple of instruments, but this doesn't fit, this doesn't give me what I am looking for, this doesn't talk to people and find out what's important. So you start doing this thing without knowing that is what you're doing. I didn't know it was called qualitative research. Actually, in Boston, there was a guy who was doing qualitative research. Then I thought, "Oh, so this is what it is." Let's name something; it is possible to go in that direction, and I started reading things that had to do with that. A lot of fumbling in the dark. (Oliva Espín, personal communication, June 12, 2015)

Moving from Boston to San Diego

Because she wanted to make a career change, Oliva decided to move from Boston to San Diego in 1990. She became a faculty member in the Department of Women's Studies at San Diego State University (SDSU) and later became a

Professor in Clinical Psychology at the California School of Professional Psychology (CSPP). Although she did not have the rich feminist environment of Boston, she believed that joining the Women's Studies Department at SDSU was one of the most influential events in her intellectual life. She recollects,

Getting here [San Diego], it suddenly felt like I was in the desert. People didn't know things that were everyday knowledge for any feminist there [Boston]. People were calling themselves "feminist" here [San Diego], and clearly, they were saying all sorts of "blah blah." But coming from psychology where you do research in a certain way, remember qualitative psychology was not accepted ... So coming from a psychology place where this is what you have to do, into a place as long [as] you were working on women it fits that purpose of the department. And yes, of course, I am doing it from a psychology perspective because that is what I know how to do. But I can do a more integrated psychology in the sense of using other disciplines. It also is because I had colleagues from history, anthropology, political science, sociology, literature, etc., I started getting in touch with ideas that are part of the feminist world in general, but are not much part of psychology. When I go do the psychology of women course at Alliant now, I go say, "How many of you have read Foucault?" Maybe one hands goes up, if it is somebody who did an undergraduate in women's studies. But for the most part, I mean people who have been very influential in the thinking of feminists and one of the books I used for the course is a women who is from New Zealand who used Foucault to try [to] understand the psychology of women and it is the only book that does that and I really, really like it. It's a very ... it gave me a perspective of a lot of different disciplines and a lot [of] different things that I wanted to get in there that are not in psychology. When I started teaching about privilege and oppression, I did a graduate course about privilege and oppression at San Diego State. You start looking at all sorts of disciplines to start talking about that thing. I learned so many things that are not psychology officially, and yet are very relevant for psychology—experiences of being privileged, experiences of being oppressed that make you who you are psychologically that come from social forces. It is not that you were crazy. It's that there was something there in the social context that made who you are. I understand psychology from a very different perspective thanks to having been in women's studies, hearing things from other disciplines that had relevance to psychology. So it is not only the multicultural and the intersectionality in the psychological sense, but it is also the interdisciplinary things that bring all these things into the understanding of psychology and the psychology of women ... (Oliva Espín, personal communication, June 12, 2015)

Writing from Experience and Curiosity

As Oliva found herself in this new environment with scholars from various disciplines, her thinking expanded and became more complex and sophisticated. Her experiences and questions led her to write the book *Women Crossing Boundaries: A Psychology of Immigration and the Transformations of Sexuality* in 1999.

The *Women Crossing Boundaries*, the 1999 book, came from doing therapy, talking to students, talking to people, people talking about their sexual or nonsexual experiences and histories in relation to whether their family expected ... that kind of thing. That was the time I stretched beyond Latinas to look at all immigrants, "Okay, let's talk about sexuality," because basically it's the same thing, "My family wants something, and I don't want that, but I don't want to break with my family." I was hearing that in so many different ways. "I want to be faithful to my parent's culture, but to do that I am going to destroy myself, where am I going to with this?" It was usually around the sexual issues where this acculturation, or whatever you want to call it, conflict intensified for women and girls. So that's why I wanted to ask those questions and find out about that. And the thing about language was also from therapy—talking to people in Spanish and they start talking about sexuality and immediately switch to English. So what is going on here? (Oliva Espín, personal communication, June 12, 2015)

The Importance of Spirituality

One area that has been very important to Oliva is her spirituality and her relationship to God or the Divine. This has been a constant in her life and a source of strength and comfort, and has never been a source of conflict or guilt for her as for many others who identify as lesbian or gay. This part of Oliva seems deeply personal and private.

I have lived most of my adult life as a lesbian, which leads many people to believe that I have no use for religious feelings since most religious institutions disapproved of my lifestyle. However, nothing matters to me more than my relationship with God. Nothing. Yet, I refused to let religious institutions and authorities determine ... determine how I should or will live. Religion is not only about rules and holy books. It is about our innermost beings, our expectations, hopes, and desires for transcendence. Spiritual beliefs have provided forms of expression for people that were otherwise excluded from the ... mainstream to express themselves. Latin American liberation theology, the Black church in the U.S., and the medieval European mystics have a lot in common regardless of the differences in centuries, geography, and social context. For me, as for many people, a relationship with the divine, whatever that is and however it's interpreted, is a source of life and freedom, not a constricting force that stifles my inner being. I have come to believe that killing the appetite for God, or alternatively the sexual drive in one's self, is a form of surrendering to and bolstering the power of patriarchal oppressive forces. (Espín, 2005)

Living in Contradictions: Intersectionality, Multiple Identities, and Social Locations

Oliva's process of understanding herself and her own life also extended to her clients and the feminist therapy she did with them. Conceptualizing the intricacies and intersections of her multiple identities and the social locations of her life remains in constant process. She relates,

The question remains how to deal with all the apparent contradictions in identity in a particular person. First, are they truly contradictions for the person? You may be surprised to know that I experienced that. If I experience any conflict, it stems from the position of those around me who want me to choose my true identity. Concretely, it is as difficult for me to deal with church teachings about my sexual orientation as it is to deal with other people, lesbians included, who think it is ridiculous and absurd to believe in anything spiritual, unless it is the God, of course. It is difficult to choose between my political commitments and my Cuban heritage because people expect me to renounce one or the other. For me, as for many others, the issue is to find room for my multiple selves, a task made difficult by the expectations that I choose one identity and stick to it. In a therapy situation, the therapist discomforts are not about not being able to pin down the client, maybe more the problem than the client's sense of multiple identities. Perhaps I'm a puzzle. But like any puzzle, if all the pieces are not in, if some pieces are discarded, there's not a complete pictures of me. (Espín, 2005)

Oliva's metaphor of a kaleidoscope where the view changes as fragments of color and light are reflected through it change is parallel to one's multiple identities, the intersectionality of the multidimensional selves, and social locations and the ongoing processes of living with the possible contradictions of these selves. In considering this, she challenges how we are situated in oppressive hierarchies and in our own actions. She further asks how we may be recreating the very oppression that we are fighting against.

The pictures inside the kaleidoscope do not exist without the fragments of colored glass that make it up. Each of my apparent internal contradictions modifies and enhances the others. And each of these little pieces of colored glass inside the kaleidoscope contributes to the beauty of the total picture. For the most part, it is still very hard to speak about some of these issues without offending someone or someone taking offense, which is not quite the same thing, or finding myself alienated, or finding myself alienated from those who do not want to hear what they interpreted as divided loyalties. Precisely because am I, I am caught in hierarchies of oppression in so many different aspects of who I am, emotional, political, and cultural communities of belonging are essential for my surviving, and misunderstanding from those communities, it's particularly painful. Because most people do not live with the awareness that we live in a context of normalized injustice, it is easy to ignore the power of horizontal oppression as an effective tool of domination. Trying to address those injustices that touch us most closely, we may end up creating similar injustices for others. We may end up becoming complicit in the oppression of others through our efforts to liberate ourselves. Those who do not fit our own category of oppression, as we think they should, become authorized as cruelly as the powerful authorize us. The individual pain is intensified by the structurally caused pain. We become unaware agents of the forces of oppression that we think we are fighting by, for example, deciding that homosexuals do not belong in our churches or do not deserve the same rights because there is chosen behavior. Um, I am now convinced that racism and nationalism derive their strength from sexism. Studying immigrants, no, it's not the cause, but they're strengthened by it. Studying immigrant women from different cultural backgrounds, I have observed over and over how women are made to carry cultural values and behaviors at the expense of their own lives. Women's bodies are policed in the name of tradition. Policing women's bodies and behaviors becomes a means of asserting superiority. It is an attempt at preserving the past ... addressing the social constant transformation. This is not just a benign manifestation of interesting traditions. It may cost some women their lives. By the same token, conflicts about sexual orientation become a territory to preserve gender structures untouched and uncontested. I know now that a lot of what we believe to be truths about color and race like sexual orientation or gender are culture-specific metanarratives that fit one group but may not fit another. (Oliva Espín, personal communication, June 12, 2015)

Conclusion

My writing about Oliva's life and contributions feels like a patchwork quilt that pieces together parts of her life. Each piece can stand on its own for the unique importance that it played in her life and for its contributions to feminism and feminist therapy. At the same time, the whole quilt in its totality is so much more ... as is the beauty and power of her life.

Selected Publications by Oliva Espín

Espín, O. M. (1984). Cultural and historical influences on sexuality in Hispanic/ Latin women: Implications for psychotherapy. In C. Vance (Ed.), *Pleasure and danger: Exploring female sexuality* (pp. 149–164). London, England: Routledge.

Espín, O. M. (1987). Psychological impact of migration on Latinas: Implications for psychotherapeutic practice. *Psychology of Women Quarterly, 11*, 489–503.

Espín, O. M. (1987). Issues of identity in the psychology of Latina lesbian women. In Boston Lesbian Psychologies Collective (Ed.), *Lesbian psychologies: Explorations and challenges* (pp. 35–55). Urbana, IL: University of Illinois Press.

Espín, O. M. (1996). *Latina healers: Lives of power and tradition*. Encino, CA: Floricanto Press.

Espín, O. M. (1997). Latina realities: Essays on healing, migration, and sexuality. Boulder, CO: Westview Press.

Espín, O. M. (1999). *Women crossing boundaries: A psychology of immigration and the transformations of sexuality*. New York: Routledge.

References

Espín, O. M. (2005). *The age of the cookie cutter has passed: Contradictions in identity at the core of the therapeutic intervention*. Keynote address at the National Multicultural Conference & Summit 2001. Alexandria, VA: Microtraining Associates.

Lewis, R. (2011). Profile of Oliva Espín. In A. Rutherford (Ed.), *Psychology's feminist voices multimedia internet archive*. Retrieved from http://www.feministvoices.com/oliva-espin/

Feminism, Therapy, and Changing the World

Miriam Greenspan

ABSTRACT

In this essay, Miriam Greenspan reviews her life's work as an early pioneer of Feminist Therapy, the influence of her birth in a displaced person's camp to parents who were Holocaust survivors, and her development as a feminist, social activist, and psychotherapist. She discusses her most influential works, including *A New Approach to Women & Therapy* (1983, 1993) and *Healing Through the Dark Emotions: The Wisdom of Grief, Fear, and Despair* (2003). She concludes with a look back at her own spiritual evolution, her assessment of the ultimate contribution of Feminist Therapy to society, the need for a wide model of therapy that incorporates the political and spiritual dimensions of experience, and the challenges that psychology and psychotherapy face in an age of global threat.

I was born in a Displaced Persons Camp in southern Germany for Jewish refugees after the Holocaust. This was my home for the first four years of my life. My father, 1 of 11 children in a *shtetl* in central Poland, left school in the fourth grade to work in order to help put food on the table. At the end of the war, he survived with one brother and one sister. The rest of his family murdered in Treblinka. My mother was from Lodz, one of five children, and was the sole survivor of her family, all of whom died in Treblinka and Auschwitz. My childhood was filled with the ghosts of my parents' dead. I was always listening to an untold story. This was no doubt the beginning of my penchant to listen to the unspoken, an art that is at the heart of good therapy.

When I was a child, my father listened to my dreams. When he asked me, "What did you dream?" I understood him to mean that my dreams were important, worthy of my complete attention, and that they contained some valuable nugget of usable information. He was extraordinarily attuned to emotion, especially for a man. My mother was more of an intellectual. She finished two years of medical school in Czechoslovakia before the war, but had to quit when the family ran out of money.

After four years of living in a refugee camp, we were allowed to immigrate to the United States and arrived in the south Bronx. My father worked in a hat factory in lower Manhattan, and my mother became a "housewife." This description, however, is like calling an Olympic swimmer a hired hand. She had a mind like a steel trap, always seeking knowledge. She taught herself English by reading books from the library. She read history, biography, and fiction. My iconic memory of my mother as I grew up was of seeing her seated on the couch completely absorbed in reading book after book about Jewish history. I was too young to understand that this was part of my mother's extraordinary effort as a survivor to comprehend the historical, economic, and political roots of the Holocaust.

My father's open heart and my mother's keen intelligence and desire to learn about the world and its inhabitants were a strong part of my upbringing. Both of them, in their youth, had been socialists who dreamed of changing the world and creating a just society without economic, sexual, or class hierarchies and inequities. When the Nazis marched into Poland, they escaped to the Soviet-ruled eastern part of the country. From here, Jewish refugees were shipped to gulags in Siberia for the crime of being "suspicious." Two years in the gulag forever cured my parents of their dream of communist utopia, but it did not remove their fundamental yearning for an end to poverty, injustice, and anti-Semitism. I inherited these proclivities from them.

My parents were kind, generous people who loved and cherished me, but growing up, there was palpable sense of shame, isolation, and unspeakable loss, the legacy of trauma survivors. My sense of 'safety' (which psychologists tend to ascribe exclusively to good parenting) had been violently destroyed by history. Being born into this family with its deeply imprinted genocide trauma set me up to be highly sensitized to human suffering and to the trans-generational impact of social violence. It also made me acutely aware of how social conditions and historical events influence the fate of families and taught me that any individual is not just a product of his or her parents, but of the world into which s/he is born. We live in the world, and the world lives in us.

It's not too far from this awareness to becoming a radical feminist activist. Once there was a social movement for women's liberation, I was in.

I was not a psychology student when I became a feminist. I was a PhD dropout who had just left Columbia University's graduate program in English and Comparative Literature. Here I was—a student with numerous awards and a full scholarship to a prestigious Ivy League university—feeling like an utter failure. I was 22 years old, depressed and adrift. The pivotal "light bulb going on" moment for me came when a friend urged me to attend something called a consciousness-raising group in New York City in the summer of 1969. Attending that first meeting didn't so much expand my consciousness as explode it. In the group, I saw my own sense of inadequacy mirrored and magnified in the lives of women as a whole. Why did women feel like failures? Why were so many intelligent, accomplished women depressed? Because we were women. We were, by definition, not good enough because we were not men and weren't treated like men and because we saw ourselves through a masculine lens. Patriarchal culture was the invisible fog that pervaded us.

Once the fog was perceived, it was impossible not to see it everywhere. The doors of perception opened to expose a world in which patriarchy not only held women back socially and economically, but enslaved us psychologically.

I spent the next few years reading the books that were essential to women in the early days of the movement: Mary Ellman's (1968) *Thinking About Women*, Kate Millett's (1970) *Sexual Politics*, Robin Morgan's (1970) anthology of writings from the movement called *Sisterhood is Powerful*, Juliet Mitchell's (1971) *Woman's Estate*, Sheila Rowbotham's (1973) *Woman's Consciousness, Man's World*, Germaine Greer's (1970) *The Female Eunuch*, Susan Brownmiller's (1975) *Against Our Will: Men, Women, and Rape*, and Andrea Dworkin's (1974) *Woman Hating*. These were the books that woke me up in the early 1970s. I joined Bread and Roses, a socialist feminist organization based in Boston. I went to rallies, demonstrations, and feminist conferences. On International Women's Day 1971, hundreds of women gathered for a march at the Boston Common, demanding equal pay for equal work, free community child-care, abortion, and birth control. This culminated in the seizure and occupation of a Harvard-owned building that we declared The Cambridge Women's Center. To this day, it stands as one of the oldest women's centers in the country. At the time, this event marked my final transformation from 'good girl' to raving radical wild woman. I knew I was breaking the law—something that horrified the obedient little Jewish girl in me. I remember being followed to my apartment in Harvard Square by undercover FBI agents (easily spotted by their dark trench coats) and being scared to death. But, my commitment to being part of a woman's revolution overshadowed the earlier conditioning in docility and proper femininity.

These heady days of the early women's movement coincided with the start of my academic study of counseling psychology and my psychology internship at Massachusetts General Hospital (MGH) in Boston, which began in 1972. That same year, I read Phyllis Chesler's (1972) *Women and Madness*, a book that made me want to storm the barricades of the psychiatry/psychology establishment and demand reparations for psychological damage to female patients (something that Phyllis actually did when she addressed the APA in 1970). Hearing Phyllis speak at Simmons College in 1973 was a riveting moment I will never forget. Brilliant and bold, a passionate, incisive revolutionary activist, she immediately became a "role model" for me. I remember thinking: "This time, there's no going back. We will change the world forever!"

My desire to become a practicing therapist grew directly out of my involvement as a social activist. I wanted to change the world, to change women's place in it, and to help women heal from the constraints and abuses of patriarchy. Being a therapist seemed like a good way to contribute to the movement, given my sensibility and skill set. For me, liberation grew not only out of changing social institutions, but out of changing consciousness.

In my interview for the internship program at the MGH Department of Psychology, I proudly declared myself a feminist (a label that, in these early years of the movement, was bound to get me branded as a bra-burning crazy woman). I felt reassured when the female psychologist interviewing me said she, too, was a feminist. I soon learned this was a misnomer. Furthering one's own career in a male-dominated institution, however laudable, is, in and of itself, not a sturdy definition of feminism. As it turned out, my two female supervisors in the program were more close-minded and punitive than their male counterparts. I was being schooled in a post-Freudian psychodynamic paradigm that, with its emphasis on individual psychopathology divorced from social context, seemed particularly damaging to women. Interestingly, it was my two female supervisors rather than the men, who took my questioning of this model to be symptomatic of my resistance to adapting to my professional role. They told me it was unprofessional to question their teachings. They said if I didn't like it, I could lump it. I was given an ultimatum: conform or leave. I learned that becoming a member of the boys' club led some women to heighten their own self-monitoring and monitoring of other women for any tell-tale signs of deviant original thinking. My revenge was to keep detailed notes on my training which later became part one—"Father knows best: The failure of traditional therapy"—of my book, *A New Approach to Women & Therapy* (Greenspan, 1983).

My husband and friends were all feminists and radical activists, and they offered the support I needed to get me through my 2-year training as a psychologist. I would come home from my internship program having learned how to diagnose a survivor of sexual abuse as a borderline personality, having observed the mind-numbing, sometimes near fatal consequences of enforced psychiatric medications, having been taught to see all patients as sick by definition—and I would rest in the arms of my five-person urban commune. Here we were engaged in fomenting what we called back then the "cultural revolution." We held weekly house meetings to explore the nature of sexism, racism, and imperialism; to understand, through self-examination, how the subjugation of people by class, gender, and race is deeply internalized by the oppressed; and to create a new kind of revolutionary 'family' that we hoped, in our earnest radical zeal, would eventually come to replace the bourgeois nuclear family in which women were socially coerced into the exploited, unpaid labor of child-rearing. My experiences as a psychology intern was often grist for our discussions about the repressive social conditioning of mental patients by psychiatric experts who enforced in this manner the kind of psychologies needed by patriarchal capitalism.

As for my own nuclear family of origin, I do remember that my beloved mother was not too keen about my being a feminist activist. She was wary and scared because she thought my feminism might jeopardize my chances of getting married. "Don't you want to get married and have children?" she'd asked me. "Sure I do, Ma, but if it doesn't happen, I don't want to feel that I've completely failed as a human being." I asked her if she could remember being a young woman in Poland. Didn't she have other ambitions besides marriage? And how was it that she never got to realize her dream of being a doctor? "My feminism, Ma, is my way of trying to do everything I can so that the dreams of women are not crushed by the world."

The tears streaming down my mother's face were my best validation. She never again questioned why I was a feminist. (In fact, much later, I remember being shocked when, in the course of a conversation we were having about the plight of women in rabidly misogynistic Middle Eastern countries, my gentle Jewish mother, at this point 93 years old, suggested that things would not change substantially for women until we were armed!)

When I finished my psychology training in 1974, I was one of a handful of women to "hang out a shingle" (way before the internet!) as a feminist therapist in Boston. Female clients immediately flocked to my door, eager for a therapist who wouldn't diagnose their stories of oppression and abuse as symptomatic of pathology. I was hungry for colleagues and met with other women in the Boston area who were transforming psychological theory and practice. For a time, I was a member of a peer supervision group in Brookline, led by Jean Baker Miller. Jean became an important mentor and one of my early champions. After reading my manuscript of *A New Approach to Women & Therapy* (Greenspan, 1983), Jean's assurance that this was just the kind of book she hoped would follow *Toward a New Psychology of Women* (Miller, 1976) gave me the confidence to go forward and get it published. I also participated in a study group with the Women's Mental Health Collective in Somerville, co-founded by Judith Herman in 1970, in which we spent endless hours discussing what was worth salvaging from conventional psychiatry and psychology and what we needed to re-invent.

Grassroots Feminist Therapy in the early 1970s became a sanctuary for women in patriarchal society, along with shelters and safe houses for battered women, rape crisis centers, women's centers, and women's health centers, all of which were being created during the same period. A growing network of feminist therapists throughout the country listened to women without imposing a conventional Freudian straightjacket on their stories of oppression, abuse, and incest. The incest survivor now had a place to tell her story and be heard. It may be inconceivable for women in their 20s now to comprehend that there was a time, just 40 years ago, when incest was interpreted in psychotherapy as an Oedipal fantasy, when rape was legal in marriage, when domestic violence and sexual harassment in the workplace didn't exist as concepts, and when victims of sexual assault thought that their only recourse was to keep it to themselves because the first thought on anyone's mind would be: you asked for it. Before the women's movement, women had no way to think about misogyny, sexism, sexual harassment, child sexual abuse, and empowerment—these were "new words" invented by the movement.

In short, Feminist Therapy was an integral part of the grassroots rebellion of women who, in the words of Robin Morgan, were saying "Good-bye to all that." Good-bye to women being seduced and exploited by their therapists. Good-bye to women being groomed in therapy to be obedient wives and breeders. Good-bye to women learning to embed their self-hatred deep within their psyches by well-meaning male therapists who diagnosed us as hysterics if we were overtly sexual or emotional. Good-bye to the ipso facto diagnosis of any angry woman as a "borderline personality." Good-bye to being treated like passive, unknowing patients by therapists who assumed they always knew what's best for their mostly female clientele. Good-bye to the distant expert therapist who interpreted a woman's need for connection in therapy as "transference," a sign of neurosis. Good-bye to therapists who failed to be accountable for their own sexism in therapy. Good-bye to all that.

Grassroots Feminist Therapy was a time of questioning all the "received givens" of the known world in the light of awakening to the realities of patriarchy. At its best, it was a time of collective inspiration, re-education, radical thinking and writing, and transformative action. On the flip side, the women's movement was not exempt from all kinds of internecine conflicts, excesses, betrayals, and foolishness. I remember being invited to be the keynote speaker at the first national conference of feminist therapists in Boulder, Colorado, in 1976 and being greeted by the female convener of the conference with the following words: "You can't be Miriam Greenspan! You're too short!" In my address, I spoke against the premature professionalization of Feminist Therapy, arguing that Feminist Therapy was still in its infancy. It was not yet a 'field.' I asked if we really wanted to be ghettoized in the APA. Did we want to agitate for change in the psychology establishment from the inside or grow our ideas and practices outside the norms of the profession? I urged the participants to consider that before we developed our own credentialing process for feminist therapists, we needed to devote ourselves more intensively to developing our own theories and practices outside the established male-dominated professional organizations. The result of all this questioning was that the conference broke into two warring factions, the more academic psychologists fighting it out with the more radical activists. I had expected to galvanize some fruitful conversations and was shocked to see the vehemence of unproductive infighting. This was my first inkling that the slogan "sisterhood is powerful," a wonderful utopian ideal, was not always actualized in practice.

I read everything I could find on the practice of therapy from a feminist perspective. At the time, there were only two full-length books I knew of that directly addressed the subject: *Feminism as Therapy* by Mander and Rush (1974), and, later, *Notes of a Feminist Therapist* by Elizabeth Friar Williams (1976). Both of these books took as their underlying assumption that what women needed in order to be liberated was to change their ideas about the female sex-role. Then voila! They could make the choice to be free! There was no radical analysis of patriarchal institutions. Jean Baker Miller's *Toward a New Psychology of Women,* published in 1976, in its clear, crystalline prose, provided such an analysis with respect to gender domination and its effects on women's psyches. It is a beautiful gem of a book that profoundly influenced my way of thinking about women. At the end of the book, Miller (1976) acknowledged that the changes she had been seeing in her therapy practice with women could not have happened through therapy alone, but were a result of the changes women were making collectively through social action. The implications for the practice of therapy of these revolutionary changes in society were enormous—a work that had not yet been done.

The work I was doing at this time was beginning where *Women & Madness* (Chesler, 1972) and *Toward a New Psychology of Women* (Miller, 1976) left off. If women's development happens in a context of gender domination and if psychiatry as an institution replicates that domination, what would a liberation model of Feminist Therapy look like in theory and practice? During the same period that Jean Baker Miller, Jan Surrey, Irene Stiver, Judith Jordan, and others were working to transform psychoanalytic theory into relational-cultural theory at the Stone Center at Wellesley College, I was working on a grassroots model of therapy practice based on the heuristic of conscious-ness-raising rather than academic research.

In *A New Approach to Women & Therapy* (Greenspan, 1983), I wanted to expose the continuing harm of traditional therapy training and practice and to set out a model of Feminist Therapy that others could build on. I saw the book as a kind of social activism in itself, hoping that it would inspire both consu-mers and practitioners of psychotherapy. I believed that Feminist Therapy was one (but by no means the only) way to address the injuries of women's oppression and chart a path of healing for women. Specifically, I wanted to expose the damaging myths of traditional psychotherapeutic practice in which I'd been trained—the myth of intrapsychic reductionism; the myth of the male expert's 'objectivity'; and the myth of the medical model itself.

I wanted to lay down a feminist framework for understanding typical female 'symptoms' of oppression such as depression, repressed anger, low self-esteem, preoccupation with what I called Woman as Body, and victim psychology. I wrote about how the so-called 'symptoms' of pathology in women could be re-interpreted as seeds of strength and how the feminist therapist could look for the resistance to oppression that was buried in these 'symptoms.' I focused particularly on the underground anger of women as a potential mobilizing force for personal and social change. The women's move-ment had 'cured' the depression, aimlessness, and powerlessness I felt starting out my adult life. I wanted to contribute to the creation of a model of therapy that could do the same for other women.

I also saw the book as a kind of handbook of training for would-be feminist therapists and hence wrote very detailed stories from my therapy practice and creatively imagined the fate of someone I called "Polly Patient" in traditional, humanist, and Feminist Therapy.

One of the main tenets of the book was that we needed to closely scrutinize the idea of professional 'objectivity' and redefine the term from a feminist perspective. Distance in therapy was not synonymous with objectivity; rather, it often masked an underlying, unquestioned sexist approach to the patient. 'Objectivity' did not have to entail a lack of meaningful emotional connection with the client. In a connection rather than a distance model of psychotherapy, the typical/traditional strengths of women—intuition, empathy, compassion, emotional ways of knowing, connection to others—could be seen as compatible with a therapeutic ethic of respect rather than distance.

In short, I presented a model in which the therapist honed her skills in using herself as an instrument of change in the service of women. One important therapeutic tool I wrote about, forbidden in conventional therapy, was the therapist's self-disclosure as a way to enhance the therapeutic alliance and augment the client's self-awareness. The self-disclosure of the therapist as a tool of therapy became the subject of a 1986 essay I wrote for the journal *Women & Therapy* called "Should therapists be personal? Self-disclosure and therapeutic distance in Feminist Therapy," which as far as I know, was the first article to discuss this subject in detail. In it, I explored the conscious, cautious, and deliberate use of self-disclosure in therapy as a discrete skill—not as a way to get chummy with the client and use her as a captive audience to meet the therapist's needs (Greenspan, 1986).

It was important to me that *A New Approach to Women & Therapy* (Greenspan, 1983) be written in my own voice, using accessible, non-jargonized language for a general audience as well as for clients and practitioners of therapy. When the book came out in 1983, it was favorably reviewed. My hopes were more than realized. I spent the next decade giving public talks at numerous conferences; college and university departments of psychology, counseling, women's studies, social work, and theology; and mental health centers and other agencies throughout the United States, Canada, and Europe. From Winnipeg and Wyoming to Nova Scotia and Maine, I experienced with gratitude the surging power of women in creating a feminist psychology of women and Feminist Therapy.

During this same period, I was solicited by Digital Corporation to serve as a consultant to management on gender issues in the workplace. I ended up leaving this lucrative position after a few years when it became clear that women seeking managerial power in the corporation were not also seeking power for the majority of women working there who were secretaries and assistants. The kind of feminism that would include women in the 'lower' echelons was not what they had in mind. More rewardingly, I served for a decade on the Editorial Board of the journal *Women & Therapy*. And, I was the first consultant in training and staff development at the Elizabeth Stone House, a new feminist therapeutic residence for women in Boston.

After a fruitful period of nearly a decade working as a feminist therapist, writer, speaker, and consultant in the field, something happened that led me to re-think all of it. The year was 1981, and the event was the birth and death in infancy of my first child, Aaron. There was no medical explanation for his brain injury during a healthy pregnancy. There was no rational explanation for the visions and dreams I had of his threatened life and death before these events happened. Most of all, there was no way, within the framework of consensually defined reality, to understand my experience of seeing his spirit when we buried him. I was an agnostic social activist, not a true believer or religious seeker. Yet, in putting my baby's body into the earth, I discovered a world charged with spirit.

I experienced firsthand a kind of suffering and grace that had little to do with social institutions, nothing to do with sexism or patriarchy. Losing Aaron re-rooted me in the sheer fact of loss and death as universal human experiences. Seeing Aaron's spirit was one of the great gifts in my life, a watershed moment that profoundly shook my entire worldview. I promised myself and Aaron that I would not deny or hide this experience for fear of being thought 'crazy.' It's not that I changed my identity as a feminist therapist. It's that I began to see the limitations of viewing reality exclusively through a radical social-analytic lens. I began to critique my own previous work and to enlarge my vision of therapy and healing.

After the 1986 birth of my third child, a beautiful daughter with multiple unexplained congenital mental and physical disabilities, my work became increasingly focused on the spiritual strengths that grow from trauma and loss. I began to run groups for female survivors of trauma and loss with a focus on facing into grief, fear, and despair and mining the dark ore of these emotions for spiritual gold. My own life continued to teach me that when we are not afraid of the dark emotions, they become transformational, giving rise to unexpected gifts of gratitude, joy, and faith in life. At the same time, ever the social analyst, I was trying to build a new paradigm of emotional ecology in which our seemingly most personal emotions are connected to their larger social and global contexts.

I began to give workshops and to speak and write about what I dubbed *healing through the dark emotions*. In 1988, I was invited by Dutch feminists to give a keynote at the International Congress on Mental Health Care for Women in Amsterdam, addressing "Feminist therapy and beyond: From the political to the socio-spiritual model of therapy," published in the anthology *On Love and Violence II* (Greenspan, 1990). They had heard of my work and hoped that my words would begin to heal the painful rifts in their own communities between the hard-core politicos and the spiritual feminists.

After thirteen years of writing, I published *Healing through the Dark Emotions: The Wisdom of Grief, Fear, and Despair* (Greenspan, 2003). I was gratified to receive the 2004 Gold Nautilus Award in self-help/psychology for "books that make a contribution to conscious living and positive social change." Once again, I took this work on the road in the form of workshops and public speaking. My work in the past three decades has been devoted to broadening our understanding of self/society/spirit and our model of therapy in the interests not only of women's liberation, but of protecting all life and the earth itself from the increasingly destructive forces of capitalism and patriarchy. In an age of ecocide, psychotherapy that ignores the ways in which the threats to life on Earth are massively psychologically denied ends up not only misunderstanding the rampant epidemics of anxiety, depression, addiction, psychic numbing, and irrational violence that plague our era, but also contributing to the mass psychology that allows us to accept the ecocidal status quo.

In the introduction to the 10th anniversary edition of *A New Approach to Women and Therapy* (Greenspan, 1993), I wrote the following about the connections between feminism, spirituality, ecology, and psychology:

> We can no longer afford to keep psychology and therapy—feminist or otherwise— separate from spiritual growth and ecological awareness and activism. Psychology and psychotherapy have often functioned as forces for adaptation to a life-denying social structure. However, they nevertheless contain the potential to widen the horizons of what is known about self and world to help us meet the real healing challenges of our time.
>
> I don't know if humans will rise to the occasion and meet these challenges. But, I do know that we in the "helping professions" cannot evade the responsibility of addressing ourselves to the global suffering of our time and the need for healing the whole. (p. xlv)

In the course of writing this essay, I have thought about what it means to be a 'pioneer' (i.e., someone who is the first to explore new territory and pave the way for others). What a pioneer does is to set out on unknown terrain without a map. We don't do this ourselves. The social movement for women's liberation pioneered a new culture, new words, and new institutions. What we accomplished was astounding, but clearly not enough. The plight of women around the world today is, in my opinion, worse than ever before, despite the advances of middle class women in the United States and Europe. All told, there is more rape, sex trafficking, female slavery, extreme misogyny, and violence against and death of women by religious fanaticism than ever before. Taken as a whole, internationally, women are worse off than they were 50 years ago. The women's revolution I longed for has not come to pass for millions of the most vulnerable women and children in the world.

This leaves me rather humble when it comes to assessing what I accomplished in the field of Feminist Therapy. I would say I helped inspire this new field and get the ball rolling. I taught countless women through my writings and in person, a model of women and therapy that they could adapt in their own unique ways. *A New Approach to Women & Therapy* (Greenspan, 1983, 1993) has been used as a textbook in programs of psychology, social work, counseling, and ministry in the United States, Canada, Europe, Israel, China, and Korea. My work on self-disclosure I think has deeply affected the practice of many therapists and become a part of a larger conversation in the field about 'dual relationships' in therapy. (See my essay "Out of bounds" in *Dual Relationships in Psychotherapy*, edited by Lazarus & Zur, 2002; Greenspan, 2002). And I'm sure (because I received dozens of letters to this effect) that I inspired a lot of women to leave abusive therapists!

My pioneering contribution was not a 'career move'! I was a small part of an uprising of women interested in overthrowing patriarchy. Ah, how I wish we had accomplished more than we did! But, we did what we could. I have never regretted a moment of it and count myself extremely lucky to have been born into an era when I could be an active participant in this 'wave' of women rising in the 1960s and 1970s. I am also lucky to have met and worked with so many extraordinary women engaged in creating a humane, socially grounded psychotherapy that respects the collective social experience, integrity, and potential for transformation of our female (and male) clients. Most of all, I am grateful to those women I've had the privilege of helping, whose hearts and courage I carry with me.

A New Approach to Women and Therapy (Greenspan, 1983, 1993), published by a now long gone division of McGraw-Hill, has been out of print for two decades. Yet, it still circulates on the internet and seems to have a kind of 'underground' presence, which I think is amusingly appropriate. For instance, after a recent talk I gave at Florida State University on the subject of "Grief in a brokenhearted world," a young woman approached to thank me for my book and tell me how much it has meant to her. Assuming she was talking about *Healing Through the Dark Emotions* (Greenspan, 2003), I asked her what was important to her about the book. Her answer was that she had read *A New Approach to Women & Therapy* (Greenspan, 1993) in a Women's Studies course at the university and how much the women in the class felt validated and charged up by the book.

I'm always delighted to hear that young women are 'charged up' reading a book that is now thirty-two years old! I would hope that my legacy to younger women coming of age today is: Don't be afraid to stick your neck out and speak in your own voice. Go out there and do what you can to change the world! Action on behalf of the world is more urgent today than ever. I hope my work as a public speaker and writer of two books and numerous articles in magazines and journals will continue to inspire others to use their gifts in the service of others and the earth.

But perhaps, in the end, my most important contribution of all was the work of Feminist Therapy itself. The Talmud says: to save a life is to save the world. All those years ago, feminism saved my life. I'd like to think that my work for the past forty years has helped save a few others.

References

Brownmiller, S. (1975). *Against our will: Men, women and rape*. London, UK: Martin, Secker & Warburg.

Chesler, P. (1972). *Women and madness*. New York: Avon Books.

Dworkin, A. (1974). *Woman hating: A radical look at sexuality*. Boston, MA: E. P. Dutton.

Ellman, M. (1968). *Thinking about women*. San Diego, CA: Harcourt, Brace & World.

Greenspan, M. (1983). *A new approach to women & therapy*. New York: McGraw Hill.

Greenspan, M. (1986). Should therapists be personal? *Women & Therapy*, 5(2–3), 5–17. doi:10.1300/J015V05N02_02

Greenspan, M. (1990). Feminist therapy and beyond: From the political to the socio-spiritual model of therapy. In A. Meulenbert M. Greenspan & M. Groen *On love and violence II: International Congress of Mental Health Care for Women* (pp. 25–43). Amsterdam, The Netherlands: The Moon Foundation.

Greenspan, M. (1993). *A new approach to women & therapy* (10th anniversary ed.). New York: McGraw Hill.

Greenspan, M. (2002). Out of bounds. In A. Lazarus & O. Zur (Eds.), *Dual relationships in psychotherapy* (pp. 425–431). New York: Springer.

Greenspan, M. (2003). *Healing through the dark emotions: The wisdom of grief, fear, and despair*. Boston: Shambhala.

Greer, G. (1970). *The female eunuch*. London, UK: HarperCollins.

Lazarus, A., & Zur, O. (2002). *Dual relationships and psychotherapy*. New York: Springer Publishing Company.

Mander, A. V., & Rush, A. K. (1974). *Feminism as therapy*. New York: Random House.

Miller, J. B. (1976). *Toward a new psychology of women*. Boston: Beacon Press.

Millett, K. (1970). *Sexual politics*. Garden City, NY: Doubleday.

Mitchell, J. (1971). *Woman's estate*. New York: Penguin.

Morgan, R. (1970). *Sisterhood is powerful: An anthology of writings from the women's liberation movement*. New York: Random House.

Rowbotham, S. (1973). *Women's consciousness, man's world*. New York: Penguin.

Williams, E. F. (1976). *Notes of a feminist therapist*. Santa Barbara, CA: Praeger.

Those Were the Best of Times, and Then...

Rachel T. Hare-Mustin

ABSTRACT

Rachel T. Hare-Mustin describes a career of feminist activism in academic life, the professions, and clinical practice in the 1970s and 1980s. She has been an advocate for changes in professional ethics and improving conditions for women. Her primary areas of influence have involved applying feminist theory to the study of gender and pointing out that the sex role model of gender differences has an inherent bias that overlooks the gender hierarchy. Women's voices are silenced, not only in the process of therapy, but in the wider society as well.

For those of us entering the field of psychology in the 1970s, we found the discipline of psychology dominated by men, including those who taught and those who were psychotherapists. Professional and academic organizations like the American Psychological Association (APA) were run by men. Women as teachers, mentors, and colleagues were rare. Female therapists were expected to work with children or act as "assistant co-therapists" to men. This is a personal account of how I tried to promote feminist ideals in my work and life.

After I received my PhD in Clinical Psychology in 1969, my first position was in the Psychiatry Department of University of Pennsylvania at the Philadelphia Child Guidance Clinic. I had married after my sophomore year at college, and then, I completed my graduate work after having four children. In the 1960s, we lived as a family in the Philippines and Africa where my husband and I each had done teaching and cross-cultural research. Our family was very active in Quaker concerns, demonstrating for civil rights, arms control, and for ending the Vietnam War. When I shifted to feminist concerns, the Quaker ideal of "speak truth to power" carried over into my life as a feminist therapist and academic.

What led me, in part, to seek a PhD when I was still raising a family was my experience working part-time at a state mental hospital in Pennsylvania. I had a Master's degree already, and I asked the chair of the Psychology Department at the state hospital if I should get a PhD. His response was, "As a woman, you need every degree you can get!" I was grateful for that advice.

When I worked at the Philadelphia Child Guidance Clinic in the 1970s, it was a very radical clinic. We were all active demonstrating together against the Vietnam War. The therapeutic staff included a number of African American friends. The systems therapy approach did not label or stigmatize patients. Problems were seen as family systems problems. The diagnostic label most frequently used was "No Mental Disorder."

One of the student interns told me students at Temple University had permission to have a seminar on sex roles if they could find an instructor. I ended up teaching the seminar in addition to working at the clinic. There were very few books or articles available on gender issues at that time. We used *The Dialectic of Sex* by the radical feminist Shulamith Firestone (1970), rather strong stuff. The students were also allowed to invite a woman for one colloquium on women's issues. They invited Phyllis Chesler. Chesler's response to the first question after her presentation was, "Why does a man always have to ask the first question?"

Concern About Ethics in Psychology

As a new staff member at the clinic, I also became acquainted with several professional groups of therapists. One organization of Philadelphia therapists invited me to be on their Ethics Committee. I became very concerned about therapists having sex with their patients. At the time, the male therapist/female client dyad was the most common dyad in therapy. I was amazed when I attended a panel at an American Psychological Association Convention where four male therapists discussed the pros and cons of sex with their patients. I subsequently wrote an article on ethical issues in sex with patients (Hare-Mustin, 1974). It was hard to get it published. When it appeared in *Psychotherapy*, it was the first article ever published in the field of psychotherapy that showed how therapists' sexual contact with patients was unethical.

The arguments being made for sex between therapist and client were like the arguments about rape—she seduced the therapist, and furthermore, she enjoyed it and benefited from it. The negative consequences of sexual contact for the patient have been well documented and include flashbacks, boundary disturbances, rage, and feelings of guilt, helplessness, and sadness.

Along with Hannah Lerman, Patti Keith-Spiegel, and others, I subsequently worked in the APA Council to change the Ethical Standards of APA to explicitly prohibit sex with patients. The Council was the APA governing body of over 100 elected representatives from divisions and states. Only in 1977, after considerable lobbying by feminist psychologists, did APA Council vote to make sexual contact with clients unethical. One of the knotty questions was how soon after therapy ended would it be ethical to have sex with a former patient—one year, five years, or never? Patti Keith-Spiegel described the problem as "You're cured, let's fuck!"

I was appointed as a member of the APA Ethics Committee in the late 1970s and subsequently served as chair. When I was chair, the committee also changed the APA ethics procedures to make them more transparent for those bringing complaints against psychologists. In those days, APA's Ethical Principles was a model for other professional organizations. Our explicit ban on sex with patients was the first in the field.

I found myself addressing the issue of therapist sex with patients again in 1992 in my article, "Cries and whispers: The psychotherapy of Anne Sexton" (Hare-Mustin, 1992). Sexton was a beautiful woman and a notable poet. Following Sexton's death, a biography appeared with the permission of her sister, Sexton's executor, that used the therapy tapes Sexton had kept of her sessions. I questioned the outcry by psychiatrists and other therapists in the media about the violation of confidentiality in the biography, but never a whisper about the sexual affair Sexton's therapist had with her. In fact, Dr. Peter Kramer, a noted psychiatrist, writing in *The Psychiatric Times* (October, 1991) about Anne Sexton's therapy, proclaimed, "She soon seduced him" (Kramer, 1991, p. 5). Whoa! Who is in charge of the therapy session here?

A Special Issue on Women and Psychotherapy

Another group I joined when working at the clinic was the American Academy of Psychotherapists. Because of my interest in women's issues, I was invited to edit a special issue of their journal, *Voices*, on a topic they had not focused on before, "Women and Psychotherapy." My introduction was "Woman's experience: The half-known life" (Hare-Mustin, 1976). Looking back on the articles that I included, I am impressed by the array of women's concerns in the mid-1970s. Here is a sample of the articles:

- "Powerlessness and women's psychological disorders" by Jeanne Marecek
- "An expanding shrink [pregnancy]" by Beth Rhude
- "Some thoughts on sexuality and supervision" by Ellen Berman
- "How women and men relate to feminist therapy" by Rachel Hare-Mustin and Rosemary Robbins
- "Assertive training in therapy with women" by Celia Halas
- "A developmental approach to marriage counseling [The Women's Walk-In Counseling Service]" by Jaquelyn Liss Resnick and Cindy Rice Dewey
- "A feminist therapy training group [Stages]" by Alexandra G. Kaplan
- "Process and power in couples psychotherapy: A feminist view" by Doreen Seidler-Feller

Finding Feminists in APA

I had left the Philadelphia Clinic in 1973 when I was recruited by the University of Delaware Psychology Department to become Director of Graduate Training in Clinical Psychology. The program at Delaware had had its APA accreditation suspended, in part because it had no women faculty teaching in the clinical program. Before I left the clinic, I remember telling the clinic director that with all the cases and training responsibilities, there was no time to think. He replied, "We don't pay you to think." Returning to academia, I hoped thinking would be rewarded.

When I first went to an APA Convention in the 1970s, relatively few women were there, since women were only beginning to enter the field in significant numbers. In the Division of Psychotherapy, Division 29, I was delighted to meet a small group of feminist therapists, such as Annette Brodsky, Jaquie Resnick, Joy Kenworthy, and others who were forming a Women's Committee in Division 29. We were defiant activists. We attended division board meetings (uninvited), organized to get on the program for presentations on women and therapy at the APA Conventions, and influenced elections to get women elected to division positions and to APA Council.

Our committee realized that many women came to APA Conventions alone, without any mentors to introduce them, and not knowing others. In my own experience as a student and in my academic career, I had never had a mentor or sponsor. Our committee established a Women's Breakfast to be regularly scheduled early in the Convention so women without a sponsor could come together and meet each other. Annette Brodsky and I became good friends and worked on feminist issues together.

One of the strengths of feminists in APA in the 1970s was that many had previously worked together on women's issues in the Southeastern Psychological Association (SEPA). It was like they had all gone to prep school together.

APA Governance, Women, and Parliamentary Procedures

When I was elected as an APA Council Representative, one day at a recess of a Council session, I was talking with two women, the APA staff member for women's issues and another active woman. The CEO of APA came by and said to us, "What is this, a conspiracy?" I concluded that for some people, a woman alone is a wallflower, two women together must be lesbians, and three women talking is a conspiracy.

How I became APA Parliamentarian in the 1970s started with a business meeting of the Division of Clinical Psychology at an APA Convention. I was then a new member of the Clinical Division, sitting alone. As an item was to be voted on, a question arose about whether there was a quorum. When the President continued with the meeting, I raised my hand and asked what happened about the quorum. He said, "Nobody called a quorum." I didn't really know much about procedures, but I said, "I'll call a quorum." They counted, and they did not have a quorum. The President had a temper tantrum, shouting, "We can't do any business, we can't approve spending, she called a quorum." I left shaken, but thought, "This is powerful stuff, I'm going to learn parliamentary procedures."

I studied up and became parliamentarian for several divisions. Then, in 1979, APA President Nick Cummings, who had been appointing women to various groups, decided APA should have a woman Parliamentarian, which had never happened before. Parliamentary procedures in APA had been rather "loose," with some people on Council using procedures improperly to run rings around others. I was chosen and became APA Parliamentarian. I served for more than 20 years, advising many different Presidents as well as Council Representatives. I saw being the Parliamentarian as a major feminist contribution, a way to make procedures transparent, and a way to make a level playing field for women as well as others. No more trickery, no more obfuscation. I had had experience in feminist groups that tried to be rule-free and collegial, and they found it just didn't work, especially in large groups, because there are always some people who take over, even among feminists. Feminist Jo Freeman (1972/3) discusses "the tyranny of structurelessness" in her article based on various experiences she had in women's groups and collectives.

Several other men were allies of feminists and became friends. A consistent supporter was Sam Osipow, whom I first met on the APA Committee on Women in Psychology. Ken Pope was an important ally to feminists working on ethical issues and women in therapy. Were men important in the feminist movement? Yes, not because they were rare, but because feminist concerns about equality in the field and in practice were not just a women's problem.

Task Force on Clinical Training and Practice

When the APA Division of the Psychology of Women, Division 35, set up a Clinical Task Force, we reviewed standards for training and practice and presented programs on "sex-fair therapy" at conventions. Sounds kind of corny now.

A big opportunity came for feminists when Standards for Accreditation of Psychology Graduate Programs were being reviewed by the National Commission on Education and Credentialing in Psychology, established by APA and other review groups like the Association for State Licensing of Therapists and the Association of Directors of Clinical and Counseling Psychology Programs. I was there to represent the Psychology of Women Division. At the end of a lengthy meeting, a steering committee of five men was appointed to continue the work. When that occurred, I raised my hand and said, "I would like to be on that committee." They were so taken aback they said, "Yes." I became a spokesperson for including "sex roles and gender" as a required area in the new accreditation standards. It was ultimately watered down, but it was a start.

During this period, those of us on the Division 35 Clinical Task Force, including Annette Brodsky and myself, were jointly presenting annual workshops at APA such as "How Not to Do Therapy" and "Are We Ready for Sex Fair Therapy?"

In 1978–1979, when I was chair of the APA Committee on Women in Psychology, we were trying to organize an APA sponsored Conference on Women and Psychotherapy with a contract from the National Institute of Mental Health (NIMH). The Project Officer at NIMH, Irene Elkin Waskow, was a strong voice in shaping the project. The conference was to be interdisciplinary and assessed both research and practice. Annette Brodsky and I co-directed the conference. In 1980, we produced a book from the conference presentations, plus additional materials (Brodsky & Hare-Mustin, 1980).

Another result of activities with feminist therapists in APA was an important article about the "therapeutic contract" that we published in the *American Psychologist,* "Rights of clients, responsibilities of therapists" (Hare-Mustin, Marecek, Kaplan, & Liss-Levinson, 1979). I was also pleased that my article about a feminist approach to therapy, "An appraisal of the relationship between women and psychotherapy: 80 Years after the case of Dora" (Hare-Mustin, 1983), appeared in the *American Psychologist* because that journal received the widest readership among psychologists at that time.

Early in the 1980s when I was on the faculty at Harvard, Cynthia Enloe and I became friends and were asked to organize a panel presentation for the Charlotte Perkins Gilman Series, sponsored by Radcliffe College. The topic we chose was "When Women Are Not Believed: A Feminist Discussion of Freud's Seduction Theory." Freud's Seduction Theory was then being debated in the media after the appearance of Jeffrey Masson's book that drew attention to the longstanding denial of sexual abuse of children. The *Radcliffe News* of June 1984 reported that our panel drew one of the largest crowds ever to the series. Cynthia, a professor at Clark University, spoke on "How and Why Women Are Silenced by State Bureaucracies," police, attorneys, courts, etc. I spoke on how women's testimony had not only been disbelieved in the courts from early times, but also how women's complaints had been disbelieved by their doctors. I had written earlier that, "the field of psychotherapy could not have flourished if it were not for the pervasive and chronic unhappiness of many women" (Hare-Mustin, 1976, p. 595).

Paradigm Change in Family Therapy

My critique of Freud's case of Dora grew partly out of my work in the area of Family Therapy. When I joined the Philadelphia Child Guidance Clinic in 1969, it was an exciting place with debates about therapy. There was a major paradigm shift then occurring in Family Therapy. Psychoanalytic Theory had been dominant among psychiatrists and other therapists up through the

1960s. Now, many family therapists were moving from psychoanalysis and Freud's view of women to understanding people as part of social systems. One of the important books was *Change* by Watzlawick, Weakland, and Fisch (1974). It pointed out that the surest way to prevent a solution was to see both sides of a question because there were always more than two sides. For me and some other feminists, the question of change and influence in therapy evolved over time into other ideas such as the social construction of meaning, the influence of power and dominant discourses in the culture, and Narrative Therapy.

I also found the transparency of the training model at Philadelphia Child Guidance Clinic a significant change. Therapy sessions were videotaped or observed through a one-way mirror (with patient permission) for staff as well as trainees. Now, we could actually see what had been happening in a session rather than just having case notes or audiotapes. Family Therapy became a truly international movement with important conferences around the world. Some of my articles were being reprinted in other languages.

In the 1970s, a group of leaders in family therapy decided to form a professional organization where they could share their work and ideas. This became the American Family Therapy Academy (AFTA). It did not get off to a pro-feminist start. The organizational meeting was held in Chicago. At this time, other professional and academic associations, including APA, were refusing to hold their conventions in states like Illinois to bring pressure on states to ratify the Equal Rights Amendment (ERA). I asked why family therapists were meeting in Chicago despite the ERA boycott. The reply was, "It never occurred to us."

I had found feminists in psychotherapy at APA, but they were mostly individually focused. I had not found feminists in Family Therapy, but I did find excitement about theory and systems of change. Yet, most family therapists still reinforced sex role stereotypes, as did other theorists like Carol Gilligan with her focus on the woman's voice. Even systems therapists viewed the healthy family in terms of sex role stereotypes. Surveys in the major clinical journals found pervasive mother-blaming by therapists for children's problems. I had undertaken a research project with Patricia Broderick, a student of mine, on attitudes toward motherhood. We published several articles that examined the idealization or demeaning of mothers, such as "The myth of motherhood" (Hare-Mustin & Broderick, 1979). I had been surprised that I was the only one in my consciousness raising group who liked her mother.

My article, "A feminist approach to Family Therapy" (Hare-Mustin, 1978), appeared in *Family Process*, the leading journal on family systems, therapy, and research. It was widely reprinted and hailed as the seminal article that launched feminist influence in family therapy in the following decades. Women therapists and trainers in family therapy began to collaborate in publishing and supporting one another to present their work. At this time,

I and some other feminists often used humor in our presentations to defuse hostility so our message could be heard. We had a workshop for several years in AFTA on "Gender and Humor." What men often found funny—those disparaging jokes about wives and mothers—was not what most women found funny.

On one occasion, I was invited to speak at an awards dinner in New York City. When I asked what was wanted, I was told, "Just take five minutes, be a feminist, tell a joke." When I got up to speak, I mentioned the request and asked, "How can you be a feminist in five minutes? Betty Friedan got ten minutes for *The Feminine Mystique*, Gloria Steinem got fifteen for *Ms. Magazine*. Besides, everyone knows that feminists don't have a sense of humor."

The first two conferences on Women in Family Therapy were organized in 1984 and 1986 by AFTA members Monica McGoldrick, Froma Walsh, and Carol Anderson. Some of us, like myself, met other women family therapists and feminists at the conferences for the first time. We had known each other's publications, but had never met. Lois Braverman and I met and became good friends, often traveling together to Family Therapy conferences such as those in Amsterdam, Copenhagen, and Oxford to speak on feminist issues.

I was known as a feminist when I became president of AFTA in 1990–1991. Of course, this did not mean that feminist therapists had become universally loved. There was a notable and sometimes fiercely personal backlash. Some men felt threatened by feminists becoming active in the professional organizations, taking space on programs, doing research on abuse of women, and questioning traditional ways of doing things. Seven feminist family therapy friends formed a support group that had mid-year gatherings at one of our homes around the country as well as getting together at AFTA meetings. Those who still remain for get-togethers are Connie Ahrons, Lois Braverman, Lee Combrinck-Graham, Carroll Dammann, and myself.

Victoria Dickerson was a feminist I first met on the AFTA Board. In our therapy, we both used a framework of how shared meanings arise and a narrative approach to Family Therapy, which was much influenced by Michael White and the group at the Dulwich Center in Australia. At Narrative Therapy conferences in Vancouver and Toronto, I met both male and female feminists from Australia and New Zealand as well as Canada.

Making a Difference

In the 1980s, Jeanne Marecek and I began to address the emphasis of psychologists on sex roles and gender differences. I was now on the faculty at Harvard, and Jeanne was at Swarthmore and active overseas doing research and teaching in Sweden and Sri Lanka. When we collaborated, I recall the problem of faxing drafts back and forth, to and from Sri Lanka, where Jeanne would get them in some form at the fax machine in the local hardware store.

Not very high tech by today's standards. We were questioning the inherent bias in assumptions of polar differences between men and women occurring in therapy and psychological research. We concluded that the "equal and opposite" point of view obscured the hierarchical differences in power and opportunities of women and men. In 1989, we traveled to Stockholm together, and each presented papers on gender at the Karolinska Institute and a women's conference.

In the area of theory, I had developed a schema that pointed out how we understand the world by comparing and contrasting. People tend to exaggerate gender differences or minimize gender differences. Jeanne Marecek and I further explained this model in a major article we published, "The meaning of difference: Gender Theory, Postmodernism, and Psychology," (Hare-Mustin & Marecek, 1988). We organized a symposium on these ideas at an APA Convention. Our book, *Making a Difference: Psychology and the Construction of Gender* (Hare-Mustin & Marecek, 1990), further explained these concepts. In addition to the chapters we wrote, the book included three chapters from psychology colleagues, Bernice Lott, Rhoda Unger, and Jill Morawski, whom we had invited to participate in the symposium.

Our work drew attention to the male as the unexamined norm in difference comparisons. The implicit question in psychology and the wider society is whether women were the same as, different from, or even as good as men. It was assumed that a woman could only be as good as a man. There was no point in being as good as a woman. We observed that if they get you to ask the wrong questions, they don't need to worry about your answers. The sex difference question had become the proverbial "wrong question."

Discourse Analysis

My interest in discourse analysis and power was the basis for an article of mine, "Discourses in the mirrored room: A postmodern analysis of therapy," published in 1994 in *Family Process* (Hare-Mustin, 1994). This article has been more widely included as a chapter in edited books about therapy than any other work of mine. I am frequently told that because of its clarity, it is still used after more than 20 years to teach therapists about discourse analysis.

What I point out is that different and competing discourses circulate in the culture. Dominant discourses are ways of thinking and talking that support and reflect the prevailing ideologies in the society. Other discourses become marginalized and disregarded. The case examples I use in the article concern gender relations: the male sex drive discourse, the permissive discourse, and the marriage-between-equals discourse. I point out how the therapy room is a mirrored room that only reflects back the discourses brought to it by the family or client and the therapist. This predetermines the content in the conversation of therapy.

Critical Psychology

Critical Psychology is an approach that in the 1990s was drawing attention to issues such as promoting social justice, shifting a focus from the individual to the larger society, and challenging the status quo. Jeanne Marecek's and my contribution to one of the first textbooks on Critical Psychology was our chapter, "Abnormal and Clinical Psychology: The politics of madness" (Hare-Mustin & Marecek, 1997).

Critical Psychology looks at how pressures from dominant institutions shape the discourse and come to influence peoples' actions. A contemporary example is how widespread anxiety after the 9/11 tragedy has been used to fuel the dialogue about national security. Disclosures about APA actions for the defense establishment have burst into awareness in 2015. These overshadow the gains many psychologists felt they had made for a more open organization, a more feminist aware organization, and an organization for the welfare of others. There is extensive evidence that starting in 2006 some top APA staff and elected leaders (ultimately being fired or expelled) colluded to modify the ethical standards and hide the action from members to allow psychologists to engage in the defense system's "enhanced interrogation techniques," now rightly identified as torture.

It is a cautionary tale, even for therapists, of how good intentions when distorted by the dominant discourses can result in bad outcomes. The worthy impulse to broaden career opportunities for psychologists in the defense establishment led to deceit and provided "legitimacy" for cruel and degrading activities. The paradox about ethics is that those involved didn't just go ahead. They behaved in an unethical manner to alter the ethics code so they could feel ethical. Psychologists who had no part in these events are trying to reconfigure APA to serve its original purpose of "promoting health, education, and human welfare."

Conclusion

As I look back to the 1970s and 1980s, I see it as a time of hope and progress for women and therapy. I became involved with a group of feminists from across the country that worked together in the academies and professional organizations to alter therapy, change the study of gender, and improve conditions for women. Of course, it wasn't all positive. At the university, I found that a feminist was rarely supported by her colleagues. For many of us, it was a lonely struggle. I had been a finalist at one university for a position. A friend there told me that despite my strong resume, what actually determined the outcome occurred when a senior faculty member said, "Oh, we don't want her, she's a feminist." That was the kiss of death.

With few exceptions, I rarely used the word "feminist" in the titles of my publications or presentations. This was a calculated choice. I wanted people to read my work and not avoid it because of the word "feminist" in the title. Using the term in the text was soon enough. My titles were often little dramas or paradoxes to invite the reader in.

Given that women and men are socialized in the same value system, not all women were sympathetic to feminists either. I recall at the University of Delaware in the 1970s, several of us were observing "Alice Doesn't Day," a day nationally set aside when women would not carry out their usual roles of helping men. Lindy Geis, a faculty member in Social Psychology, always kept a pot of coffee for all of us in her office. When Sam asked for coffee, Lindy said, "Sorry, Sam, it's Alice Doesn't Day." To which another woman faculty member said, "I'll get coffee for you, Sam."

Problems in getting one's papers accepted for publication often occurred, but seemed worse for feminists. Although Jeanne Marecek's and my paper on "The meaning of difference," submitted to the *American Psychologist*, received two glowing reviews, the editor kept asking for changes. We made some changes, but finally said, "Enough!" Or an editor would delay a decision, such as how the editor of *Family Process* did with my paper on "Discourses in the mirrored room." When I inquired, he said it was on his desk and he was thinking about it. It was finally published with virtually no changes three years later.

I realize that my life course was different from most feminist therapists. Raising a family of four children was a happy time, but it meant I often had to get home to the family. I did not have as large a network to rely on as some because I did not have the time to spend with colleagues. It probably contributed to my being more direct, like saying, "I'll call a quorum," and "I would like to be on that committee." I, too, had been socialized as a female to be nice, so such moves were always done with trepidation. It did take courage. Being a feminist means you have to be courageous.

What happened to the feminist movement? We didn't realize how difficult a change to feminism could be in daily life. Women and men interact intimately in families and often love each other. The dominance of traditional discourses holds sway in the home as well as the workplace. We all watched Women's Studies programs became programs on Gender Studies–equal and opposite, much less threatening. Some feminists shifted to working on multiculturalism as that area emerged.

Does bias still exist? In 2015, a Nobel Laureate in London stated that female scientists should be segregated from male colleagues because women cry when criticized and are a romantic distraction in the laboratory. (He was forced to resign.) This recalls a statement some years back by a prominent Democrat who asserted that women's "raging hormones associated with their lunar periods" made women unsuitable for executive positions in government, business, and national crises. He would not feel safe in an airplane piloted by a woman. Congresswoman Patsy Mink is reported to have responded, "And what's your excuse?"

There were good times, and there were hard times. Challenging the accepted order of things was not easy. The support of feminists for each other made it possible for me. My life and work were enriched by colleagues in several different organizations. Those were the best of times. But, revolutions often become co-opted and fade from prominence. Feminism remains an unfinished project. The feminist movement deserves more than five minutes. Times change, but feminist goals are still worth promoting and achieving.

References

Brodsky, A. M., & Hare-Mustin, R. T. (Eds.). (1980). *Women and psychotherapy: An assessment of research and practice.* New York: Guilford Press.

Firestone, S. (1970). *The dialectic of sex.* New York: Morrow.

Freeman, J. (1972/73). The tyranny of structurelessness. *Berkeley Journal of Sociology, 17,* 151–164.

Hare-Mustin, R. T. (1974). Ethical considerations in the use of sexual contact in psychotherapy. *Psychotherapy: Theory, Research, and Practice, 11,* 308–310. doi:10.1037/h0086370

Hare-Mustin, R. T. (1976). Woman's experience: The half-known life. *Voices: Journal of the American Academy of Psychotherapists, 12*(3), 4–5.

Hare-Mustin, R. T. (1978). A feminist approach to family therapy. *Family Process, 17,* 181–194. doi:10.1111/j.1545-5300.1978.00181.x

Hare-Mustin, R. T. (1983). An appraisal of the relationship between women and psychotherapy: 80 years after the case of Dora. *American Psychologist, 38,* 593–601. doi:10.1037//0003-066x.38.5.593

Hare-Mustin, R. T. (1992). Cries and whispers: The psychotherapy of Anne Sexton. *Psychotherapy, 29,* 406–409. doi:10.1037/h0088543

Hare-Mustin, R. T. (1994). Discourses in the mirrored room: A postmodern analysis of therapy. *Family Process, 33,* 19–35. doi:10.1111/j.1545-5300.1994.00019.x

Hare-Mustin, R. T., & Broderick, P. C. (1979). The myth of motherhood: A study of attitudes toward motherhood. *Psychology of Women Quarterly, 4,* 114–128. doi:10.1111/j.1471-6402.1979.tb00702.x

Hare-Mustin, R. T., & Marecek, J. (1988). The meaning of difference: Gender theory, postmodernism, and psychology. *American Psychologist, 43,* 455–464. doi:10.1037/0003-066x.43.6.455

Hare-Mustin, R. T., & Marecek, J. (Eds.). (1990). *Making a difference: Psychology and the construction of gender.* New Haven, CT: Yale University Press.

Hare-Mustin, R. T., & Marecek, J. (1997). Abnormal and clinical psychology: The politics of madness. In D. Fox & I. Prilleltensky (Eds.), *Critical psychology: An introduction* (pp. 104–120). London: Sage.

Hare-Mustin, R. T., Marecek, J., Kaplan, A. G., & Liss-Levinson, N. (1979). Rights of clients, responsibilities of therapists. *American Psychologist, 34,* 3–16. doi:10.1037/0003-066x.34.1.3

Kramer, P. D. (1991, October). Said the poet to the analyst. *Psychiatric Times,* p. 5.

Watzlawick, P., Weakland, J. H., & Fisch, R. (1974). *Change: Principles of problem formation and problem resolution.* New York: Norton.

The Proud and Productive Life of a Red-Diaper Baby: Judith Herman

Kayla Weiner

ABSTRACT

Judith Herman is a feminist psychiatrist, political activist, intellectual, and writer. Her work in the field of abuse and trauma spans decades. Her work is informed by generations of prolific thinkers, teachers, writers, and social/political activists. Her groundbreaking work, in turn, is informing future generations of feminists, political activists, and clinicians.

As I began examining the life of Judith Herman, I found myself smiling and cheering for her. Though the trajectory of our lives landed us in different places, we share a similar cultural and political/social history with the exception of her position as a "Red-Diaper Baby." Kaplan and Shapiro (1998) describe this phrase as a term for a child of parents who were members of the United States Communist Party (CPUSA) or were close to the party or sympathetic to its aims. More generally, the phrase is used to refer to a child of any leftist radical parent regardless of that parent's past partisan affiliation (or the affiliation of the child). I find it particularly refreshing to connect with someone who brings her social activism to her profession, and I am delighted to share what I have learned about her.

Part of the information herein comes from the original manuscript of Judith's recent chapter about her mother, the psychoanalyst/psychologist Helen Block Lewis (1913–1987), in Salberg and Grand's *Wounds of History: Repair and Resilience in the Trans-Generational Transmission of Trauma* (Herman, in press). (This chapter is an expansion of a memoir of Herman's mother published in *Psychoanalytic Psychotherapy* in 2013). I highly recommend reading this for a more extensive understanding of their personal and professional relationship. I have also included information from her Epilogue for the 2015 edition of her groundbreaking book *Trauma and Recovery*. In addition, I viewed a filmed interview done in 2000 with Harry Kreisler for his *Conversations with History* series, and Judith and I spoke on the phone to flesh out points and to clarify positions. Whenever possible, I have used her own words to best describe her beliefs.

Formative Early History

Judith's path in life was set by prior generations of left leaning intellectuals and social activists. In a tribute to her mother, Judith gives a very vivid picture of these influences. She writes:

> My mother was ... brilliant, original, and ahead of her time as a professional woman ... intellectually fearless and she did not suffer fools gladly. ... Her story really begins a generation earlier, with the story of her father ... [who] fled to this country from Riga, Latvia in 1887, at the age of 17, after he was arrested for reading revolutionary literature. Though he had studied to become a rabbi like generations of his forefathers ... [he was in] the clothing business while studying English and saving money to go to medical school. Eventually he opened a general practice on the Lower East Side [of New York City]. (Herman, 2013, p. 528–529).

In the same paper, she states:

> Like Helen, my father was the American-born child of Jewish immigrants with modern American ideas about education and careers for women. Both mother and father were ambitious for me and placed enormous emphasis on intellectual achievement. In that domain of life, both she and my father were unfailingly supportive. When, as a college student, I confided my wish to follow in her footsteps and become a psychologist, she told me to go to medical school instead. "You'll have more power that way," she said, and of course she was right. And of course, though I didn't realize it then, she also wanted me to follow in the footsteps of her adored father, John Block, who died before I was born [for whom Judith is named]. (Herman, 2013, p. 530)

In 1953, Judith's parents were both called before the U.S. Senate Permanent Subcommittee on Investigations (colloquially known as the McCarthy Committee for its Chairman, Sen. Joseph McCarthy) Her father stated that he had never been a member of the Communist Party and therefore was not blacklisted, but her mother refused to answer questions about her membership, citing her constitutional right under the 5th Amendment, and consequently was blacklisted within academia. This denied her the opportunity to become a researcher and professor, which had been her goal. Judith notes that her mother never renounced her leftist beliefs and supported Judith's participation in the Civil Rights and Anti-war Movements. Helen did not, however, understand the Women's Movement until much later in her life. For Judith, feminism was her true passion to "call into question all the deep structures of patriarchy." She says, "I wanted to be part of the "longest revolution, challenging women's subordination in all its domains: production, reproduction, sex, and child rearing" (Herman, 2013, p. 530).

Judith is very clear that her heritage as the granddaughter of Jewish immigrants fleeing oppression and as the daughter of leftist intellectuals who suffered political persecution significantly influenced her journey. In our discussion, she posited that being a part of an oppressed people fostered an empathy for others. The injunction to make the world better (*Tikkun Olam* is the Jewish concept of healing the world) combined with her intellectual capacity to connect ideas led her to take action politically, socially, and professionally.

Training

In writing of how her schooling had an impact on her political awareness and feminist consciousness, she states:

> My four years in medical school (1964–68) hastened my feminist awakening. Here for the first time I truly experienced what it was like to be in a minority. Women constituted 10% of my medical school class. Lectures often included openly derogatory comments about women; these were considered to be humorous. My female classmates and I learned to ignore these slights or to laugh along with the rest of the class; after all, we were a token presence, often reminded that we should be grateful to be admitted at all. (Herman, in press, p. 7)

She continues:

> My first experience of frank discrimination, when I applied for internships, also taught me to know my place in the world. Despite my success in an elite medical school, I was told flatly, on more than one occasion, "We don't take women." After all, it was explained, if hired, I would be taking a coveted position away from a man who, as a breadwinner, deserved it far more than I. And anyway, I'd probably just go and get pregnant and all that medical training would be wasted on me. And anyway, what about "that time of the month?" (Herman, in press, p. 8)

She goes on to say:

> By the time I was ready to begin my psychiatric residency training (1970–73). I was also ready to join a consciousness-raising group. My feminist awakening coincided with the beginning of my professional career, and profoundly shaped the path that career would take. The safe space of the psychotherapy office had many similarities with the free space of the [woman's] movement, and as my women patients revealed their secrets, I listened with a new awareness of woman's condition. My first two patients, admitted to the hospital after suicide attempts, disclosed histories of father–daughter incest. It was not hard to see the connection between their despair and their early initiation into the life of a sexual object. I wrote in my journal: "in patriarchy the father maintains the right to sex with his daughter in the same way that the feudal lord maintains the *jus primae noctis* with his subjects." Incest seemed to me like a paradigm of women's sexual oppression. (Herman, 2013, p. 530)

In 1975, Judith and Lisa Hirschman submitted a paper describing their observations of 20 patients who reported histories of father–daughter incest to a new women's studies journal (see Herman & Hirschman, 1977). She says,

> A year elapsed between the time the paper was accepted and the time it was published. During that year, the paper was copied and passed from hand-to-hand, and soon we started getting letters from women all over the country, saying: "I

thought I was the only one," or "I thought no one would believe me," or "I thought it was my fault." By listening to women, and daring to publish what we found, we had become catalysts for a transformative moment, when crimes long hidden were revealed. (Herman, 2013, p. 531)

This was a major impetus for the disclosure of abuse by women and children all over the country. It took internal fortitude and commitment to continue to speak out in the face of powerful institutional denial. Judith wrote:

> In hindsight, I realized that along with the inspiration of the women's movement, it was the example of both my parents that enabled me to venture to write down and publish my observations. (Herman, 2013, p. 531)

At this point, Judith became the flag bearer for abused and oppressed women and men by researching, writing, speaking, and teaching. She became a trailblazer, conceptualizing the implications of abuse and trauma and creating methods of treatment for survivors.

Feminist Biography

Judith's extensive contributions to feminism and psychology are grounded in her ability to examine her experiences and allow these observations to cross-fertilize. In so doing, she expands the particular to the universal. The following is a classic example of this talent.

Judith's parents employed a housekeeper, always an African-American woman. She reported that her mother tended to have very warm relationships with the women who served her family; nevertheless, these relationships also were highly orchestrated. Friendly conversations always took place in the kitchen, for example, never sitting in the living room. And though we all ate the same food that the maids prepared, they never ate with us at the same table. The unspoken rules of both gender and racial segregation were observed without question.

Judith, who in her own words, became an "outside agitator" in the Deep South, as part of what was known as "Freedom Summer" continues:

> I witnessed far more extreme rituals of racial segregation, enforced by murderous violence. Clearly, the tyrannical oppression of Jim Crow was of another order of magnitude from the genteel conventions I had observed in my privileged upbringing. What these conventions shared, however, was the unconscious acceptance of elaborate social rules dictating that the dominant group was entitled to deference and service, and the intense emotional reactions that seemed to result whenever these entitlements were challenged even in the slightest degree. (Herman, in press, p. 7)

Judith believes "consciousness-raising" at the beginning of the Women's Movement was the major force to have created change for women. Herman cited the importance of Kathie Sarachild's leading role in the consciousness-raising movement in the 1960s and 1970s as especially influential. Judith stated in her interview with Harry Kreisler in 2000 that Kathie Sarachild's inspiration for women's groups acted as the initial form of organizing and questioning. Once women had a place free of fear and shame to tell their stories and share their experiences, there could be no going back. Judith continues:

> With personal testimony, women uncovered the coercive methods by which male dominance is enforced. It soon became apparent that rape and domestic violence were a common part of women's lot. Over the following decades, these initial discoveries led to large-scale epidemiological studies documenting the worldwide pandemic of violence against women. (Herman, in press, p. 5)

In our discussion about the importance of consciousness raising (CR), she said, "it totally revolutionized" the fields of psychology and psychiatry. She agrees with Sarachild's idea of CR as an empirical method to allow women to understand our condition for social political and sociological reasons. She went on to say:

> We had to actually study ourselves and testify about the reality of our lives because we were invisible even to ourselves. We were not able to name our condition until we actually testified about it. We were in a situation where our psychology as it regards women was a medieval scholasticism. It was by way of CR that we developed our knowledge about gender-based violence and not just the fact of it, but the political analysis. We came to understand that ultimately a subordinate group is not subordinate because it is inferior, stupid or "too emotional" but is kept subordinate by means of (the superordinate) male domination and financial subordination. (Herman, in press, p. 5)

In the Epilogue to the latest 2015 edition of *Trauma and Recovery,* she states:

> Internationally, the UN now recognizes violence against women as the most common human rights violation in the world, and a Special Rapporteur is appointed to gather information on violence against women in each member country.

> In 2009, Yakin Erturk, then the Special Rapporteur, summed up the progress she had seen:

> Traditional patriarchy has slowly but systematically been ruptured at different paces in various parts of the world. Applying a human rights perspective to violence has created a momentum for breaking the silence around violence, and for connecting the diverse struggles across the globe. (Herman, 2015, p. 22)

Feminist Scholarship

Judith's 1987 work, "Recovery and verification of memories of childhood sexual abuse," described a group of patients who reported periods of partial or complete amnesia followed by delayed recall (Herman, 1987). She documented the ways that these patients were able to obtain independent corroboration of their memories. Many clinicians clung to her words, especially those in the 1990s when there was a groundswell questioning the validity of her work. Clinicians who were then working with clients with what was formally called "dissociative amnesia" and popularly known as "repressed memory" depended on her wisdom. Despite a fierce backlash against so-called "false memories," fostered by the media, retrograde professionals, and attorneys for accused perpetrators, her work stood the test of time and helped to establish the scientific literature on trauma and memory. Others helped the growing number attesting to the discoveries of gross abuse by individuals and institutions and by testifying and establishing laws protecting the victims of violence. Because of Judith and many others, many adult survivors of all forms of abuse can now seek redress.

Feminist Practice

Treatment modalities for working with abuse/trauma survivors have been adopted and adapted by many individuals and institutions, but not enough. Judith writes in relation to a program designed to coach new parents on ways that are conducive to developing a solid attachment to their children:

> Given the enormous medical, psychiatric, and social costs of childhood trauma, and the availability of prevention programs that have proven their effectiveness, common sense would dictate that such programs ought to be made available immediately to all young mothers and their babies, or at the very least to those at high risk. But as the history of the trauma field has shown repeatedly, increasing scientific knowledge and raising public awareness are only the first steps in efforts to end violence. Moving from awareness into social action requires a political movement strong enough to overcome pervasive denial, the passive resistance of institutional inertia, and the active resistance of those who benefit from the established order. (Herman, 2015, p. 21)

She adds,

> In trauma treatment studies, success is usually measured by reductions in PTSD symptoms. Though most would agree that this criterion is a necessary measure of success, it is hardly sufficient. The goals of psychotherapy are far more ambitious than this; we aim more broadly for the restoration of a life worth living. (Herman, 2015, p. 26)

Another contribution of Judith's relies on the way she is able to broaden concepts. She writes:

> The concept of mentalization, or "holding mind in mind" offers a way of explaining complex relational ideas both to patients and to therapists. In a worksheet for patients at the Menninger Clinic, psychologist Jon Allen demystifies the concept, explaining that mentalizing means "being aware of your own thoughts and feelings as well as the thoughts and feelings of others.... [This] includes not only empathy

for others, but also empathy for yourself. "He describes the "mentalizing style of psychotherapy" as "conversational, informal, commonsensical, and engaged" (Allen, 2003). He also suggests that another name for mentalization-based treatment could be "plain old therapy." (Herman, 2015, p. 32)

Judith adds,

The "plain old therapy" approach is in fact a highly sophisticated form of treatment, built on a vast evidence base, which demonstrates that the single most powerful predictor of therapeutic success is the quality of the relationship between patient and therapist. Many years ago, psychologist Carl Rogers and his followers showed that relational qualities of the therapist like accurate empathy, nonjudgmental warmth, and genuineness are among the strongest predictors of good treatment outcome. By contrast, the particular method or technique of therapy counts for relatively little. When competing treatments are compared with one another in well-designed studies, no one method shows clear-cut superiority. (Herman, 2015, p. 32)

In describing her latest iterations of thinking, Judith wrote about her collaboration with her mother. She says,

Recently, my work on trauma has brought me back to the subject of shame. At this late date, I, too, have become a "shamenik." Helen formulated shame as the reaction to rejection and unrequited love. It seems to me that shame is also an inherent reaction to social subordination. The implications of this idea are still unfolding. In general, psychology suggests that human beings innately desire relationships of equality, or mutuality, along with life and liberty. In the trauma field, it suggests that conceptualizing post-traumatic stress as a disorder of fear is far too limited; shame is so central to the experience of victimization that it might be equally useful to conceptualize the post-traumatic reaction as a disorder of shame. (Herman, 2013, p. 533)

Looking Back

Judith's research, writing, and speaking about the impact of interpersonal violence validated abuse victims everywhere. Institutional betrayal by government, hospitals, and other systems of power is what she and many mental health providers are experiencing as we currently face the state of mental health treatment in this country. Judith is disheartened by the lack of funding, which has desiccated programs designed to help trauma survivors as well as all in need of mental health services. The mentally ill are now cared for in jails where they are recycled between the streets and returned back to prison. Both Judith and I bemoaned the state of affairs and hope there might be the political will to make changes.

In the Epilogue of the newest 2015 edition of *Trauma and Recovery*, she writes:

One of the great pleasures of my teaching career has been to see ... a model adopted and developed by a new generation of clinicians. Recently, a grant from a private foundation enabled us to develop and publish a practice guide ... [we] translated a wealth of clinical craft from an oral culture to a written one. As one of the grand-mothers of the project, I got to *kvell* when the book was published. *Kvell* is a Yiddish word that means literally, to overflow, like a fountain or a spring, and figuratively, to feel joy at the accomplishments of the next generation. (Herman, 2015, p. 276)

Judith has made remarkable contributions to the field of feminist psychology, including, but not limited to, her understanding of gender based violence, conceptualizing the complexity of survivors and their responses to trauma and the development of a comprehensive method of treatment that has demonstrated great success. Her wealth of writings (see selected list of publications below) have been innovative and revolutionary. Keeping in mind all she has done, I asked her of what she was most proud. Her response was classic "Herman" as I have come to know her. She said:

It is hard to separate one thing from another. It is sort of seamless in my mind. I just put one foot in front of the other and whatever my work was at the time, one idea developed out of what came before. (J. Herman, personal communication, September 7, 2015)

And what a cloth she has woven.

Judith lives by the words of wisdom given to her by her mother who told her to "stay engaged" in life. In our interview, she said she believes that activism is an antidote to despair. "I have tried to follow her {Helen's} advice to the best of my ability … Witnessing the lives transformed in this process of recovery is what enables us old timers, the practitioners of plain old therapy, to keep on keeping on" (Herman, 2015, p. 276).

References

Allen, J. G. (2003). Mentalizing. *Bulletin of the Menninger Clinic, 67*, 91–112.

Herman, J. L. (in press). Trauma and recovery: A legacy of political persecution and activism across three generations. In J. Salberg & S. Grand (Eds.), *Wounds of history: Repair and resilience in the trans-generational transmission of trauma*. New York: Routledge.

Herman, J. L. (2013). Helen Block Lewis: A memoir of three generations. *Psychoanalytic Psychology, 30*, 528–534. doi:10.1037/a0034580

Herman, J. L. (2015). Epilogue. In J. L. Herman (Ed.), *Trauma and recovery* (3rd ed., pp. 248–276). New York: Basic Books.

Herman, J. L., & Hirschman, L. (1977). Father–daughter incest. *Signs: Journal of Women in Culture and Society, 2*, 735–756.

Herman, J. L. & Schatzow, E. (1987). Recovery and verification of memories of childhood sexual trauma. *Psychoanalytic Psychology, 4*, 1–14. doi:10.1037/0736-9735.4.1.1

Kaplan, J., & Shapiro, L. (1998). *Red diapers: Growing up in the communist left*. Champaign: University of Illinois Press.

Dis-Illusioning Psychology: Epistemology and the Contextual Psychology of Ellyn Kaschak

Natalie Porter

ABSTRACT

Ellyn Kaschak is a pioneer feminist therapist whose contributions to feminist theory, practice, education, and advocacy have spanned the globe over the past 40 + years. From being a founder of one of the first feminist counseling services in the country in the early 1970s, Kaschak has influenced decades of feminist, family and multi-cultural therapists through her teaching and countless others through her feminist epistemology and theory development and the Mattering Map. This article describes Kaschak's life and work and the lasting contributions she has made to the field of feminist psychology.

Upon receiving the APA Committee on Sexual Orientation and Gender Diversity Award for Outstanding Contributions in August 2015, Ellyn Kaschak remarked to the audience, "This work was my means of survival. It doesn't feel right to accept an award for something I did to save my own life." The inscription of the award summarizes the many contributions of Ellyn Kaschak, work that began in the early 1970s and has flourished since. The inscription reads:

In recognition of her scholarship, leadership, advocacy. Among the first to write and speak about the complexity of gender and sexuality, women, feminist theory, domestic violence, ability, and privilege with attention to race and nationality, Kaschak's enduring contributions include the Mattering Map for understanding intersectionality and numerous books and articles, including *Engendered Lives: A New Psychology of Women's Experience*, and recently, *Sight Unseen: Gender and Race through Blind Eyes*. Kaschak's contributions extend to the Spanish and Portuguese speaking worlds, elevating the visibility and credibility of the psychology of women, LGBT psychology, and gender studies. Attesting to her influence are many invited presentations in the international arena, 20 years as editor of Women & Therapy, her role as an advisor to the Vice President of Costa Rica and as a research consultant in the Netherlands and Yugoslavia. As reflected in her work, Kaschak recognizes her privileged identities and advocates for the powerless and voiceless with grace and good humor, while also equipping others to do so.

Color versions of one or more of the figures in the article can be found online at www.tandfonline.com/wwat.

Kaschak's work is creative, insightful, and thought provoking and has made LGBT psychology and the psychology of women more dynamic.

Put in that context, it could be said that Ellyn Kaschak saved not only her own life, but the lives of many others. Add to the inscription that her writings, therapy and teaching initiated her lifelong inquiry into epistemology and represent the culmination of this inquiry, and a picture of Dr. Kaschak's significant contribution to the field of feminist therapy emerges. The Women's Counseling Center in San Francisco represents the beginning of these contributions, and Figures 1–3 document the origins of the organization. I interviewed Ellyn Kaschak on June 12, 2015, and her history and perspectives are quoted throughout.

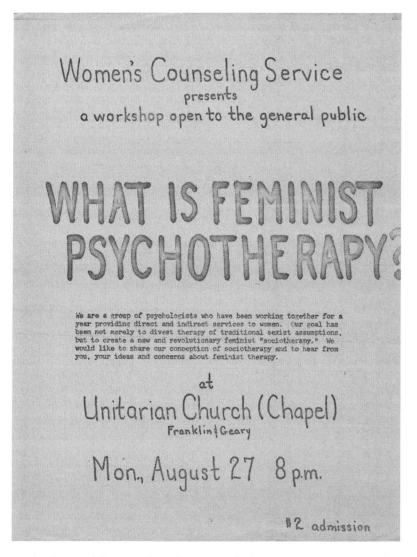

Figure 1. Flyer for a workshop on "what is feminist psychotherapy?" at Women's Counseling Service.

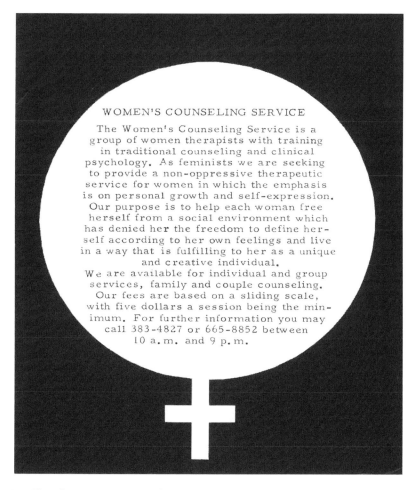

Figure 2. Flyer for Women's Counseling Service.

Becoming

The Early Years

In accepting the APA CODG award and in other venues as well, Ellyn Kaschak speaks often of the ordinary life. She has reflected on winning an award for living an ordinary life; she has described feminist therapy as the understanding of the ordinary lives of women; and she has written that her grandparents immigrated to the United States to escape the brutality, anti-Semitism, and poverty rampant in villages and cities of Russia in search of an ordinary life (Kaschak, 2010). Rarely is "ordinary" spoken of as aspirational in contemporary North American culture, and I have come to understand that "ordinary" in these contexts includes a pogrom-free life, a violence-free life for women, an authentic life where one is free to be oneself. It also, on another level, exposes the ordinariness of all these experiences of abuse, violence and colonization. In much of the world, this definition of an ordinary life, in the first sense, remains

Figure 3. Flyer for workshop on sociotherapy: a feminist alternative for all women at Women's Counseling Service.

extraordinary. For Kaschak, her expectation that she could create this life for herself was also extraordinary. From early childhood, she fought for a life as she saw fit to live it, a life different from those who had gone before her and different from those around her, much to their consternation. As a child, she was admonished, ridiculed, and coerced to conform by her own family, but Ellyn described herself as a "warrior of resistance" from earliest childhood.

Ellyn grew up in the Borough Park section of Brooklyn and then later on Long Island, the eldest daughter of first generation Jewish parents, whose own parents had emigrated from Eastern Europe. From immigrants to first generation, New York accents and clerical jobs had replaced the old world dialects and grueling piecework factory labor. The details of her family and her life growing up are eloquently depicted in "Somewhere Else" (Kaschak, 2010); here, I will provide her observations about this period rather than repeat the earlier account. In that article, she claims herself to be culturally Jewish rather than Jewish in a religious sense. As a young child, she accompanied her grandfather to shul and sat next to him until her growing up required that she be shut out in the women's section. As I read this narrative, I reflect on Ellyn's experience, my own, and the lives of other women I know. Feminism was birthed through these experiences of being shut out of shul, barred from the altar, forbidden rabbinical training or the priesthood, in short, a denial of spiritual, intellectual, and social power.

Ellyn described her childhood as being strongly gendered both within her family and in the larger society; being sequestered at religious services is a metaphor as well as a real experience. Nevertheless, she would not be easily contained and roamed the streets of Brooklyn with her best friend, Bruce, and later those of Long Island with her newer friend, Arlene. She found her way to the local libraries, and to the train that would carry her to the museums and theaters of Manhattan, even as a pre-teen. She did so in spite of the restraints she experienced as a girl and the punishments she endured for frightening her mother with her boldness. "When I visited the Village, I would stop at a newsstand and buy copies of *The Realist* and *The Ladder*, and sneak them onto the subway and home hidden in the latest issue of *The New Yorker*" (E. Kaschak, personal communication, June 12, 2015).

When it came time to form an adult relationship, she chose marriage to the young man she had dated all through college: "Living outside of that frame seemed to me like it would be a bleak existence. Literature was replete with women who suffered because they did not conform and did not marry. I read *The Group* by McCarthy. I did not want my life to be the tragic life of the writers there; I didn't want to end up alone in an anonymous New York."

The push for gender conformity was strongest in her family:

My parents didn't want me to go to college, something they would not have been against had I been a boy. I insisted and went anyway. After all, how could they stop me? However, in an apparent compromise, I brought home a husband and the week that I got my B.A., I also got what we called at that time the MRS. Degree.

Nevertheless, the theme of not fitting in resonates throughout Kaschak's story, a theme of being from "somewhere else" (Kaschak, 2010, p. 7), perhaps from the "Williamsburg section of Mars" (Kaschak, 2010, p. 5).

Education and the Fundamentals of University Life in the 1970s: Racism, Sexism, and Homophobia

So, what is the ordinary life? Is it the ability to live life authentically and unencumbered by prejudice as Kaschak's earlier comments would suggest? Or is it a life typified by racism, sexism, anti-Semitism, violence, sexual harassment, and homophobia? These experiences are, in fact, the more ordinary ones. The extraordinary resides in whether and how one challenges them for oneself and for others. The bookends of this section are education, during which Ellyn experienced the panoply of "isms" that educational institutions and faculty offered women at that time, prominent among which were sexual harassment and other ways of not being taken seriously as colleagues or students. These were the typical experiences of the time that shaped a generation of women. Ellyn's responses to this "education" influenced that generation of women to resist and rebuild.

"I wanted to study and understand individuals and cultures, to speak many languages and to walk many foreign streets to hear them spoken. It was my Brooklyn writ large" (Kaschak, 2010, p. 8). Ellyn's first choice for university was Cornell, "but they had a Jewish quota; another Jewish student was accepted from my high school so I knew I would not be." She enrolled at Harpur College in the SUNY system. Although she knew she wanted to be a psychologist early on, she majored in Russian and Russian literature because the program at Harpur was purely Skinnerian and rat-focused in the 1960s. Ellyn was interested in the human species. She simultaneously took psychology courses at NYU to prepare for studying psychology in graduate school. She adds, "In many ways, Dostoevsky and Chekhov were my first psychology supervisors. They taught me more about human nature than the behaviorists ever did" (E. Kaschak, personal communication, June 12, 2015).

Days before graduation, Ellyn married her long-time college boyfriend. Now, everything appeared idyllic—from the outside:

> I married him, I thought, forever, but it was not to be. I could not be satisfied with a life that felt empty, but looked perfect. I wanted authenticity and so I had to go for it despite the loss and disapproval. I ultimately left the marriage and began a very different relationship with another female graduate student. It was a heart-wrenching decision, but it wanted to happen.

Ellyn enrolled in the master's program at George Washington University and was graduated first in her class. She then applied to the PhD program, but was told that they did not accept women at that level because it was a waste of their resources.

Instead of studying, Ellyn found employment as a school psychologist, giving three test batteries a day to "problem students" (read as "Black and Brown"):

> My first consciousness about racism occurred in the Washington, DC inner city schools, where I quickly saw that the kids I was testing could not get higher than a 60–70 on the IQ test of the time, based on its gender and culturally biased questions. I had very little political analysis at the time. I, too, was just trying to survive. Yet, I was so upset by this experience that, when I left the position to return to school, I removed all my reports from the files and eventually burned them. I was frightened and told nobody, yet I had to do something and nothing else occurred to me. Working with those students brought me to political consciousness and changed my life. I am grateful to them for that and I still regret that I could not do more in return. (E. Kaschak, personal communication, June 12, 2015).

When she began to be involved in feminism, Ellyn sought diversity from the start. It was not only a matter of principle and of ethical practice, but of interest and different perspectives. "It is a mistake to say that the first American feminists where all White. Our groups were all diverse by intent. Otherwise, what was consciousness about?"

Ellyn eventually returned to graduate study at Ohio State University, where they were building a more progressive program that included women and men of color. This was roughly the time that Title IX had become law, and universities and graduate programs had to start taking women students. Nevertheless, this seemingly progressive program turned out to have an all-White male faculty, which inevitably led to more struggle.

During Ellyn's second year there, she participated in a consciousness-raising group. Ellyn describes "the aha" of an almost immediate transformation that occurred for members of the group. The students requested a course in the Psychology of Women, but there were no faculty capable of teaching it. The students were provided the opportunity to organize and teach the course themselves. "Phyllis Chesler's [1972] *Women & Madness* and Naomi Weisstein's [1968] essay, "Kinder, Küche, Kirche as Scientific Law: Psychology Constructs the Female, influenced us significantly." That volatile year of study ended with student protests, tear gassing, and the early closing of Ohio State following the shooting of students at the nearby Kent State by the National Guard.

Ellyn explains that the political beliefs of the male faculty did not insulate the women students from sexual harassment: "They still expected that you would have sex with them if they chose you" (E. Kaschak, personal communication, June 12, 2015). Ellyn described an incident where her Ohio State advisor sexually assaulted her when he visited her internship site: "He insisted on staying at my apartment, claiming he didn't have the money to stay in a hotel. He took me to the best restaurant in San Francisco, got drunk, and then assaulted me. When I struggled, he did stop, but never spoke to me again. I had to find a new dissertation advisor." Ellyn recounted incidents of sexual harassment that occurred in the early years of her academic position at San Jose State. By then, she had felt it necessary to refine her skills of refusal, as if it was her responsibility to emerge from these situations unscathed: "I wouldn't directly refuse the person, which would have had negative consequences, but instead change the topic permanently, as if I had no idea what they were proposing. I developed a pre-Internet form of ghosting, but it also made me into something of a ghost."

Ellyn went from Ohio State University to the Palo Alto Veterans Administration Hospital for internship training. The VA had a historical association with the Mental Research Institute that attracted interns because of the intellectual confluence of anthropology, systems thinking, and family therapy. The Institute was founded by Don Jackson, who passed away in 1968, and at the time Gregory Bateson, Jay Haley, Paul Watzlavick, Charles Fisch, and Virginia Satir were still affiliated to various degrees. By this time, the interns were most exposed to their work via consultation and workshops. Their daily work involved mostly adult male patients and a strong representation of schizophrenics, psychopaths, substance abusers, and child molesters.

Kaschak marks her lifelong enthusiasm for epistemology being ignited by her experiences there, while other fires were dampened or extinguished.

> I resonated most with Bateson, who had a brilliant and interesting mind and was very much the absent-minded professor. The fact that they [MRI group] were contextual

stayed with me, although they only took the context as far as the family boundaries. Only Bateson took things further, but never to gender. I found them all to be very patriarchal in different ways, although I would not have called it that then.

I already did not like the manipulative approach of Jay Haley. I soon wrote a major paper on how his branch of systems work had a lot in common with behaviorism in its external manipulation of behavior [See Kaschak, 1990]. I wanted a psychology that included, but was not limited to, the internal experiences of each individual, along with the larger context. Behaviorism and systems approaches seemed to me to focus on context to the exclusion of self. This was the beginning of my interest in epistemology. None of my professors at Ohio State knew anything about it, and I had never heard of it. Yet I started to see all the commonalities between behaviorism and systems theory, and I started inventing it for myself. The epistemology was instantly more interesting to me than the actual practice of therapy.

Haley's work was also homophobic, and I had gotten stuck on an example he gives in his book *Strategies in Psychotherapy* that a homosexual can never be satisfied because he wants "a real man" and anyone who goes with him is not. The theories could still function with impunity while incorporating homophobia and the sexism of mother-blaming (e.g., the schizophrenogenic mother; the refrigerator mother). Yet I was still using the double bind theory in the *Sociotherapy* (Kaschak, 1976) article I wrote (E. Kaschak, personal communication, June 12, 2015).

Engendering San Francisco's Early Feminist Therapy Collective

The 1970s was a time of radicalization in the San Francisco Bay Area, and Ellyn reported a fast-growing awareness of the issues. Although training at the Palo Alto VA by day, by night, she was part of a new movement in San Francisco where traditional patriarchal, heterosexist and White values were being critiqued and rejected: "The Abortion Coalition was addressing the rights of women to choose, and lesbian and gay groups were active in developing radical theory, as well as securing civil rights" (E. Kaschak, personal communication, June 12, 2015).

In *Angle of Repose,* Wallace Stegman (1971) labeled the cultural divide for those reaching adulthood in the late 1960 to 1970 period not as a generation gap, but:

> ... a gulf. The elements have changed, there are whole new orders of magnitude and kind ... My grandparents had to live their way out of one world and into another or into several others, making new out of old the way corals live their reef upward ... [They believed] in the life chronological rather than in the life existential. ... [The new generation believes] Post-industrial post-Christian world is worn out, corrupt in its inheritance, helpless to create by evolution the social and political institutions, the forms of personal relations, the conventions, moralities, and systems of ethics appropriate to the future. Society being thus paralyzed, it must be pried loose. (p. 3)

For Kaschak, this sentiment included psychology.

I was beginning to feel, as were others that I had to invent the psychology I had been looking for. I began to meet with other women, including Sara Sharatt, Sue Cox, and sometimes Dolores Jimenez and others, with the goal of developing a theory of feminist therapy. Two of these women were bicultural and bilingual because our goal from the beginning was to include women of color and diverse perspectives on feminism and on therapy. I obtained an MFT license in 1972, as did some of the others, and we opened for business as the Women's Counseling Service of San Francisco. How did it begin? We tacked up announcements of our opening all over the city with the words, "What is feminist therapy? Come find out." We thought that maybe 10 people would show up, but 200 came. We were as shocked as they were. Soon enough, grassroots women's organizations began opening up, rape crisis centers and abortion clinics. The slogan, "If she tells you it happened, it happened" became ubiquitous. We questioned everything about traditional therapies and would not accept any provided "truths" without scrutiny. We examined all therapy techniques for complicity in oppression. We aimed for equal power between client and therapist. We were learning by doing. For example, we negotiated fees and session length, the latter of which I would not do again. We learned right alongside our clients. (E. Kaschak, personal communication, June 12, 2015)

Ellyn described her interest in the psychology of the ordinary, not in the concept of psychopathology. She was motivated by understanding what women's "ordinary" lives are like and by making the invisible visible. "I soon realized that the 'real' aspects of women's lives often remain invisible to ourselves and others." Ellyn wrote an article on therapy, "Sociotherapy: An ecological model for psychotherapy with women" (Kaschak, 1976), as her first attempt at capturing the contextual nature of these lives. It foreshadows her later work.

Life as a Feminist Professor and Therapist

Ellyn's wish to remain in the San Francisco Bay Area was fulfilled when San Jose State posted a position for someone with expertise in Community Psychology and Family Therapy. The University was close enough to San Francisco and to her Counseling Women practice that she could maintain it. Because being an outsider was the norm, Ellyn reported that she wasn't worried about not fitting in. "My humor was an important tool—one needs to see the irony" (E. Kaschak, personal communication, June 12, 2015). The community psychology program seemed to her to be a good match, reasonably radical and recruiting students of color from various local communities. She fit in with them more than with the faculty, an experience she described as common throughout her academic career. For example, she relates the story of a talk she gave in 1972 at CSPP about feminist therapy: "The all-male faculty completely lost control. They were screaming at me, comments like, 'You cannot let a prospective client choose her therapist (one of our basic tenets), because it is the neurosis that chooses.' It was exhilarating but terrifying. The disrespect for women clients and therapists was frightening. We could not permit it any longer."

Kaschak described the university climate as anti-feminist in those early years. Issues of ethnicity were gaining traction, but there was no overlap in that the students or faculty committed to anti-racism were not interested in women's issues. "So I trained 35 years of graduate students at San Jose State to be feminist therapists without naming it as such. Teaching a new generation of therapists was a very efficient and effective way of making change."

Ellyn also struggled with the promotion and tenure process at San Jose State, not unlike her contemporaries across the country. She reported that the department chair fought her being promoted and would remove materials from her dossier before the committee could review it. When students organized a protest about her treatment, the Chair blamed her for inciting them. Ellyn prevailed over time, receiving tenure and promotions all the way to Professor, because of her teaching record, her publications, and engagement in national psychology organizations. She initiated international research early on, working with Sara Sharratt (Kaschak & Sharratt, 1979) to develop a Latin American Sex Role Inventory in Spanish and norming it in Central and South America. Kaschak and Sharratt presented at several Inter-American conferences at that time and eventually introduced a bicultural adaptation of feminist therapy in Costa Rica. Sharratt, it should be noted, is a native Costa Rican, and Ellyn is bi-lingual and bi-cultural as well.

Ellyn continued to practice therapy herself until 1993 and continued throughout her career training and supervising student therapists. She continued to expand her notions of feminist theory and therapy. For Ellyn, therapy was a lab to test theoretical ideas. She developed the Mattering Map (1992, 2010, 2011) based on her therapy experiences, as she became more aware of the importance of context and complexity for each client. Not only is context important, but which ones are important to the client (categories) are fluid and can morph from moment to moment:

> I grew up in a family with little reality and truth. I often got punished for seeing and commenting on what I saw with my own eyes. The appeal of therapy to me was that I could see what I believed to be true and say it out loud. The next question, of course, was what to do about it. The Mattering Map came about as a way to assess individuals in a way that matters to them rather than with mainstream psychology's test batteries. What is their context? How does it change? The Mattering Map recognizes the fluidity of people's identities and the contextualized ways in which we actually live. (E. Kaschak, personal communication, June 12, 2015)

Legacy: International Feminist Therapist, Teacher, Mentor, Activist, and Scholar

When asked what she sees as her legacy, Ellyn's response is that, "Psychotherapy gives people back to themselves for the first time. You learn that you have a right to exist, to be exactly who you are. I learned that alongside others" (E. Kaschak, personal communication, June 12, 2015).

My view of her legacy is less humble. The work that Ellyn Kaschak initiated in the early 1970s, such as the early development of feminist therapy in Northern California and one of the first groups nationwide, the integration of lesbian and gay concerns into therapy, the integration of feminist thinking into family therapy, and the start of a 35-year academic career where she educated burgeoning family therapists to be community, race, and gender aware blossomed into national influence over the next decade and continues today. Several areas that reflect the legacy of Dr. Kaschak include her scholarship, particularly from an epistemological framework; her feminist therapy model; the Mattering Map; her national leadership in feminist, anti-racist, and LGBT advocacy; and her teaching and advocacy within the United States and internationally.

Teaching

Ellyn has been a master teacher and mentor for her entire career. During the span of her 35-year faculty career at San Jose State University, she chaired the Marriage and Family Graduate Program for 10 years and directed the Family Counseling Service for 20. She has also been sought after as a "master" professor by most of the San Francisco Bay's clinical psychology programs and has taught in many of their programs. Ellyn's involvement with mentoring students in these roles is impressive and many of her relationships longstanding. For example, while teaching a feminist therapy course in the doctoral clinical program at the California School of Professional Psychology, Ellyn worked with several students in submitting journal articles on feminist therapy themes and engaged them in editorial work for *Women and Therapy*. These activities changed the course of their careers for several of these young professionals. At San Jose, she has been responsible for the education and professional training of literally thousands of students, who provide therapy services throughout California.

Teaching and Advocacy in Costa Rica and the University for Peace

During a Fulbright period in Costa Rica, Ellyn, along with Sara Sharratt, offered a post-graduate course for practicing therapists on feminist theory and feminist family therapy in Costa Rica. Ellyn described this work as the first introduction to feminist therapy in Costa Rica.

She served as advisor to Vice President Odio Benito of Costa Rica on gender issues for several years and worked to improve the quality of health and mental health care in Costa Rica. Odio Benito has called Ellyn "an honorary Costa Rican." She introduced cancer support groups and improved treatment regimens for women there. She has been key in bridging the gaps between U.S. feminism and feminism in more developing countries, an understanding that has been essential for growth on all sides. She also served as an advisor to Odio Benito when she served as a judge on the World Criminal Court. During this time, Judge Odio Benito was one of two members of the criminal tribunal in Yugoslavia credited with succeeding, for the first time in world history, in having the World Criminal Court include sexual assault and rape as war crimes. Judge Odio Benito has described Dr. Kaschak's influence as an advisor, by which she means the kind of influence that has profoundly improved the status and well-being of women around the globe.

Ellyn continues to work in Costa Rica on gender issues and, most recently, through teaching at the University for Peace in Ciudad Colon. Her focus has involved a transnational approach to addressing gender and peace for students from around the world.

Leadership in National Arenas

Ellyn's leadership and advocacy have been significant in both the United States and internationally. She is a Fellow of six APA divisions; is past president of the Feminist Therapy Institute; and former chair of two APA Committees, the Committee on Women in Psychology (CWP) and the Committee for Lesbian, Gay, Bisexual, Transgender Issues (CLGBT). She also served on NOW's National Committee on Mental and Physical Health. Internationally, she was one of the earliest feminist therapists in Costa Rica, where she lectured and advocated for women. She served as a member of the planning committee for the UN Decade for Women Conference in Nairobi. A fuller picture of her contributions in these areas follows.

Committee on Women in Psychology

Ellyn's early bilingual and bicultural work, as well as her pioneering practice in feminist therapy, soon came to the attention of the APA Committee on Women in Psychology (CWP), then 6 years old. Ellyn was appointed for a 3-year term from 1981–1983, serving as the chair in 1982–1983. Accomplishments of the CWP during those years included: establishing an ad hoc Committee on Underrepresented Groups in the Publication Process in conjunction with the Publication and Communications Board to increase the involvement of women and ethnic minority psychologists in APA journals, developing a slate for CWP of openly identified lesbians to ensure their representation and supporting the APA Committee on Gay Concerns, supporting the formation the APA Committee for Children, Youth, and Families, and sponsoring the first Directory of Hispanic Women in Psychology (American Psychological Association Committee on Women in Psychology (APA-CWP), 1993).

Feminist Therapy Institute

Founded in 1980 by and for experienced feminist therapists in order to further theory and practice, the Feminist Therapy Institute (FTI) met annually for about two decades. Between 30 and 60 diverse women met together and presented and critiqued their latest work and writings. Kaschak chaired FTI for 3 years, including at its tenth meeting, a time when the organization was experiencing growing pains and the conflicts of exploring difficult issues and intersections such as racism and homophobia, along with sexism. After a fractious meeting the year before, Ellyn restored the unity of the group and their engagement in constructive self-reflection about these social justice priorities. Her remarks, "Loving in the War Years," (Kaschak, 1991) refocused the group on working together to fight societal oppression of women, and many members attributed the subsequent unification and thriving of the Institute to her words and leadership.

APA Committee on Lesbian, Gay, Bisexual, and Transgender Concerns (CLGBT)

Most recent advocacy leadership involved being a member and subsequently chairing the Committee on LGBT Concerns of the American Psychological Association. Again, Ellyn's focus was on tackling fractious and often unspoken issues such as the divisions between the gay, lesbian, and transgender members, as well as those between the People of Color and White members. Accomplishments during the year of her serving as Chair included working on International LGBT issues, particularly focused on Uganda and other African countries where lives were in jeopardy, and in the area of Aging for LGBT populations.

Scholarship

Ellyn's contributions to feminist theory and scholarships have been significant. Her writings in the areas of feminist epistemology and the deconstruction of patriarchal social structures are at the core of the field. As the Editor for *Women and Therapy* for the last 20 years, Ellyn has addressed some of the most important applied feminist psychological issues of this decade, such as women and war, feminism and spirituality, domestic violence in lesbian relations, third wave feminism, contemporary approaches to feminist therapy, ethics in therapy, the intersectionality of gender and race/ethnicity, women and disability and chronic illness. In some issues, she has gone where other feminists "fear to tread" in providing an analysis of feminist therapy private practice or in addressing the ways in which even feminist therapists may avoid addressing adequately the moral issues and personal and social responsibility inherent in their work with clients. Her work is comprehensive, unsentimental, and clear-headed. It calls for each of us to become involved, whether in our own scholarship, our own self-evaluation of our practice, or our self- reflection about our own complicity with racism, sexism, classism, homophobia or other oppressions. It takes away the lens that allows us to live in a dualistic, simple world and forces us to see the world through a more complex lens where even feminists and feminist therapists must continually assess their perspectives and practice.

Engendered Lives

In *Engendered Lives: A New Psychology of Women's Experience*, Kaschak (1993) gave us a revolutionary framework with which to truly understand the nature of the gendered world. This work received both the AWP Distinguished Publication Award and the Critics' Choice Award of the American Educational Studies Association and has been adopted nationally and internationally in Women Studies as well as psychology courses. This book continues to be an important resource for many in their teaching and scholarship.

In the text, Kaschak (1993) argues that female bodies are gendered from birth with a profound impact on women's selves because they are living in a society in which " ... the masculine defines the feminine by naming, evaluating, containing and invading it" (p. 5).

> In this highly perceptive, original book, she reworks the myth of Oedipus, which she interprets as not just a story about a cursed son (as Freudians maintain), but a family drama involving King Oedipus's dutiful daughter Antigone, conceived through incest in a patriarchal society. Using modern women's "Antigone complex" as a starting point, she develops a psychological model designed to help women reconnect with themselves and other women, to go beyond being defined by men, subject to protection and violence, to adulation and humiliation. (Publisher's Weekly, 1992)

The Mattering Map

The Mattering Map is an epistemological and contextual approach to understanding the psychology of being human. It recognizes the "full complexity of being human, the dynamic interaction of all aspects of existence and the inseparability of our most empirical perceptions from our human system of perception and our systems of perception from those of influential others" (Kaschak, 2010, p. 6). It repudiates the boundaries between inner and outer experience and encompasses the multiplicity of all experience, perceptions, contexts, cognitions, and feelings as they shift and unfold continuously in time and space (Kaschak, 2013). The Mattering Map is a way to capture what matters for each individual and a "model of meaning making, of what matters in psychological life" (Kaschak, 2010, p. 9). Kaschak continues:

> Mattering subsumes and contains what are named the cognitive and the affective, the psychological and the sociological, the individual and the cultural. Additionally

mattering is inextricably intertwined with matter, each of which shapes the other through the processes alternately named genetics, biology, psychology, culture or human experience. It is, at the same time, a meta-concept and the glue of all human experience. Mattering is what unites diverse aspects of the context into patterns that repeat themselves sufficiently to be designated in our human minds as significant and it is what connects us to each other so irrevocably. As much as matter is a sine qua non of our material existence, so is mattering of our psychological, spiritual and cultural aspects. (p. 10)

About the Mattering Map, Kaschak explained that it represents the culmination of her shift to focusing on epistemology rather than therapy orientations per se. This shift is rooted in her early move from behaviorism to systems thinking, which emphasized complexity, context, and questioning the categories.

I have questioned the categories my entire life: What are we saying when we say, LGBT? What does it mean across all contexts and circumstances? Psychological categories are too concrete. Even when we say we are deconstructing a category, we still are too rigid. I have emphasized fluidity. I think of it as Dis-illusioning— pulling the mask back. For example, when people ask if I am a Jew, my answer is that it depends ... . It depends on what the person is asking, am I a religious Jew, a cultural Jew, am I white, non-white? This notion of fluidity has culminated with the mattering map for me. It is a map of a mind for any individual. (E. Kaschak, personal communication, June 14, 2015)

Sight Unseen

Sight Unseen: Gender and Race through Blind Eyes (Kaschak, 2015) is a groundbreaking contribution to our understanding of the role of vision as a crucial way of knowing. Kaschak (2015) illuminates the epistemology of vision—the fundamental role vision plays in developing and shaping knowledge—and demonstrates that vision manifests as an epistemology prior to that constructed of language and of words. Although "seeing" may be a function of neurology, vision is organized by social and interpersonal meanings. As it is pre-linguistic, vision is also largely unconscious in sighted individuals, learned before the person could put words to the experience. Through studying persons without sight, the epistemology of vision is revealed. Lacking the experience of sight and vision, blind persons must put words to visual concepts. This ethnomethodological approach sheds light on the development of the complexities of identity and critical race and gender theories through the in-depth narratives presented of persons without vision. It produces deep insight into the role and function of visual knowledge in constructing gender, sexual orientation, and race.

The text's main argument is that vision is the first "language." It plays a central role in our understanding of who we are and of the world we live in. The epistemology of vision occurs prior to verbal language and is shaped by experience and social context. It impacts our understanding and interpretations of most ordinary experiences and reactions. Because these interpretations typically fall outside of our awareness, they are resistant to change. They influence central aspects of our identity without us "seeing" or knowing their roots or their impact.

Kaschak (2015) argues that only by studying individuals where vision is absent and comparing them to sighted individuals can we explore how vision impacts our understanding of ourselves and our worldviews. As Kaschak (2015) asks, "Are such crucial human characteristics as gender and ethnicity, race and sexual orientation discoveries or inventions of a species dependent on sight? How would we categorize each other, how would we discriminate were it not for the details of vision transmitted to our human brains?" (p. 3). By exploring the lives of men and women who have never seen, Kaschak (2015) has illuminated some of the other pathways that transmit bias. She skillfully demonstrates the attribution error that we all commit, " ... each of us constructs a life, a worldview out of what is possible for us to see and names it reality when it is instead only possibility" (p. 7).

Recognition

Ellyn may insist that she is merely living her life, putting one foot in front of the other in a march to stamp out patriarchy. Perhaps the day-to-day unfolding of this life's work does seem "ordinary" in the making. Perhaps this attitude reflects the culmination of her Buddhist practice that each day is life fully present, engaged, and meaningfully. However, when viewed from the outside, the breadth and depth of the contributions seem hardly like leading the simple life. Ellyn has been recognized with many awards for her contributions. In 1993, she received the Distinguished Publications Award from the Association of Women in Psychology; in March 2003, the Feminist Therapy Institute honored her for her pioneering work in feminist therapy and theory at their annual conference. She received the APA Committee on Women in Psychology's Distinguished Leadership Award in 2004, the APA Society for the Psychology of Women's Heritage Award in 2005, the APA Society of International Psychology's Denmark-Reuder Award for International Gender Studies in 2008, and the APA Society for the Psychology of Women's Carolyn Wood Sherif Award in 2011.

More Manna

They Keep Stealing Our Stuff

In discussing the legacy of feminist theory and therapy, the good news is that is has been incorporated into mainstream psychology; the bad news is that it has been incorporated. Ellyn makes the point that the work of feminists has become highly visible, while the feminist sources have remained invisible. The theories and practices have been largely usurped by others and incorporated into most theoretical orientations without credit to their origins. Feminist theory has morphed into contemporary narrative therapy, trauma theory, inter-subjective psychotherapy, and largely attributed to the work of men within these orientations.

> Feminists get credit for bringing up issues of gender and then it gets co-opted and the field we developed gets 'colonized' by others. Basic early tenets, such as "Listen to women and believe what they say," sound almost quaint now because our ideas spawned whole fields of study and legal action. Whatever I know I learned in the "fields of our field. I see what we have done as a revolution and a liberation movement, not a therapy intervention." (E. Kaschak, personal communication, June 12, 2015)

What Do You Want Your Obituary to Say?

I don't have to be remembered ... but I want them to get the story right if they do. On one level it is a story that seems very ordinary. I am just doing what any other woman would do ... and it seemed ordinary because feminism was so central to my life; it was the air that I breathed. But it is important for people to realize that in 1974 one had to be intrepid to do this work. A difficult childhood actually helped me to learn how to do this.

When I step out of feminist circles—even to LGBT groups, I realize how much sexism still exists. It is shocking. My entire world, my professional life, academic life, social life, even spiritual Buddhist life, emanates from a feminist perspective.

I think what I would like my obituary to say is, "She did her best." (E. Kaschak, personal communication, June 12, 2015)

On Feminism and Buddhism

"Buddhism is complete deconstruction or 'dis-illusioning.' My feminist vision is strongly influenced by Buddhism, which I consider the most profound human psychology ever realized." (E. Kaschak, personal communication, June 12, 2015)

Ellyn is truly one of the pioneers in feminist theory, scholarship, and therapy. However, she is also one of its stalwarts, continuing to make significant contributions that are growing with the field, shaping it, and encouraging us to explore, shift, and grow every day.

References

American Psychological Association Committee on Women in Psychology (APA-CWP). (1993). *Two decades of change*. Retrieved from http://www.apa.org/pi/women/committee/decades-of-change.pdf

Kaschak, E. (1976). Sociotherapy: An ecological model for psychotherapy with women. *Psychotherapy: Theory, Research and Practice, 13*(1), 61–63. doi:10.1037/h0086487

Kaschak, E. (1990). How to be a failure as a family therapist. In H. Lerman & N. Porter (Eds.), *Handbook of feminist ethics in psychotherapy.* New York: Springer Publishing.

Kaschak, E. (1991). *Loving in the war years.* Opening remarks at the 10th Annual Meeting, Feminist Therapy Institute, Oakland, CA.

Kaschak, E. (1993). *Engendered lives: A new psychology of women's experience.* New York, NY: Basic Books.

Kaschak, E. (2010). The mattering map: Morphing and multiplicity. In C. Bruns & E. Kaschak (Eds.), *Feminist therapy in the 21st century.* New York: Taylor & Francis.

Kaschak, E. (2013). The mattering map: Confluence and influence. *Psychology of Women Quarterly, 37*(4), 436–443. doi:10.1177/0361684313480839

Kaschak, E. (2015). *Sight unseen: Gender and race through blind eyes.* New York City: Columbia University Press.

Kaschak, E., & Sharratt, S. (1979). Sex roles and androgyny in Latin America: A psychological perspective. *Reportorio Americano,* Spring 1979.

Publisher's Weekly. (July, 1992). *Engendered lives: A new psychology of women experience.* Retrieved from http://www.publishersweekly.com/978-0-465-01347-0

Stegman, W. (1971). *The angle of repose.* New York: Penguin Books.

Hannah Lerman: My Feminist Journey

Hannah Lerman

ABSTRACT

This is a description of the journey Hannah Lerman sees herself as having taken to become a feminist, feminist therapist, and feminist psychologist, and what she sees as her contributions to feminism along the way.

I am an only child and was very shy during my childhood. I was often lonely and came to view myself as an outsider and an observer of life. It was not pleasant at the time, but I think that this has stood me in good stead, both personally and professionally. It has certainly contributed to what I do in psychotherapy and to how I have developed my ideas in my writing.

I was my father's daughter. He was the most significant person in my family to me. He was, I have always thought, brilliant, and in my eyes, he knew everything. He was relatively uneducated, but he read a lot and was self-taught. As a child, I idolized him. Later, I came to realize that he was not particularly emotionally sensitive. He had lived a very full life by the time he met and married my mother when he was in his 40s. He boasted that he had been in 46 of the 48 continental states of the United States. He had been a labor organizer and a radical leftist member of the International Workers of the World (known as the 'Wobblies'). He would occasionally mention that he had participated in a Free Speech fight without explaining what he was talking about. I only learned later how dangerous such a situation was. He had worked as a coalminer in Pennsylvania, a freight handler on the docks on the West coast, and had worked on the Hoover Dam in Nevada, all before he came back to New York and met my mother. In my early years, he worked as a freight handler on the New York New Haven and Hartford Railroad and was the union shop steward. In later years, I have always regretted that I never sat him down in front of a tape recorder and learned more about the details of what he had done and where he had been.

He met my mother after he moved into a rooming house that was run by her mother and "became involved" with her. He had come to the United States from Russia early in the twentieth century and his older sister who had come with him lived in New York. His not-so-flattering story was that he didn't feel that he could get out of marrying my mother because of the nearby presence of his sister.

Although both my father and mother were of Jewish backgrounds, his relationship to Judaism was much less conventional than hers. He had been brought up in a religious Jewish household in Russia with his sister and several brothers. He had been the baby of the family. He had had an orthodox Jewish upbringing, but he had moved away from that after he came to the United States. His sister, my Aunt Fannie, remained religious during her lifetime and was quite active in the sisterhood connected with her synagogue in the Bronx.

My mother, on the other hand, was born in the United States to parents who had come from Poland. Her religious background was relatively conventional. Her father died when she was relatively young. She was the maid of all work in her mother's boarding house, and according to my father, he took pity on her after he met her there. She was also uneducated, but also uninterested in intellectual activities. I think that after I showed my own intellectual interests, she didn't know what to do with me or how to relate to me. I, on the other hand, was ashamed of her during my childhood. I cringed at her bumbling attempts to talk to my friends and when I saw her handwriting.

My father would go through the house, giving it the white glove treatment and criticizing my mother unmercifully when he found any dust. Until my teens, I didn't realize that my mother was as good a housekeeper as most and that my father's demands were the real problem. My mother would take it and take it and then periodically erupt to my father. I vividly recall one fight between them when I was about 8 years old. We lived on the fourth floor of an apartment building in the Bronx. My mother was threatening to jump out of the window. I was sitting nearby and crying. After the argument was over, my father saw my distress and tried, in his way, to comfort me. He said, "You know how your mother is" in an attempt to enlist me on his side. I still don't know why I knew that I shouldn't take sides, although internally, I was on his side. I just didn't respond.

My father had high hopes for me. In New York, there were Regents' State scholarships. He was sure that I could get one, but I didn't. He would accuse me of "dissipating my brain" when I wanted to go somewhere with friends rather than study. However, I always read everything that I could get my hands on. My father taught me to read before I got to kindergarten, and I went to one of New York's great neighborhood public libraries regularly throughout my childhood. When the time came for me to go to high school, I applied to several special high schools. I didn't get into the Bronx High School of Science, but I did get into Hunter College High School.

I am very glad that I went there because I got a very good education. However, it was an all-girls school at the time and going there definitely did not help my social life. There was a very distinct difference at the time between the friends I had in my neighborhood and those that I had in school. In the neighborhood group, I was the "Dictionary" and answered questions for all on a variety of subjects. At school, I found other girls who were as smart as or smarter than I was. Several of my high school teachers had doctorates. I did not realize until later that they were working in a high school because they were probably not able to get employment in a college or university at that time.

I am still grateful that I lived in New York. My family didn't have much money, and I could not have gone to college, except where the city colleges were free. I lived at home during my undergraduate years. I do remember that I spent about one whole year mentally chewing on the question of whether I was going to college because I wanted to or because my father wanted me to go. Ultimately, the answer I arrived at was that it didn't matter. I knew that my father wanted me to go to college, but I realized that I also wanted to go. I did have some feeling that if I ever left college at any point, I wouldn't be able to go back. Fortunately, I never had to actually face this.

I worked part-time throughout my undergraduate years. I learned how to type in high school, although I didn't know shorthand. I worked in a variety of office jobs during those years. In the summers, I would apply for a full-time job and swear that I would stay permanently, although I knew that I wouldn't. At one point, I made $50 a week. That was more than my father was making at the time!

As I have said, I read everything. At one point, I kept a record of what I read for about a year. I was reading more than one book a day for most of that period. I read fiction, of course, especially science fiction, but I also read nonfiction. I still remember, because it was somewhat embarrassing, when I asked at the reference desk in the public library for the Kinsey Sex Report on males. I was about 12 at that time. Later, when I was in college, I read Simone de Beauvoir's *The Second Sex* (De Beauvoir, 1961). I then walked around telling everybody that she agreed with me.

I was married briefly just after I got my bachelor's degree. I met Bart at City College. He was somewhat older than I was. He had been in the military and had served in Germany just after World War II. He was not Jewish. I knew this would upset my mother. I enlisted my father's aid in telling my mother, and it worked out. Bart was a militant atheist. I was (and am) an agnostic. I didn't think that this particular difference was something to fight about—but he did. We got married by a Justice of the Peace in Yonkers because I wasn't old enough yet to get married in New York City itself. My parents and one of his friends were present. The ceremony was remarkable because the judge's telephone kept ringing throughout. I was afraid that he was going to stop and answer it. Eventually, someone else came into the room and answered it instead. I was to move into Bart's apartment in midtown Manhattan. After the ceremony, we moved my books. One of our first fights was about my copy of the King James Bible. He didn't want a bible in the home. I said we could put it in the closet, saying that it was beautiful literature, etc. When we moved my books, it was on top of a pile that I was carrying down to the car. I didn't realize until later that my father had colluded with Bart and had taken the bible off the pile of books I was carrying. I got it back three and one half years later after Bart and I divorced.

At the time, he was still an undergraduate at City College. I enrolled in the Master's Program in Psychology there and continued my schooling there for the next year and one half. One of my jobs was to sit in the reception chair during evening classes and basically direct traffic. One evening, late in a term, one of the students in an Introductory Psychology course came to me and asked me to teach the class as the instructor wasn't present. She, I knew, was a physiological psychologist. They had finished discussing all the chapters in the book, except for two: one on physiology and one on culture. I thought that I could handle discussing the chapter on culture. However, I made two immediate mistakes. When I stood before the students, I told them that they could leave it they wished to. No one left at that moment. Next, I said basically, "You have read the chapter. Ask me questions." Following that, every single student in the class filed out the door. It was quite a long time after that before I felt comfortable standing in front of a class again.

After Bart graduated, we both enrolled in graduate programs at Michigan State University, me in psychology and him in physics. I spent five glorious years in East Lansing, Michigan. The teachers affiliated with the Psychology Department, especially those in the counseling center where I interned, were truly interested in the development of the students. I need to thank Bill Kell and Josephine Morse, especially, for all that they gave to me. This was where I grew up in emotionally and intellectually. During some of these years, I was in psychotherapy myself at the counseling center. I was able to conquer my anxiety and depression during this period. I also divorced my husband before I got my Master's degree.

I dedicated my doctoral dissertation "To those who helped me grow" (Lerman, 1963). Of course, I meant some of the faculty, but I also meant some of my fellow students. Since I was married while I was in graduate school, I experienced some conflict between being able to study and my marital obligations. I recall, before a holiday party, having to iron my husband's shirt rather than do my own schoolwork and resenting it bitterly.

I knew, however, the very first time that I sat down with a therapy patient that this was the right work for me. I worked part-time for 3 years in the VA psychology intern program. The first year was at Battle Creek VA Hospital where I did psychological testing. The second year was at Dearborn VA Hospital where I worked in the TB ward. The third year was at the VA Outpatient Clinic in Detroit. Two significant memories from this last year stand out. The first was about the partitioned cubicles in which we saw clients at the

Detroit clinic. The walls were very thin, and there was no soundproofing. It was literally possible not to know for sure if you were responding to something your client said or if it was from the client being seen in the next cubicle. The second involved a weekly seminar that we participated in. The leader was a male psychoanalyst. A psychiatrist presented his case notes on his psychoanalytic psychotherapy with a client. The problem was that he presented about sessions that had occurred about 2 years previously. As I recall, the material we heard and discussed was never anywhere close to being current. Neither the psychoanalyst nor the presenting psychiatrist ever seemed to be the least bit bothered in any way about this fact.

The last 2 years, I worked in the Michigan State Counseling Center. This was the best experience that I could possibly have had. The faculty members of the program were caring and supportive. This was where I really learned how to do psychotherapy. It was shortly after the end of World War II. Many students were returning GIs who were older than the typical college student. I had one such client who did whatever he could to make the sessions other than psychotherapy. I was somewhat vulnerable because I was in the process of divorcing my husband. One day, he remarked about the fact that I was wearing a different shade of lipstick than I had before. I was totally disarmed by this comment and had trouble recovering. Later, I had an emergency supervision session with Dr. Kell at his home about my experience. Another member of the counseling center staff walked in during our session and commented: "I see that you have discovered his anger."

My doctoral years coincided with the years that the United States was involved in the Vietnam War. My father wrote to me regularly, complaining that I was not protesting and demonstrating against the war. I was with him in spirit, but I never became involved. I was sympathetic, but was not involved in any political activity at all during those years. My immediate reaction to what I learned about Sigmund Freud was negative. In fact, my original idea for my doctoral research was to investigate Freud's idea that women's super-egos were less well developed than those of men. I did a pilot study, but couldn't find a suitable test instrument and then switched to another topic. The idea for my book about Freud came out of that original project. I envisioned synthesizing the material about the psychological development of women from psychoanalysis, academic psychology, sociology, and any other branch of study that contained any significant material. I did not return to this idea until many years later.

Although my personal experiences in graduate school were positive primarily because of the nurturing people at the counseling center, I recall an APA convention party one year in which one of the male psychology department faculty members expounded on the foolishness of enabling women to get doctoral degrees. His reason was that they would get married and leave the field. I had female professors as well as male professors and did not experience much overt discrimination. There were a few other female students as well. All the interns who worked at the counseling center, male and female alike, used whatever psychological concepts we were learning to put each other down, "analyzing" each other regularly in a brutal manner. My later reaction to this was to deliberately never comment to anyone other than a client about whatever I felt I learned about a particular person's psychological state, whether they were a fellow student, friend, or colleague. I have found that not all psychologists or other mental health workers have chosen to operate similarly.

After receiving my doctoral degree in 1963, I took a job at Topeka State Hospital in Topeka, Kansas. My experience of living in Topeka was surreal for a city person like myself. I was in rural Kansas, a totally different place from anywhere else I had ever been. Topeka was the state capitol of Kansas. Besides the legislators with whom we had almost no contact, the only other intellectual group around was at the Menninger Foundation that was still situated there. Because no theater in Topeka showed foreign films, the Fellows of the Menninger Foundation organized a private set of film screenings that took place in a junior high school building every few weeks during the fall and winter. Generally, the films that were shown were several years old. The running joke in the psychiatric community was that if you hadn't already seen any of the films in the current year's screenings, you had been in Topeka too long.

These screenings were a major social event for the psychiatric and associated community. You had the chance to talk to someone you had been trying to reach by telephone during the work week and learn who was going with whom (and which twosomes had broken up). The major problem was the small size of the community. I recall one weekend when the film showing was on Friday evening, there was a lecture by Gardner Murphy on the Menninger campus on Saturday morning, a chamber music concert at the local college on Saturday evening, and a Blintze Brunch at the Jewish Temple on Sunday morning. If you went to all of these events (and there wasn't much else to do), you saw approximately the same people at each one. The best thing about Topeka's psychiatric community, however, was that anyone who was anybody in the psychiatric and psychoanalytic fields came through the city and gave a lecture that was free and open to all.

I learned a great deal in Topeka. The first thing was how to take on the persona of being a psychologist. At the first ward meeting to discuss patients, the psychiatrist who was leading the meeting asked: "And what does the psychologist think about this?" I almost looked around to see who he was referring to before I realized that he meant me. The people who came to lecture also taught me a great deal.

As I have said, the community was small, and everyone in it knew everybody else. This was one of the biggest differences from what I had experienced growing up in New York City. In Topeka, it was not possible to be anonymous in almost any part of your life. At one point, I dated a male psychologist who worked at the local VA hospital. He lived across the street from a psychiatrist who worked at another section of Topeka State Hospital, the one where yet another male psychologist who was my very good friend also worked. It felt as though everybody knew every single thing about you.

Most of the work was diagnostic work. Topeka State Hospital followed the format of the Menninger Foundation. It was usually about two or more weeks after a patient was admitted to the hospital that they were given a diagnosis. I did not realize at the time how unusual this relatively leisurely process was. I was also given a few outpatients to do psychotherapy with. They were long time patients who were assigned to the new staff, psychology interns, and psychiatry residents who generally stayed in Topeka only a few brief years. One man who was my patient guessed before I told him that I too would be leaving Topeka. He had experienced such changes before as most of his prior therapists had been students of one type or another.

I stayed about three and one half years before I left and took a job in Los Angeles at the Los Angeles County–USC Medical Center's Psychiatric Unit. I had my first experiences here in supervising psychological interns. The overall process was far different here than that I had known in Topeka. There was always a massive influx of patients. We did not have the luxury of spending two weeks on diagnosis. We had to get patients stabilized and ready to move on as soon as possible. The heartbreaking problem, however, was that there were few resources available for patients after they left the psychiatric unit.

There were many opportunities in Los Angeles. I trained at UCLA as an encounter group therapist during the height of that particular phase. I also worked at the Los Angeles Free Clinic during the height of the psychedelic era. We would see clients who were on bad acid trips and write on our records that they were "anxious" without any additional details. I supervised a group of intake workers, all of whom were also volunteers. Some were "Acid Heads" themselves. One highlight of this experience was when we participated in a group LSD session using some of the original Sandoz "acid" that one of the intake workers had on hand. It took place at someone's secluded house in the Hollywood Hills. I learned some significant things about myself during this experience. I also learned that the Acid Heads in the group had considered me to be a potential problem during the experience because I seemed "uptight." After we took the acid, one woman brought out a set of color photographs of flowers. After I looked at them for a while, the flowers seemed to come out at me from the photos. The experience had begun. I resolved some issues related to a recent relationship breakup during the session, experienced what I came to call a latent toothache (a tooth problem that began evident later), but about which I was somehow aware during the acid session, and dealt with several other issues as well.

My overt journey toward Feminism began in early 1971. I was asked to join a presentation that would take place later that year at the Association for Humanistic Psychology meeting (This was held in conjunction with the American Psychological Association Convention in Washington, DC that year). The symposium was *The Sexes Today: With the Past Recast*. I took on the task of presenting about Sigmunda Freud (Lerman, 1971). Other people reversed the work of other scientists and philosophers. I enjoyed writing this paper more than any other that I have ever written. I went to the library of the Los Angeles Psychoanalytic Society to read and, with secret glee, enjoyed the librarian's assistance. In the paper, I wrote about Alfreda Adler, Karla Jung, and Karl Horney. This work reignited my earlier interest in reviewing all the different available literatures about the development of women. It was shortly after this that I began to work on the book that became *A Mote in Freud's Eye: From Psychoanalysis to the Psychology of Women* (Lerman, 1986). My intent was, as I have already mentioned, to review many avenues of study. I actually did end up doing some of this, but focused most specifically on Sigmund Freud.

The woman who invited me was Theodora Wells who wrote *Woman—Which Includes Man, of Course: An Experience in Awareness* (Wells, 1972). This was one of the first of the experience pieces that circulated via copying machine and postal service during the early days of the second wave feminist movement in the psychological and mental health communities. It was the inspiration for the symposium that I mentioned above and was a role reversal piece, something that was very popular in these circles for quite a while.

Shortly after this experience, a woman arrived in Los Angeles who had been a social worker in New York. She initiated a consciousness-raising group for women therapists that I attended weekly for several years. It was an experience that changed my life. I had been part of the way toward being a feminist before this experience, but this was the experience during which it all crystallized. I still remember my negative reaction when someone in the group called me a feminist before I was ready to accept that term.

What feminism did for me was to tap into my vaguely socialist views and integrate me into a whole female feminist person. I had never taken part in any kind of demonstration before this time and had never stood up for any idea, although, of course, I certainly had had opinions. I felt as though feminism had reached down into the essence of my very being and my socialist roots, twisted the elements, and integrated me into a whole being during the approximately year and a half that I attended the consciousness-raising group. This was so very far from being merely an intellectual change in me.

After a time, three other therapists and myself organized a group called Feminist Psychological Associates and gave presentations at professional groups for other mental health professionals about feminist issues. One of my memories from this time was a woman psychiatrist whose reaction to our discussion of the feminist movement was: "What is going to happen to love?" When I think about this today shortly after the Supreme Court's decision about marriage equality, my answer is "It's doing just fine."

While I worked for Los Angeles County, I also maintained a small private practice. During this period, I moved my office and sent out announcements to the psychological community. I included that my practice was that of a feminist therapist. The year was 1972. Apparently, I was the first person in the Los Angeles area who identified herself as such. Shortly thereafter, I received a letter from the Los Angeles Society of Clinical Psychologists about this. I answered with a letter that included references. I don't think that at any time, before or since, have I ever written a letter that included references. The LASCP thanked me for my letter and suggested that I might better have described myself as specializing in women's problems. I am now sorry that I did not carry this correspondence further in response to these comments. I have kept this correspondence ever since. At times, I have used it in presentations to groups.

During the 1970s, I was involved with the establishment of a new freestanding school of psychology in Los Angeles. This became the California School of Professional Psychology, and I became its first Dean of Student Affairs. While I was pursuing feminism outside of my work here, I worked in a setting that might now be called anti-feminist. I was one of four deans. Announcements in the form of memos to faculty often were sent out in my name as if I were the only decider. I was as much as told that because I was a member of the administration, I should not interact much with the other psychologists who were members of the faculty. I, unfortunately, accepted this and became emotionally isolated in this setting. The dynamics of the administration were undemocratic and ultimately involved coups that, during this time, got rid of female personnel. Hedda Bolgar, Astrid Beigel, Rona Fields, and I were ultimately casualties and were kicked out of the organization. At a later time, men who were involved in the early days, including Arthur Kovacs and Nicholas Cummings, the founder himself, were also removed.

When I was forced to leave, it turned out to be very good for me personally. I had presented my first major paper at an APA convention in 1974. It was entitled "What happens in Feminist Therapy" (Lerman, 1976) and has since been republished. I was now able to work more intensively on my Freud book and was free to also get involved in APA feminist women's politics in the Division of the Psychology of Women and the Association for Women in Psychology. I helped to establish a women's section within the Division of Psychology of APA and used some of what I had learned about psychological politics from my time at CSPP in my interactions within APA. At that time, focusing on women's issues was sometimes contentious within APA, and the path was not always easy. My first recollection about power came during a meeting of Division 29's Executive Board where I was representing the women in the division. I do not recall what the issue was. I do recall that when I said in response to the issue, "The women won't like that," the men looked at me and nodded. I was envisioning an army of women behind me as I spoke. I don't think I have ever felt so powerful, either before or since this event.

I was a founding member of the Feminist Therapy Institute. We originally formed this group because we wanted a place to talk to one another about what we were doing in psychotherapy. At the Association of Women in Psychology during this period, those of us who were interested in Feminist Therapy often presented what we came to consider as presentations in Feminist Therapy 101. A group of us met in Lenore Walker's hotel room at the 1980 APA convention. We racked our brains and came up with a group of names of women who we believed were feminist therapists and invited them to a meeting that was held in Vail, Colorado (off season). The requirement for attention was that you had to present to the group. When we met, we sat indoors in one of the most beautiful spots in the United States for three days without going outside, except for meals and sleep, and listened to one another present. It was quite exhilarating. Many of these presentations were eventually published in *Handbook of Feminist Therapy* (Rosewater & Walker, 1985).

My book, *A Mote in Freud's Eye: From Psychoanalysis to the Psychology of Women,* was published in 1986 (Lerman, 1986). This, as I have indicated before, was the ultimate result of my original idea to review and attempt to synthesize all the available theories and research about the psychodynamic development of women. I also wrote a number of other papers, mainly on the topic of Feminist Therapy and other women's issues during the 1970s and 1980s.

Earlier, I had run some group sessions in what was the first women's building in Los Angeles. One member confided in the group that she had been sexually abused by her prominent Beverly Hills psychologist. I helped her take her case to the Los Angeles County Psychological Association. There were no formal legal mechanisms available at the time to deal with such a complaint. She came to an APA convention in Hawaii and presented her story. Members of the Association for Women in Psychology heard her and went to the APA President, Leona Tyler. APA's Task Force on Sex Bias and Sex-Role Stereotyping in Psychotherapeutic Practice resulted from this presentation. They published the results of a survey of psychologists who were therapists (Brodsky & Holroyd, 1981) and also published *Guidelines for Therapy with Women* (Task Force on Sex Bias and Sex Role Stereotyping in Psychotherapeutic Practice, 1978). Later, I became part of a taskforce of the California State Psychological Association that did some of the earliest research about the prevalence of sexual abuse by therapists. We asked for information from subsequent therapists about their clients who had been sexually abused by their prior therapists. This was published in 1983 (Bouhoutos, Holroyd, Lerman, Forer,

& Greenberg, 1983). Also, in 1984, I completed the first edition of my bibliography about the literature about sexual abuse by psychotherapists (Lerman, 1984/1991). This was originally available through the Association of Women in Psychology. When I completed the second edition, it was available through Division 29 of APA, the Division of Psychotherapy. I have continued to collect literature about the subject and want to make an ongoing bibliography available eventually as a database through a website.

Meanwhile, the Feminist Therapy Institute (FTI) met yearly. As a group, we began interested in issues related to the psychodiagnosis of women as the fourth edition of the American Psychiatric Association's Diagnostic and Statistical Manual was in preparation. For a while, we even had a subgroup of the FTI that was primarily devoted to this topic. Some of us even picketed the American Psychiatric Association's convention in Washington, DC the year the DSM-IV was published. The major issues that we were concerned with at the time were the diagnoses of Self-Defeating Personality Disorder, Pre-Menstrual Disorder, and Paraphilic Rapist. Self-Defeating Personality Disorder was a diagnosis to be given to individuals who stayed with abusive partners. Lenore Walker pointed out that this was not a personality disorder, but a situational issue. The issue for Paraphilic Rapist was the possibility that rapists would not be punished because their behavior had been pathologized. A number of us became quite interested in diagnosis at this time. It had not played much part in our thinking before this. The power of formal diagnosis, however, became clear to many of us around this time. Later, I published my second book, *Pigeonholing Women's Misery: A History and Critical Analysis of the Psychodiagnosis of Women in the Twentieth Century* in 1996 (Lerman, 1996).

In the 1990s, the major part of my practice was going out to consult in nursing homes throughout the Los Angeles area. Suddenly, the rules for what psychologists were allowed to do changed, and we were no longer able to see clients with major psychiatric disorders. This change was made only for the extreme Western part of the country. I understand that the changes were later reversed, but I had already moved to Las Vegas where I have continued to do some of the same type of work. I picked it because a cousin lived there. It was also a place where I could continue to consult to nursing homes.

Las Vegas is a very strange place conceptually for a feminist to live. I exist here because I have no contact of any kind with the tourist and entertainment part of the city. Apart from that, the city and its people are very similar to any other city, although it took me a while to learn this. I have continued to go to nursing homes and now also direct psychology dissertations at Walden University online and have a small practice in my home. When I began working at Walden, I was thankful to be able to get back in touch with psychology in general. In nursing homes, I only saw nurses and social workers and rarely saw other psychologists.

I still get recognized for my earliest feminist paper and my Freud book. However, I consider my annotated bibliography of the literature about sexual abuse by professionals to be my most important work. I feel as if I went with the flow of the second wave of the Women's Movement, so to speak, and let it carry me. I am mostly comfortable with the way things turned out and am glad that I was open to what was going on around me. I am also very glad to have had the experience of meeting the very special women that I met along the way. I am glad to be a therapist. That is my calling. However, the part of me that is a scholar has always regretted that I couldn't devote more time to that side of things. After 30-some years working in nursing homes, I have begun to think about writing about this setting. Most people don't know what nursing homes are like, and there is much that could be done to make them better (Vladeck, 1980). There is much for a feminist in particular to say.

References

Bouhoutos, J., Holroyd, J., Lerman, H., Forer, B. R., & Greenberg, M. (1983). Sexual intimacy between psychotherapists and patients. *Professional Psychology, Research and Practice, 14*, 185–196. doi:10.1037/0735-7028.14.2.185

Brodsky, A., & Holroyd, J. (Eds.). (1981). *Report of the task force on sex bias and sex-role stereotyping in psychotherapeutic practice. Women and Mental Health*. New York: Basic Books.

De Beauvoir, S. (1961). *The second sex* (H. M. Parshley, Trans.). New York: Bantam Books (Original work published 1949).

Lerman, H. (1963). *A study of some effects of the therapists' personality and behavior and of the clients' reactions in psychotherapy* (Unpublished PhD dissertation). Michigan State University.

Lerman, H. (1971). *Depth psychology according to Sigmunda Freud. In the sexes today: With the past recast*. Symposium conducted at the ninth annual meeting of the association for humanistic psychology, Washington, DC.

Lerman, H. (1976). What happens in feminist therapy. In S. Cox (Ed.), *Female psychology: The emerging self* (pp. 378–384). New York: St. Martin's Press.

Lerman, H. (1984/1991). *Sexual intimacies between psychotherapists and patients; An annotated bibliography of mental health, legal and public media literature and relevant legal cases* (superseded by second edition, 1991). Phoenix, AZ: Division of Psychotherapy of the American Psychological Association.

Lerman, H. (1986). *A mote in Freud's eye: From psychoanalysis to the psychology of women*. New York: Springer.

Lerman, H. (1996). *Pigeonholing women's misery: A history and critical analysis of the psychodiagnosis of women in the twentieth century*. New York: Basic Books.

Rosewater, L. B., & Walker, L. E. A. (Eds.). (1985). *Handbook of feminist therapy*. New York: Springer.

Task Force on Sex Bias and Sex Role Stereotyping in Psychotherapeutic Practice. (1978). Guidelines for therapy with women. *American Psychologist, 33*, 1122–1123. doi:10.1037// 0003-066x.33.12.1122

Vladeck, B. C. (1980). *Unloving care: The nursing home tragedy*. New York: Basic Books.

Wells, T. (1972). *Woman—Which includes man, of course: An experience in awareness*. Los Angeles, CA: Theodora Wells.

Harriet Lerner: A Feminist Voice From the Wheat Fields

Harriet Lerner

ABSTRACT

Harriet Lerner, a Menninger-trained psychologist, has published widely in scholarly journals and for a general audience. Her twelve books include *The New York Times* bestseller, *The Dance of Anger*, and she blogs for *Psychology Today*. In this chapter, she shares her personal and professional evolution as a feminist theorist, psychotherapist, and writer.

I was born in Brooklyn, New York, on November 30, 1944, the younger of two daughters. My grandparents on both sides were Russian Jewish immigrants, and my parents, first-generation Americans, were high school graduates. Brooklyn was a wonderful city to grow up in, and quite affordable back then. I spent my early childhood in places that were a subway token away, like the Brooklyn Public Library, The Brooklyn Museum, and the Brooklyn Botanical Gardens.

Achievement was next to Godliness as far as my parents were concerned. My father talked about "my daughters, the doctors" while we were still in strollers, and we knew we'd get PhDs. the way other kids knew they'd go to elementary school. Perhaps this was too much of a good thing, but it pushed against the constraining gender roles of the day.

I decided to become a clinical psychologist by the time I entered kindergarten, and I never veered from this goal. My early career choice probably had something to do with the fact that my mother put my sister and me in therapy before the age of three. Back then, most folks considered therapy a last resort for the mentally ill, but my progressive Jewish mother thought it was a learning experience. Our family was poor, but my parents had a health insurance plan that let us have therapy for a dollar a session. Our pediatrician (none other than Doctor Benjamin Spock) was a similar bargain.

Gender Roles

When I grew up, the rules of the game were clear and simple. Men were to seek their fortune, and women were to seek men. A man's job was to make something of himself in the world, and a woman's job was to find herself a successful man. Boys were supposed to "be someone," and girls were supposed to "find someone."

"Finding someone" or just aiming to be popular required a fair amount of pretending. Back then, pretending was as natural as breathing and as ordinary as good manners. Advice to women and girls explicitly prescribed male dominance while implicitly warning women that men were weak. The paradoxical notion that women must strengthen men by relinquishing their own strength was everywhere.

In one popular book, *Help Your Husband Stay Alive* (Lees, 1957), the author wrote: "What is humiliating about being under a man—whether in business, in government, or any role of life … if it is clear to you that he is only on top because you are holding him up?" (p. 14). Despite my precocious career plans, I took such messages to heart. When a sixth-grade teacher advised us girls that it was endearing to misspell big words in notes to boys, I consulted my dictionary to be sure of my misspellings. The unconscious rule for women of my generation was this: *the weaker sex must protect the stronger sex from recognizing the strength of the weaker sex lest the stronger sex feel weakened by the strength of the weaker sex.*

Most women bought into that, even if they weren't aware of it. It took me a long time to appreciate the enormous unconscious power of the paradoxical rule behind the cultural teaching that women should strengthen men and our bond with them by relinquishing our own strength—that to do otherwise, or simply to be ourselves or to take up a woman's cause, was unfeminine, unlovable, castrating, destructive, and threatening to men. We didn't consider the terrible cost to our lives—and to men's lives, too—when we behaved not as authentic women, but as Gloria Steinem has put it, like female impersonators (Gorney, 1995).

The Women's Movement

I was living in New York and then Berkeley during the heady days of the second wave of feminism. I was a graduate student, and my response to the Women's Movement was, "What does this have to do with me?" My mother was the boss of the family I was raised in. I was getting my PhD, and no one had discriminated against me as a woman. What was all the kvetching about? If women didn't like standing over the oven, they should get out of the kitchen. Looking back, I think I was sleepwalking or perhaps in a coma.

In 1972, my psychologist husband and I moved from Berkeley to Topeka, Kansas, where we completed our post-docs in clinical psychology and subsequently joined the staff of the Menninger Clinic. There, in the land of patriarchy, necessity became the mother of comprehension. I quickly "got" feminism, which had not yet arrived to Topeka. This was back in the day where women who were dissatisfied with their prescribed role of wife and mother were seen as imitating or envying men. Narrow and constricting ideas about female psychology were reified as truth and treated as scientific facts of the day. When women didn't fit the theories, it was the women and not the theories that were called into question.

For a long time, I was the only feminist voice at Menninger, and I was so intense about trying to convince my colleagues that I quickly became encapsulated in a role (the "women's libber") that made it impossible for me to be heard. I had a major contribution to this problem, being young and zealous, and failing to make wise choices about how and when to say what to whom. It took me a long time to learn to choose my battles and to stop dissipating my energy trying to change my colleagues.

Menninger was an institution large enough in size and spirit to tolerate differences, and I had many wonderful teachers and supervisors. Looking back over my more than three decades as a staff psychologist, I'm enormously grateful for my experience there. It was a place where people took their work seriously (there wasn't much else to do) and encouraged me to do the same. Had I stayed in Berkeley or New York, I doubt I would have made the contributions that I ultimately went on to make.

I also had difficult times. Some colleagues were quick to interpret my thinking as an expression of my pathology rather than simply disagree with my feminist ideas. I wore long earrings from Berkeley and was told by one supervisor that this was seen as a reflection of penis envy. As Carol Burnett once said, humor is tragedy plus time. It wasn't funny to me back then.

Here's an illustration of the worst of it. Early in my career, I wrote a professional paper challenging Freud's theory of penis envy—turning it on its head, if you will, with a focus on male envy of women. The paper was accepted, but then rejected, and later accepted again by the Menninger Bulletin, the scientific journal of the Menninger Clinic. During the time when the paper was flatly rejected for publication, the following written exchange took place between a well-known senior Menninger psychiatrist and Dr. Karl Menninger.

11-7-1978

Dear Dr. Karl,

I was a bit surprised and greatly pleased to learn of your change of view regarding the Bulletin's publishing of the Lerner paper on "penis envy."

Frankly, Dr. Karl, I am sick and tired of these mother-hating viragos exposing their so-called feminist pathology in purportedly scientific papers and trumpeting about the very "penis envy" which lies at the root of their miseries. And God help the children they produce!

In any case, I am gratified that you and I are indeed together on this one.

With kindest regards,

Donald B. Rinsley, M.D. (H. Lerner, personal communication, November 7, 1978)

When I opened the inter-office envelope addressed to me and found this note, I was flung sideways in my chair. I took it to the senior editor of the journal and protested. I was devastated and furious, but also grateful to the anonymous secretary who took the risk to leak it to me. The editor of the journal, also a psychologist, was sympathetic, and the paper entitled *Envy and Devaluation of Women* was ultimately published. It was translated into several languages and received considerable positive attention.

When this article was published, feminist psychiatrist Teresa Bernardez reached out to me from a long distance. She had been on the staff at Menninger, but left before I arrived. She called to invite me to present with her at a professional meeting. In addition to her friendship, she generously introduced me to her vast network of feminist friends and colleagues, which included Jean Baker Miller who wrote the classic book, *Toward a New Psychology of Women* (Miller, 1976).

These two women, Teresa Bernardez and Jean Baker Miller, had a major influence on my work. I remain grateful to both of them and miss their presence among us. Teresa Bernardez wrote the first paper on the subject of female anger, which inspired me to write *The Dance of Anger* (Lerner, 2015/1985). Jean Baker Miller encouraged me to write accessibly in plain English, even as she warned me that I might lose credibility as a scholar among my colleagues. They were both generous and collaborative. I was quickly blessed with a wonderful and expanding network of long-distance feminist colleagues and friends who supported my work during difficult times and showed me a new meaning of intellectual community and camaraderie among women.

The shift from professional to popular writing was more difficult than anything I could have imagined. People who think it's simpler to write simply have never done so or have never done it well. First, I had to unlearn everything I had learned as an academic writer. Second, I was forced to face my unclarity. If I wrote, for example, "The child became the carrier of the mother's unconscious projections," my editor would say, "What is this? What exactly is happening between this mother and child, and describe it in plain English please!" When I was forced to explain, say, the family emotional process in plain language, I was confronted with what I did not know and what had been obscured by abstraction.

While I remain allergic to jargon and obfuscating language, I value the academic papers that I've published. Some are feminist and systemic revisions of psychoanalytic theory and practice, and others are pioneering contributions to female psychology and development. Many of these works are reprinted in my book, *Women in Therapy* (Lerner, 1994).

Feminist Understanding

At the heart of feminism, as I began to understand it, was the struggle for truth telling. Feminism encouraged women to go the hard route, to fly in the face of all that had been prescribed for us regarding possibility and place, to say nothing of good manners. It required protesting the exclusion of women and other marginalized groups from public life and to stop colluding with the objectification, diminishment, and invisibility of women. This required that we be wide-eyed, alert, and outspoken rather than compromise clarity, truth, and honor. Feminism helped us to pay attention to who had a seat at the table and who was rendered silent or invisible. The fact that all major institutions that generated power, policy, or wealth were run by men no longer seemed like the natural order of things.

Before the consciousness raising groups in the sixties, women I knew, myself included, did not begin to tell the truth about female experience—not even to ourselves. The Women's Movement, drawing on insights from the Civil Rights Movement, brought about an epistemological revolution whereby women respected our own truths above what the dominant group said to or about us. Indeed, we questioned the very nature of truth. We asked, "Who says what's true about women? How does it benefit them? What would be different if we created new truths?" We examined how issues of gender and power shape what we take to be real and true.

Of course, men also pretend, and as a dominant group, White men have created for themselves many dehumanizing forces that block them from acting and reacting from an authentic center. But, there are many categories of pretending in which men will not participate. Men will not pretend, for example, that words like "she" or "chairwoman" could ever truly include them. Men will not pretend that the works of womankind represent humankind. Men will not fail to notice when they are excluded from a particular subject, event, discourse, or governing body. The list could go on. In these ways, women might learn from men.

My Practice as a Therapist

As a therapist, I work to create a safe space in which people can begin to remember, to give voice to the unspoken, and to be courageous about facing their own truths and inventive about opening up difficult truths with other people. The subject of authenticity is at the heart of both feminism and therapy. Both include challenging what others tell us about ourselves and learning to pay passionate attention to our own experience, to the stories of other women, and to the voices of those women and men we have learned "don't count."

Mental health professionals owe a countless debt to pioneering feminists and to the Women's Movement. Many therapists who don't identify with feminism or begin to understand it are oblivious to the fact that broad social change profoundly influences what therapists do in consulting rooms and what our clients bring to us.

Consider the secret of sexual abuse. As recently as the early 1970s, experts estimated only one to five cases of incest per one million people. Now, we hear this story in great numbers. Why weren't we hearing these stories back then? Did the cultural context deny women the capacity to remember? Did women remember and not tell? Did they tell their therapists only to be disbelieved? However, you see it. Something changed the cultural climate that determined what can be said, what can be remembered, told, believed, and even imagined. We all have multiple possibilities, potentials, and stories that our context makes more or less possible. Although the connections aren't always obvious, the personal and political are inseparable.

A few of the feminists outside of our profession who had the largest influence on my work were Audre Lorde, Adrienne Rich, and Gloria Steinem. I dedicated my fourth book, *The Dance of Deception* (Lerner, 1993) to the memory of Audre Lorde who taught us that women have gained nothing from silence. Her slender book, *The Cancer Journals* (Lorde, 1980), should be required reading for all. Adrienne Rich's book, *Of Woman Born* (Rich, 1976), and her text, Lies, *Secrets, and Silence* (Rich, 1979), are classics. Rich, who was also a renowned poet, told the truth incisively, urgently, and uncompromisingly. And, Gloria Steinem is Gloria Steinem.

Contributions as a Feminist Pioneer

My original training was in psychoanalytic theory that, back in the day, was a linear, backward "whodunit" game which ended up pointing the finger in mother's direction. The implicit assumption was that the mother is the infant and child's environment, especially during earlier stages of development. The epistemological framework assumed that what happens to a child is largely the product of who the mother is and what she does and does not do.

Like many other feminist pioneers, some of my early work challenged this intense preoccupation with maternal power and the mother–child dyad (back in vogue now with attachment theory) and widened the lens setting. My later publications viewed female psychology and all key relationships from a systemic perspective in which the field of observation and inquiry is within the reciprocal, circular patterns and triangles maintained by all family members. My work demonstrated the importance of viewing female development through the broadest possible lens that looked at the complex circular interconnectedness between the individual, family, and culture, while keeping in mind that the special strengths and vulnerabilities of women are inseparable from the psychology of subordinate group functioning.

The Dance of Anger

The Dance of Anger (Lerner, 2015/1985), first published in 1985, has sold several million copies. It has had a great influence in helping women use anger as a vehicle for change rather than staying stuck in relationships characterized by too much intensity, distance, or non-productive fighting that goes nowhere. The book takes complex theory about how relationships operate and translates it into simple prose without simplifying. Rescuing women (and men, too) from the swamps and quicksands of difficult relationships is what I do best. My commitment to writing in clear and accessible prose is reflected in all my work.

The Dance of Anger (Lerner, 2015/1985) was my first book, and bringing it to life wasn't easy. At the time I wrote it, my colleagues believed self-help was low-level stuff, and my first publisher (who did believe in the power of books to change lives) fired, re-hired, and fired me again. It was then followed by five years of rejections, during which time, I never stopped writing. I will never forget that long stretch of frustration and sorrow when I sat hunched over a gray typewriter (the speediest technology of the day) with scissors and scotch tape as my cutting and pasting editing tools. Now, the loving and generous messages from readers span four generations. I'm humbled and grateful to know that The *Dance of Anger* (Lerner, 2015/1985) has helped so many people and its message continues to resonate.

Being A Feminist Therapist

Rather than calling myself a "feminist therapist," I identify myself as a feminist and a therapist. I prefer to say that feminist theory, like family systems theory and all of my life experience, informs my work. Feminism is an important filter through which I see the world, but the term "Feminist Therapy" says little about how I actually work, or worse, it mistakenly implies that I work in a similar way other feminist therapists. It seems more accurate to say that I am a feminist, that this perspective guides my clinical work, and that a feminist perspective is essential in enlarging my thinking and practice.

Prefixing ourselves ("I do feminist therapy" or "I'm a feminist therapist") is a practice that merits more conversation. You won't find a psychologist saying, "I will now present a paper from my White male perspective," unless, of course, he happens to be presenting at a women's conference. Nor will you find a college course titled "White Male History." As philosopher Minnich (1990) notes, the dominant group isn't prefixed but is rather taken to be the "generic human" whose particular truths speak for all of us. Move down the hierarchy and you'll note that the greater the marginalization, the greater the number of pre-fixes. For example, a brochure on my desk says, "Black women writers at work." It is a panel of four black women. If it were four White women, it would just say, "Women writers at work." If it were four male writers, it would say, "Writers at work" We prefix what is marginalized and subordinate, but not what is dominant, thus continuing the confused notion that dominant un-prefixed groups are what is essential and real. We all speak from a particularized perspective that excludes more than it includes so dominant groups might take a lesson and pre-fix themselves. "This panel of White male heterosexual psychologists will now discuss the future of marriage."

Feminists and Other Mentors

I could not begin to name the countless women whose courageous voices have made such a difference to me over the past 40 years. This would include nearly all the contributors in this issue, with a special nod to Miriam Greenspan and Judith Jordan who I am privileged to call my friends.

In addition to those I've mentioned by name, my Menninger friend and colleague Marianne Ault-Riché included me as an equal partner in two vital projects she originated at Menninger—our early women's workshops in the Topeka community (*"Talking Straight and Fighting Fair"*) and our *"Women in Context"* conferences series at Menninger. I'm particular grateful to Menninger social worker Kay Kent for teaching me systems concepts and helping me to apply Bowen Family System theory to my life and work. *The Woman's Project in Family Therapy,* which consisted of Betty Carter, Peggy Papp, Marianne Walters, and Olga Silverstein, made spectacular contributions to issues of women in families, and I put their work on my reading lists. Monica McGoldrick, a generation younger than these women, is a force of nature. She is an untiring pioneer in honoring diversity and teaching therapists how to bring issues of gender, culture, and class into our work. All of these women are social workers, and what I've learned from them is incalculable.

I'm also grateful for my contemporary psychology cohorts who continue to bring social activism and current social concerns out of the consulting room and the world. Mary Pipher is a well-known example of this. Less know is psychologist Jeffrey Kotler who in addition to writing over eighty books is an extraordinary activist whose project has saved the lives of countless Nepalese girls, while inspiring his students and others in our field to do nothing less than change the world. My agent/manager, Jo-Lynne Worley, has enhanced and supported my writing and speaking career since we teamed up in 1990. I have long counted on her unflappable patience, enduring friendship, unfaltering competence, and her steadfast belief in my work.

To young therapists who don't identify with feminism, I would say this: I know the "F word" makes many young people twitchy, but if you know your history, you will be proud to call yourself a feminist and grateful for what my generation has made possible for you. There is no "post-feminist" era and no resting place in the struggle to create a just and safe world for women. Violence against women and threats to reproductive freedom are greater than ever before. As therapists and mental health professionals, we can't afford silence.

I encourage young women to stay awake and to speak out. Everyone's voice makes a difference, even if you don't know it. Five people may speak out and not be heard. But, the sixth person is heard because of the previous five. Each act of courage counts. And sometimes, we need to speak and act, even if we are discounted, because it is important to speak and act. In addition to our individual efforts, nothing is more powerful than joining together collectively as a social and political force to be reckoned with.

What would psychotherapy look like in a world where women were fully represented and valued in every aspect of language, politics, and culture? It is impossible to imagine. We can only long for and work toward that unrealized world where the dignity and integrity of all women, all human beings, all life, are honored and respected.

Harriet Lerner: Selected Early Articles

- The hysterical personality: A woman's disease (1974).
- Parental mislabeling of female genitals as a determinant of penis envy and learning inhibitions in women (1976).
- Girls, ladies, or women? The unconscious dynamics of language choice (1976).
- Adaptive and pathogenic aspects of sex-role stereotypes: Implications for parenting and psychotherapy (1978).
- Internal prohibitions against female anger (1980).
- Female dependency in context: Some theoretical and technical considerations (1982).
- Special issues for women in psychotherapy (1983).
- Work and success inhibitions in women: Family systems level interventions in psychodynamic treatment (1987).
- Female depression: Self-sacrifice and self-betrayal in relationships (1987).
- A critique of the Feminist Psychoanalytic contribution (1988).
  (Note: All of the above articles are reprinted in Lerner, H. (1994). *Women in therapy* (reprint edition). New York: Harper & Row).

Harriet Lerner: Selected Books

- *The Dance of Anger,* 1985 (re-issue 2015)
- *Women in Therapy*, 1988
- *The Dance of Intimacy*, 1989
- *The Dance of Deception*, 1993
- *Life Preservers*, 1996
- *The Mother Dance*, 1998
- *The Dance of Connection*, 2001
- *The Dance of Fear*, 2004
- *Marriage Rules*, 2012
- *Why Won't You Apologize?*, 2017

References

Gorney, C. (1995, November/December). Gloria. *Mother Jones.* Retrieved from http://www.motherjones.com/politics/1995/11/gloria

Lees, H. (1957). *Help your husband stay alive.* New York: Appleton-Century-Crofts.

Lerner, H. (1993). *The dance of deception.* New York: HarperCollins.

Lerner, H. (1994). *Women in therapy* (reprint edition). New York: Harper & Row.

Lerner, H. (2015). *The dance of anger.* New York: William Morrow. (originally published 1985)

Lorde, A. (1980). *The cancer journals.* Iowa City, IA: Aunt Lute Books.

Miller, J. B. (1976). *Toward a new psychology of women.* Boston, MA: Beacon Press.

Minnich, E. (1990). *Transforming knowledge.* Philadelphia, PA: Temple University Press.

Rich, A. (1976). *Of woman born: Motherhood as experience and institution.* New York: Norton.

Rich, A. (1979). *On lies, secrets and silence: Selected prose, 1966–1978.* New York: Norton.

Blowing in the Wind: '70s Questions for Millennial Therapists

Jeanne Marecek

ABSTRACT

Psychotherapy came in for a drubbing by the Women's Liberation Movement of the 1960s. Indeed, some movement members declared that Feminist Therapy was an oxymoron. Despite the antipathy, feminists in the mental health professions borrowed practices, ethical ideals, principles, and goals from the Women's Liberation Movement to create innovative models of therapy. This progressive impetus came to an abrupt halt with the sweeping re-medicalization of psychiatry in 1980s and the corporatization of medicine that followed thereafter. As the landscape of psychotherapy changed, so too did the founders' vision of Feminist Therapy. Drawing on interviews with feminist therapists, I examine some of these changes. I close by asking about the conditions of possibility for feminism in therapy today.

Every history of the past is constructed from the vantage point of the present. I look at the beginnings of Feminist Therapy through the lens of the present; I cannot do otherwise. Stories are not copies of reality; they are "edited versions" of it (Magnusson & Marecek, 2015). When we tell stories about the past, we rely on memories, which are always colored by the present. Our understandings of the past change as new events and experiences lead us to adopt new perspectives. Stories always smuggle in moral judgments of the events and the actors. As you'll see, I make no effort to scrub such judgments out of my stories.

I chose my stories with an eye to highlighting the contrasts between then and now. My first story is about my graduate training just as the sun was setting on the era of "womanless" psychology. The second story focuses on the Women's Liberation Movement in the United States and the gestation and birth of Feminist Therapy in the womb of that movement. The third story spans a longer time period. From the eighties to the present, the mental health professions have been buffeted by drastic ideological and material changes. Few, if any, feminist therapists have escaped those changes. My third story, then, is about the conditions of possibility for Feminist Therapy in the decades since the 1970s.

In the Academy

Today, the sheer presence of women in psychotherapy and the centrality of their contributions as researchers, clinical theorists, and organizational leaders makes it next to impossible to imagine the near-womanless state of psychology in the late '60s. During my graduate training, I went through 4 years of study, several practica, and an accredited internship in clinical psychology without encountering any female instructors, mentors, or clinical supervisors. That was the norm, and though it seems incredible in hindsight, I did not find this absence of women notable or objectionable at the time.

I entered graduate school while the Vietnam War was raging. The U.S. military was conscripting young men by lottery; deferments for graduate education were far from assured. War or no war, the members of the psychology department needed workers to run rats, pigeons, and college students through their experiments. To assure a supply of labor, they admitted an unprecedented number of women into the class—almost one-third of the incoming class. (Previously, the rate of admissions for women seemed to have hovered between zero and one.) At the welcome event for new students, the Director of Graduate Studies—seemingly oblivious to the presence of female students—took pains to reassure those present that this unusual gender composition was only a temporary aberration. Once the war ended, things would revert to normal. As it turned out, his promise went unfulfilled. History (and Title IX) intervened.

Some of the male faculty members actively resisted the intrusion of female graduate students into what had been a boys' club. One senior social psychologist ruefully opined that once he took female students into his research group, there could no longer be Friday afternoon beer-drinking sessions, Thursday night poker games, or Saturday fishing trips. On top of that, men would no longer be able to curse. An eminent psychoanalyst and personality theorist wanted to bar female students from his classes. Women, he said, were not capable of doing therapy. He was told that he had to enroll women. He did, but he insisted that they take seats out of his line of vision. How ironic that the history of his field is replete with distinguished female writers and practitioners. Could it be that he had never heard of Karen Horney, Anna Freud, Frieda Fromm-Reichmann, Clara Thompson, or Melanie Klein?

In this insular and rarified corner of the academy, words like sexism, feminism, sex discrimination, lesbian, or even sex difference were not in the lexicon. Training in clinical psychology was entirely psychoanalytic—theories of psychopathology (*pace* Norman Cameron!), projective tests for assessment, and psychodynamic psychotherapy. Psychoanalytic theory was the sole framework within which mental disorders and normal development were defined and understood. It was the sole framework within which we students learned to carry out assessments, and the sole framework within which therapy was conducted.

In the Real World: A Tidal Wave of Feminism!

Outside my graduate school bubble, women were on the move, and gender relations were in upheaval as women questioned everything. In the United States, people by the thousands pored over *The Feminine Mystique* (Freidan, 1963). In the UK, *The Female Eunuch* (Greer, 1970) was raising a firestorm of controversy. Freud's ideas about women came in for an unrelenting drubbing at the hands of feminist thinkers (e.g., Firestone, 1970; Gilman, 1971; Koedt, 1970). We feminists in psychology read *Women and Madness* (Chesler, 1972). We handed around mimeographed copies of *Psychology Constructs the Female* (Weisstein, 1968) and *Training Woman to Know Her Place: The Power of a Nonconscious Ideology* (Bem & Bem, n.d.). (Photocopy machines, let alone pdfs or email attachments, did not yet exist.)

In those days, feminists pursued a double agenda. One sector pressed for women's rights, that is, changing the legal status of women. This sector included bureaucratic organizations as NOW, Women's Equity Action League (WEAL), and the National Women's Political Caucus. The other sector pushed for women's liberation, that is, the transformation of cultural beliefs about women and personal relationships. By the mid-1970s, the ideological distinctions between equal rights and women's liberation had blurred. A profusion of organizations of women from particular backgrounds (e.g., the National Association of Black Professional Women and the Older Women's League) and occupations (e.g., the Association for Women in Psychology, Sociologists for Women in Society) had emerged, pursuing varied agendas.

What was the take-home message for me as a young feminist and, by then, an assistant professor? First, women *qua* women constituted a political interest group, and as a political interest group, women could command a presence in the public arena. Second, solidarity among women was necessary to force societal change. I witnessed this solidarity in the form of mass demonstrations (such as the New York Radical Feminists Speak-Out on Rape in 1971) and protest marches (such as pro-choice rallies in Washington leading up to the passage of *Roe v. Wade*). I witnessed the power of this solidarity on a local scale when women on my own campus united to press a class action suit concerning unfair hiring and promotion practices.

Feminists' Dis-Ease with Psychotherapy

The litany of psychoanalysts' sexist and mother-blaming pronouncements about women did not sit well with many feminists of this era. Many drew upon the ideas of the left-leaning Radical Therapy and anti-psychiatry movements. In their most extreme form, these ideas denied that mental disorders were other than politically useful labels. Such labels protected entrenched social arrangements and power structures. As Ellen Herman noted in her cultural history of psychology, the feminist critique of psychotherapy,

> dovetailed neatly with the core propositions of anti-psychiatry: that the medical establishment had inappropriately usurped authority over vital social issues, including gender and sexuality; that psychotherapeutic practice harmed women by teaching that their problems were personal and intrapsychic rather than social and relational; that the neutral language of testing, diagnosis, and treatment concealed clinicians' complicity with male domination and their determination to make women adjust to sexism; that "mental health" was nothing but shorthand for gender conformity; that faith in experts (especially male experts) was counterproductive because experience—not expertise—imparted deserved authority. Only women could liberate themselves. (Herman, 1995, pp. 286–287)

This hard line appeared frequently in the writings of radical feminists of the sixties. Carol Hanisch, for example, declared:

> The very word "therapy" is obviously a misnomer if carried to its logical conclusion. Therapy assumes that someone is sick and that there is a cure, e.g., a personal solution. … Women are messed over, not messed up! We need to change the objective conditions, not adjust to them. Therapy is adjusting to your bad personal alternative. (Hanisch, 1969, p. 3)

Dorothy Tennov (herself a psychologist) deemed psychotherapy to be "monstrous," an "opiate," and an "agent of patriarchy." Her book, *Psychotherapy: The Hazardous Cure* (Tennov, 1975), was only a trifle more generous. Mary Daly (1979), the radical feminist theologian, went the farthest, arguing that psychotherapy of any sort was "mind rape." In therapy, Daly (1979) believed, women were infected with disease, not cured of it. How then would therapists who were feminists move past the idea that Feminist Therapy is an oxymoron? By taking a detour through consciousness-raising.

Consciousness-Raising and Women's Liberation

Consciousness-raising (CR) groups were the hallmark of the Women's Liberation Movement. Whether hip young singles or suburban mothers, women across the United States came together in small group meetings to explore and analyze their experiences. CR theorists were adamant that the groups were not support groups or therapy groups, but vehicles for cultural and personal transformation. This is how Carol Hanisch (the woman who coined the phrase "The personal is political") described the transformative power of consciousness-raising.

> First and foremost is consciousness-raising, which has been THE radical organizing tool for women's liberation … We saw how it made things clearer—how it resulted

in the higher levels of determination and courage and willingness to take risks that people have when they are sure they are right and when they know that others feel the same. (Hanisch, 1999, p. 3)

Feminist consciousness-raising groups were modeled after the practices of a number of revolutionary movements. As in such revolutionary struggles, creating the broad base of support necessary to succeed depends on creating a broad-based critical consciousness (Echols, 1989). For example, the campaigns of Chairman Mao's revolutionary brigades, for example, organized "speak bitterness" (*su ku*) sessions in order to incite serfs to revolt against feudal landlords. Similarly, *conscientizacao* (conscientization) was a central practice in the peasant liberation movements in the Caribbean and Latin America, intended to arouse dissatisfaction among the oppressed (Freire, 1970/1984). In the Civil Rights Movement in the American South, activists encouraged African Americans to come together to testify to the oppressive conditions of their lives.

In circumstances in which subordination has been naturalized, change first requires critical consciousness—the recognition of unfair treatment. In consciousness-raising groups, the everyday experiences of the members were the focus of discussion. As those experiences were brought forward, group members could draw connections that revealed the common aspects of women's condition in society. Further analysis enabled members to see how those experiences were embedded in sociopolitical structures and cultural beliefs. This is what Hanisch meant by "making the personal political." With raised awareness, group members would be ready to mobilize for change (Kravetz, Marecek, & Finn, 1983). To quote Carol Hanisch again, reflecting back on her CR experiences:

It was through consciousness-raising—using the wealth of women's collective experiences—that we were able to make these major theoretical leaps that helped us organize ourselves and made us able to organize others effectively. Consciousness-raising helps women to understand our oppression in concrete ways and makes every woman's life experience a part of the analysis. (Hanisch, 1999, p. 3)

Grassroots Feminist Organizations

The 1960s were a time of progressive social movements that challenged the status quo and agitated for social change. Progressive movements included the Civil Rights Movement, the Black Power Movement, student movements such as SDS and SNCC, and the anti-war movement. Some movement members defied the law, and some engaged in civil disobedience. Encounters between the protestors and the state sometimes were violent. One example was the shootings by the National Guard of unarmed college students at Kent State during an anti-war protest in 1970. Another was the "police riot" during the anti-war protests surrounding the 1968 Democratic National Convention in Chicago. Alienation from and distrust of the state ran deep among members of these movements and among youth more generally.

Many feminist activists shared this distrust of the state and of the established institutions, most of which were male-dominated. This distrust led feminists to develop grassroots organizations and social service agencies of their own (Ferree & Martin, 1995; Kravetz, 2004). Run by women for women, these organizations not only delivered services to women; they also engaged in public information campaigns and advocacy for women's issues. Some, like Jane—a grassroots abortion service on Chicago's Southside— flouted the law. In Philadelphia, where I was living, feminist agencies included a service for women who were separating and divorcing (which soon re-invented itself as a service for women in violent relationships); a safe house for battered women; a rape crisis center; a women's health center, which provided abortions as well as low cost medical care; a hotline providing information and referrals regarding contraception, sexuality, and pre-natal care; a feminist legal center that engaged in litigation, advocacy, and education; and a collective that offered therapy groups for women. It has become the custom to slam the Women's Liberation Movement as exclusively for White middle class women. But in Philadelphia at least, all these organizations had a strong commitment to ethnic diversity and mainly served low-income women. Kravetz (2004) reported a similar commitment to diversity and inclusion in the feminist agencies that she studied in Wisconsin.

These women-run agencies adopted a number of feminist principles. Among the staff, decision-making was collaborative and democratic. The organizational structure was nonhierarchical; some organizations operated as collectives. The service models they developed focused on the crises or situations for which their clientele sought help. Agencies that offered counseling emphasized group work as a means through which women could share their wisdom and life experiences with one another and join together to support each woman's efforts to change. In this way, the group experiences validated women's perspectives and their competence at managing their lives. In addition, group work often included elements of consciousness-raising— that is, clarifying how women's experiences were connected to the societal subordination of women.

Building Feminist Therapy on the Shoulders of Movement Activism

Despite the denunciations of psychotherapy from some quarters of the movement, feminists who were therapists held onto the hope that psychotherapy could foster the women's liberation. Although CR theorists saw CR as the politically informed *replacement* (or even *antidote*) for therapy, the pioneers of feminist therapy drew upon CR as the template for a new form of therapy (Brodsky, 1973). Consider what Diane Kravetz and I wrote in 1977,

> Feminist therapy reflects the conviction that personal change and sociopolitical change are inextricably linked. Thus, in feminist therapy, identifying sexism and its effects on the client and other women is an important active ingredient of the treatment process … . The relationship between the goals of treatment and social change is emphasized … (Marecek & Kravetz, 1977, p. 326)

Feminist therapists also entertained ideas about therapy outcomes (and, by extension, mental health) that were based in movement politics and CR theory (Klein, 1976). For example, some therapists held that clients should come to endorse feminist beliefs; others thought clients should come to engage in feminist activism; some spoke of female solidarity. For some, becoming angry about societal injustices was a positive outcome of therapy.

The first feminist therapists also drew upon the principles and practices of the alternative service agencies I described above. One such principle was a commitment to what they termed "self-help" (that is, helping women to discover their strengths and take responsibility for making changes in their lives). Feminist therapists also experimented with ways to diminish the authority of the therapist, for example, by using contracts or co-writing case notes (Hare-Mustin, Marecek, Kaplan, & Liss-Levenson, 1979). Other feminist therapists promoted models of therapy in which the therapist limited her role to that of a facilitator, placing responsibility for many of the functions usually undertaken by a therapist on the group members (Johnson, 1976; Kravetz & Marecek, 1976). The purpose behind these models was to curb the therapist's power and to foster women's respect for and trust in one another.

Outsiders on the Inside? Feminist Therapists and the Mental Health Establishment

Psychotherapy as it existed in the seventies no longer exists. It has not "evolved" nor is its new form a reflection of scientific progress. Rather the transformation came about as a result of the broad-scale re-ordering of the political economy of mental health. The conditions of possibility for Feminist Therapy today bear little resemblance to those of the seventies.

In the seventies, ideas about the social causes of suffering—racism, poverty, sexism, and unemployment—fell on receptive ears. Feminist Therapy was but one effort among several kindred efforts to rethink mental disorders. Examples are innovations in family therapy at the Philadelphia Child Guidance Clinic, the communications theories of the Palo Alto Group, and the experimental therapeutic community of R. D. Laing. The seventies supported both political critique and bold experiments in treatment. The Community Mental Health Center Movement (a part of John F. Kennedy's

Great Society initiative) supported grassroots mental health centers in low-income urban settings; these centers were tasked with developing programs of prevention and early intervention, as well as treatment.

Ronald Reagan's election in 1980 marked an abrupt and extreme swing toward social and fiscal conservatism. Almost immediately, the rug was pulled out from under progressive initiatives. The federal government wiped out funding for the community mental health program. The National Institute of Mental Health (NIMH) cut off funds for research on poverty, unemployment, social class, and urban problems. A new doxa was proclaimed; mental disorders were brain diseases, which were largely inherited.

In the same year, the DSM-III was released. The DSM-III entailed a sweeping revision of psychodiagnosis. The categories of mental disorders were re-engineered to mimic the categories of biomedical diseases. As is well documented, this re-conception was not grounded in science; it was purely pragmatic (Horwitz, 2002; Wilson, 1993). With corporatization and managed care barreling down on medicine, psychiatry had to re-invent itself as a *bona fide* medical subspecialty if it were to have a viable financial future. Clinical psychologists leapt right onto the ersatz-medical bandwagon, with textbooks and training materials re-written to conform to the new reality. Even a college sophomore in an Abnormal Psychology course would get the new message. The APA invented new monikers for clinical psychologists like "behavioral health care providers."

Describing psychological suffering as if it consisted of disease-like entities exemplifies what is called medicalization. When psychological suffering is re-described as a medical condition, it then is subjected to medical scrutiny, diagnosis, and treatment. This effectively frames psychological suffering as residing "inside" the person and depoliticizes it. That is, if the putative causes of suffering are chemical imbalances, childhood experiences, dysfunctional cognitions, and the like, factors that lie "outside" the person—such as social inequality, poverty, gendered subordination, and difficult living conditions—are rendered invisible (Hare-Mustin & Marecek, 2009).

Mimicking biomedical diagnoses, the DSM-III defined mental disorders in terms of lists of symptoms. Such symptom criteria reduce human experience and personal difficulties to a series of sub-personal parts. Diagnosing under the DSM-III (and DSM-IV and DSM-5) does not comprehend a person; it instead portrays a collection of sub-personal parts. In the 1980s, this way of thinking about clients and their troubles became the "new normal." One student of mine, for example, reported with disdain that the patient intake forms she was required to fill out at her practicum site allotted "only" eight spaces for diagnoses. I have watched a senior clinician conduct an intake interview by barking out a checklist of symptoms and demanding yes/no responses from the client. (And this while the clinician faced the computer screen, not the person.) A student in an advanced psychotherapy class questioned why I had assigned a book with the title *Change* (Watzlawick, Weakland, & Fisch, 1974). What, she asked, does "change" have to do with psychotherapy? Therapy, for her, was about curing symptoms.

In the Institution: Psychotherapeutic Culture

How do feminist therapists practice in a regime of a medicalized psychotherapeutic culture? Has this regime changed the way that feminist therapists work and think? As far as I know, there has been next to no systematic research on this question. Although we did not have this specific question in mind, a large study of self-identified feminist therapists that Diane Kravetz and I carried out in the mid-1990s offers some beginning answers.[1] When we asked therapists to describe what made therapy "feminist," they spoke of the therapist's personal qualities, often invoking feminine stereotypes. Feminist therapists, they said, were "nurturing," "softer," "less judgmental," "compassionate," and "respectful of women's ways of doing things" (Marecek & Kravetz, 1998a). Few seemed to connect Feminist Therapy with emancipatory goals for women.

Many of the feminist therapists in the study centered their ideas about Feminist Therapy on "PTSD" and "trauma" (Marecek, 1999). Several took pains to identify PTSD as the quintessential feminist diagnosis. Some regarded "taking the trauma history" as the proper feminist approach to assessment. Yet, others preferred to make liberal use of PTSD diagnoses because "PTSD means you are normal." Yet, the diagnostic category PTSD is a medicalized diagnosis. Although the term gestures toward an external cause of suffering, PTSD, like every other diagnostic category, is defined in terms of a set of "inner" symptoms; little reference is made to the external stressor (Summerfield, 2001). Moreover, at present, traumatology is awash with claims about neurobiological causes of PTSD, "body memory" of trauma, and pseudo-neuroscientific treatment regimes.

As psychotherapists well know, the material basis of therapeutic practice has further altered the conditions of possibility for feminist therapy. Managed care systems, with their overarching mandate to cut costs, control the delivery of mental health care. As Philip Cushman and Peter Gilford said,

> Whoever controls the delivery of mental health care—by determining such things as the definition of mental disorder, triage criteria, and the nature and length of proper treatment— inevitably and deeply affects society-wide understandings of health and illness, the possibilities and limits of human nature, and thus what is believed to be proper and good. (Cushman & Gilford, 2000, p. 985)

Managed care organizations often require therapists to specify treatment goals in terms of symptom reduction. Such goals involve modest improvements in narrowly defined target behaviors and often they are formulated to be quickly attainable (Cohen, Marecek, & Gillham, 2006). By definition, the "inside" of the person, not the social surround, the larger social structure, or the political economy, is the target. Carol Hanisch's (1969) complaint that "Therapy is adjusting to your bad personal alternative" comes to mind. What of the therapy outcomes that Feminist Therapy pioneers proposed in the 1970s? Would an insurance company authorize a goal of helping a woman develop a feminist consciousness? Or a goal of instigating a client's righteous anger over unjust treatment?

Feminist therapists have always been concerned with "the reparative psychological redistribution of power inside and outside the therapy relation" (Bruns & Kaschak, 2010, p. 189). But this places today's feminist therapists in a difficult position. Under managed care, the power to define the terms of the therapy lies in the hands of the managed care organization. Patients are figured as the compliant recipients of the therapist's expert knowledge and techniques. When the therapy relationship is an asymmetrical triangle, wherein is the possibility of redistributing power?

W(h)ither Feminist Therapy?

In the 1970s, members of the Women's Liberation Movement accused mainstream psychotherapists of imbuing treatment with sexist ideology. Mainstream therapists, on the other hand, accused feminist therapists of imposing their ideology on clients. In a certain sense, both were right; psychotherapy is inescapably a value-laden enterprise. Today, discourses of "health" (as in "health service provider"), "science," and "evidence" are invoked to occlude the value-laden nature of therapy (Marecek & Kravetz, 1998b). However, psychotherapy appears to be value-free only insofar as it is aligned with the values of the dominant culture (cf., Skoger & Magnusson, 2015).

I opened this essay by saying that histories are re-presentations of past, constructed from the vantage point of the present. The history I tell here is no different. But my history is also oriented toward the future. Although the political culture of the seventies cannot be revived, I tell this history with the hope of stirring debate and reflection. The medicalization of psychological suffering is now thoroughly embedded in both popular culture and therapeutic culture. For some, it is just the way things are, not one description of things out of many possible ones. Can we nonetheless recoup the emancipatory goals of Feminist Therapy?

Note

1. Although all these therapists identified themselves as feminist therapists in the screening interview, most of them did not declare openly themselves as feminist therapists to their colleagues or their clients. Some said they had openly used the label feminist therapist in the past.

References

Bem, S. L., & Bem, D. (n.d.). *Training the woman to know her place: The power of a nonconscious ideology*. Pittsburgh, PA: KNOW Press.

Brodsky, A. M. (1973). The consciousness-raising group as a model for therapy with women. *Psychotherapy: Theory, Research, & Practice, 10*, 24–29. doi:10.1037/h0087537

Bruns, C., & Kaschak, E. (2010). Feminist psychotherapies: Theory, research, and practice. In J. Chrisler & D. McCreary (Eds.), *Handbook of gender research in psychology*, (pp. 187–219). New York: Springer.

Chesler, P. (1972). *Women and madness*. Garden City, NY: Doubleday.

Cohen, J., Marecek, J., & Gillham, J. (2006). Is three a crowd? Clients, clinicians and managed care. *American Journal of Orthopsychiatry, 76*(2), 251–259. doi:10.1037/0002-9432.76.2.251

Cushman, P., & Gilford, P. (2000). Will managed care change our way of being? *American Psychologist, 55*, 985–996. doi:10.1037/0003-066x.55.9.985

Daly, M. (1979). *Gyn/ecology: The metaethics of radical feminism*. Boston: Beacon Press.

Echols, A. (1989). *Daring to be bad: Radical feminism in America 1967–1975*. Minneapolis: University of Minnesota Press.

Ferree, M. M., & Martin, P. Y. (1995). *Feminist organizations: Harvest of the new women's movement*. Philadelphia, PA: Temple University Press.

Firestone, S. (1970). *The dialectic of sex: A case for feminist revolution*. New York: William R. Morrow.

Freidan, B. (1963). *The feminine mystique*. New York: Norton.

Freire, P. (1970/1984). *Pedagogy of the oppressed*. New York: Continuum.

Gilman, R. (1971, January 31). The feminist-liberation case against Sigmund Freud. New York Times Magazine, 10.

Greer, G. (1970). *The female eunuch*. London: Harper Perennial.

Hanisch, C. (1969). *The personal is political*. Retrieved from http://www.carolhanisch.org/CHwritings/PIP.html

Hanisch, C. (1999). *Some thoughts on what's wrong with feminist theory today and what it will take to make it successful again*. Retrieved from http://www.carolhanisch.org/Speeches/CJH%20Marist%20Speech%206.11.99%201.pdf

Hare-Mustin, R. T., & Marecek, J. (2009). Clinical psychology: The politics of madness. In D. Fox, I. Prilleltensky & S. Austin (Eds.), *Critical psychology: An introduction* (pp. 105–120) London: Sage.

Hare-Mustin, R. T., Marecek, J., Kaplan, A., & Liss-Levenson, N. (1979). Rights of clients, responsibilities of therapists. *American Psychologist, 34*, 3–16. doi:10.1037/0003-066x.34.1.3

Herman, E. (1995). *The romance of American psychology: Political culture in the age of experts*. Berkeley, CA: University of California Press.

Horwitz, A. V. (2002). *Creating mental illness*. Chicago, IL: University of Chicago Press.

Johnson, M. (1976). An approach to feminist therapy. *Psychotherapy: Theory, Research, and Practice, 13*, 72–76.

Klein, M. (1976). Feminist concepts of therapy outcome. *Psychotherapy: Theory, Research, and Practice, 13*, 89–95. doi:10.1037/h0086493

Koedt, A. (1970). *The myth of vaginal orgasm*. Retrieved from www.uic.edu/orgs/cwluherstory/CWLUArchive/vaginalmyth.html

Kravetz, D. (2004). *Tales from the trenches: Politics and practice in feminist service organizations*. New York: Rowan and Littlefield.

Kravetz, D. F., Marecek, J., & Finn, S. E. (1983). Factors influencing women's participation in consciousness-raising groups. *Psychology of Women Quarterly, 7*, 257–271. doi:10.1111/j.1471-6402.1983.tb00839.x

Kravetz, D. F., & Marecek, J. (1996). The personal is political: A feminist agenda for group psychotherapy research. In B. DeChant (Ed.), *Women and group psychotherapy: Theory and practice*, (pp. 351–369). New York: Guilford.

Magnusson, E., & Marecek, J. (2015). *Doing interview-based qualitative research: A learner's guide*. Cambridge, UK: Cambridge University Press.

Marecek, J. (1999). Trauma talk in feminist clinical practice. In S. Lamb (Ed.), *New versions of victims: Feminists struggle with the concept*, (pp. 158–182). New York: New York University Press.

Marecek, J., & Kravetz, D. F. (1977). Women and mental health: A review of feminist change efforts. *Psychiatry, 40*(3), 323–329.

Marecek, J., & Kravetz, D. (1998a). Power and agency in feminist therapy. In I. B. Seu & M. C. Heenan (Eds.), *Feminism and psychotherapy: Reflections on contemporary theories and practices*. London: Sage.

Marecek, J., & Kravetz, D. (1998b). Putting politics into practice: Feminist therapy as feminist praxis. *Women & Therapy, 21*(2), 17–36. doi:10.1300/j015v21n02_02

Skoger, U., & Magnusson, E. (2015). What makes feminist knowledge legitimate for therapists? A study of Swedish child psychotherapists. *Feminism & Psychology, 25*(25), 489–505.

Summerfield, D. (2001). The invention of post-traumatic stress disorder and the social usefulness of a psychiatric category. *BMJ, 322*, 95. doi:10.1136/bmj.322.7278.95

Tennov, D. (1975). *Psychotherapy: The hazardous cure*. New York: Abelard.

Watzlawick, P., Weakland, J., & Fisch, R. (1974). *Change: Principles of problem formation and resolution*. New York: Norton.

Weisstein, N. (1968). *Kinder, küche, kirche as scientific law: Psychology constructs the female*. Boston, MA: New England Free Press.

Wilson, M. (1993). DSM-III and the transformation of American psychiatry: A history. *American Journal of Psychiatry, 150*, 399–410. doi:10.1176/ajp.150.3.399

Sara Sharratt: Global Feminist Pioneer

Ellen Abell and Claudia Pitts

ABSTRACT

Sara Sharratt is a psychotherapist, a scholar and an activist, whose contributions to feminist therapy and social activism are innumerable. Some of her most salient work was during the years she spent witnessing and giving voice to countless victims at war crime tribunals in the former Yugoslavia, the stories of which are recounted in her published works. As a global feminist pioneer, Sharratt has dedicated her life to insuring that the voices of women throughout the world be heard, in order that justice and peace might prevail.

Sara Sharratt was born and lives in Costa Rica. She is small of stature, but not of spirit. Sara is a feisty feminist and always ready to stand up for girls and women when it is necessary. Unfortunately it has been necessary too many times throughout her life, but she has met the challenge.

The interviews with Sara Sharratt were conducted via the Internet and embellished slightly by those who know her better than I. She spoke to me from her office on the campus of the University for Peace, where she is currently Academic Dean. It is a tropical campus in Ciudad Colon, built by the United Nations and serving students from all nations. Despite only being able to see her via a small screen, the bigness of Sharratt's personality was immediately evident. As we began to discuss her history, it quickly became clear that this would be no ordinary interview because she has truly lived an extraordinary life.

Early Life

Sharratt's parents were Jewish immigrants. Her mother and father both immigrated to Costa Rica from Poland just before the start of World War II, thus escaping the fate of many other relatives and friends at the hands of the Nazis. Costa Rica was one of the countries that accepted immigrants at the time and so, as Sara was growing up, she lived in a small community of Polish Jews planted right in the center of the country of Costa Rica, where most citizens had never even heard of a Jew and really didn't care to understand these different looking Europeans who spoke a language so different from Spanish. Yet this Costa Rican anti-Semitism was far preferable to the death camps. She is the oldest of three children and is the only daughter.

> I am a first-generation Costa Rican and was raised and schooled here. I only came to the United States when I was 17 to attend George Washington University and first had to learn English, which I did at Georgetown University. My mother sent me away to stop me from marrying a non-Jew, which I proceeded to do in Washington, DC. This was a different man, as I am nothing if not flexible. (S. Sharratt, personal communication, November 17, 2015)

Many of the Jews in Costa Rica thrived economically and her parents were among this group. The pattern is a familiar one. Her father began as a door to-door peddler in the countryside and eventually opened his own store in San Jose, where the whole family pitched in and worked when they could. Her family moved with two other Jewish families to an exclusive neighborhood that was quite distant from the Jewish ghetto, an intentional choice made by her parents, which Sharratt never quite understood. "We had Catholic friends, attended high Jewish holidays, and belonged nowhere" (S. Sharratt, personal communication, November 17, 2015).

Sara recalls having witnessed and experienced the effects of discrimination in her early childhood and saw her parents engulfed in oppressively restricted lives as immigrants and as a very traditional couple in an arranged marriage. She realized quite early that did not want that life for her self.

When asked about her mother's influence on her life and her development, she was quick to acknowledge the profound impact her mother had on her life. Sara recalls her mother's obsession with romantic love and men, and her father's apparent indifference. "I was very aware of male privilege. My mother craved love from men, which made me feel as a young kid that women were not as important" (S. Sharratt, personal communication, November 17, 2015). Sara reflects on how the women of her mother's generation dared not to contradict traditional mores. Although many of them were quite intelligent, they were denied an education beyond middle or high school. Sara's mother was able to return to school later in life. In her 50s, she began her middle school education and eventually completed her Master's degree in Social Work, at which time she began to work with women in Costa Rica who had breast cancer. Her mother eventually died from this very disease. With obvious sadness, Sara recalls how she misses her mother every day of her life.

While living as a child in Costa Rica, Sara remembers experiencing strong anti-Semitism during a decade in which there was a Nazi-friendly government. She states:

> I read books that [typical] adolescents did not read. I read all of the books of Wilhelm Stekel, a well-known member of Freud's psychoanalytic circle, during

my early adolescence. I learned much later in my life that he had invented all the case histories and was kicked out of the Psychoanalytic Association. Yet the stories somehow spoke to me and fueled my interest in psychotherapy and the human mind. (S. Sharratt, personal communication, November 17, 2015)

Education

Dr. Sharratt holds a doctorate in Clinical Psychology from Southern Illinois University. Sara's graduate school experience was in the late 1960s and early 1970s, a time of tremendous social and intellectual upheaval in the United States, although she was still receiving training in very traditional behaviorist and psychodynamic approaches. In graduate school, she was among those who began to question the ways in which masculinist approaches both blamed and pathologized women for the very abuses that were beginning to be revealed at an alarming rate. She already had a strong commitment to social justice that was not fully congruent with the traditional training she was receiving.

She described how she began to become involved in the emerging field of feminist psychology:

In the early 1970s, I was living in San Francisco and was working in an outpatient setting, Mission Mental Health, where most of the clients I saw were bi-lingual and bi-cultural. They were, at the time, mostly from Mexico, but as a Spanish-speaking therapist, I was expected to work with them. I had come to California to do my clinical internship in family therapy at the Palo Alto V.A. [Veteran's Administration Hospital] and so was able to work with entire families and not just with individuals. This was considered more culturally appropriate at the time. By this time, the biases in the field were starting to be discussed in the literature by early theorists such as Phyllis Chesler, Naomi Weisstein, and others. (S. Sharratt, personal communication, July 10, 2015)

She goes on to say:

I had no formal mentors as regards feminist psychology, but eventually found like-minded women. One of these women was Ellyn Kaschak, who went on to become a notable Feminist Pioneer herself. We met in Washington, DC, where we were both pursuing a master's degree in the same program. Later, in 1972, we reunited in California and were instrumental in founding the Women's Counseling Service of San Francisco, with several other feminist therapists, including Sue Cox and Pat Grosh. (S. Sharratt, personal communication, July 10, 2015)

She was aware, at the time, that there were two other collectives developing feminist therapy in San Francisco and that there were collectives being formed in several other major U.S. cities, including Boston, New York, Philadelphia, Washington, DC, Los Angeles, and "probably some others." Clearly, it was a concept, which was resonating for women all over the country and eventually the world.

In later years, Sharratt became a professor at Sonoma State University in California where she taught marriage and family therapy with a cross-cultural emphasis. In an echo of earlier days, she founded "Chrysalis," a psychotherapy center for women and their significant others. It also served as a training center for feminist psychotherapy and is still operating today.

In 1985, Sharratt was awarded a Fulbright scholarship to create a master's degree program and an introductory women's studies program in Costa Rica. She returned, for a time, to Costa Rica to create and direct those programs. As a result of the success of these programs, Ellyn Kaschak (who was also deeply involved in the project) and Sara Sharratt were able to train a generation of Costa Rican therapists in feminist family therapy. This Master's program in Women's Studies was the first conjoint project of both main Costa Rican universities and a first in Latin America. It was a huge breakthrough in Costa Rica and many Costa Rican therapists, female and male, were more than ready for it.

Sara is proud to say that she was the first feminist therapist who taught gender studies and feminist psychotherapy in Costa Rica and was the main consultant in creating the first Master's program in gender studies in Latin America. In her current position as Dean of Academic Affairs at The University of Peace, a UN mandated university, she is able to work closely with students from more than 100 countries. Sara proudly remarks that graduates from their programs work in "NGOs, with women and children, or return to academics; they become peace educators and work for human rights and women's rights" (S. Sharratt, personal communication, July 10, 2015). In this and so many ways, Sharratt is passing on the legacy of her remarkable life's work. And although her work enables her to live in Costa Rica, in actuality, Sharratt says "she is everywhere."

Feminist Biography

In 1972, when she was living in San Francisco, Sara Sharratt and several of her colleagues held one of the first known feminist psychology conferences. She was surprised, then and now, by how many women showed up for it. These numbers provided validation to her and to her female clients, and "lives were changed."

> We told women that it was okay to have needs of their own. We normalized their feelings rather than pathologizing them. Many of the women who were experiencing depression had endured sexual abuse and we challenged the victim blaming and the notion that they 'asked for it.' (S. Sharratt, personal communication, July 10, 2015)

She recalls,

> Around 1972, four of us, all psychologists, after that first conference, began talking about feminist issues as part of our discussions on women and mental health.

Ellyn Kaschak was one of them, and Pat Grosh and Sue Cox, who had written a book called *Female Psychology* (Cox, 1976), which I remember strongly impacted me at the time. We began to meet and talk about challenging these misogynist assumptions and normalizing women's depression. We had to unlearn all that we had learned and begin to understand the fact that as far as psychology was concerned, women didn't exist. (S. Sharratt, personal communication, July 10, 2015)

When asked how she found the courage to challenge these long held assumptions at a time when no one was talking about these issues, she said,

It was not a question of courage. I discovered that the injustices that my own mother and I had experienced were becoming more broadly recognized. I could not turn away nor did I want to. It was a question of integrity and ethics and my own sense of justice. (S. Sharratt, personal communication, July 10, 2015)

Sharratt warmly credits her colleagues and friends who were also working towards these understandings.

Of course, I couldn't have done it without them. There was a collective force that developed, a new perspective that I was drawn into. The time was right, and I was there. I became one of the first women in the States to talk about and conduct research in women's studies, integrating gender into psychology. Women, as a group, and my students, in particular, knew something was wrong. They were relieved to have a place to talk about these things. I was lucky to know other feminists intimately, and I saw the positive impact we were having with women who were labeled depressed, etc. The women got much better! It was very helpful to see women improve. (S. Sharratt, personal communication, July 10, 2015)

Feminist Scholarship

Dr. Sharratt is the author of two books, along with Ellyn Kaschak, *Assault on the Soul: Women in the Former Yugoslavia* (Sharratt & Kaschak, 1999), and *Gender, Shame and Sexual Violence: The Voices of Witnesses and Court Members at War Crimes Tribunals* (Sharratt, 2011). She explains that the first book grew out of her association with the Tribunal for the former Yugoslavia. The second book was a direct result of her work with the International Criminal Court in The Hague. She's worked with various judges of the international courts as well as having worked directly with the women who had testified about sexual and gender violence at that high court. She also worked with women who testified in Sarajevo, Bosnia Herzegovina where a number of the gender violence cases had been transferred. She was strongly affected by the attitudes and biases of the judges and prosecutors toward victimized women while researching and writing these books. In fact, she found their attitudes profoundly shocking. "Saying that they were sexist does not even begin to expose the indifference and cruelty" (S. Sharratt, personal communication, July 10, 2015).

Sara spent years in courtrooms listening to the testimonies of victims of war crimes. When asked how she was able to listen to these horrific stories day after day, she said simply, "I don't really know. I was compelled to do it. I could not turn away. My training in clinical psychology helped with the interviews, but I was continuously shocked by the information I heard" (S. Sharratt, personal communication, July 10, 2015).

She explains the goals of her writings,

> Tribunal courts and laws are not enough. We must teach children something very different because, by the time they are judges and lawyers, it is too late. I heard the President of the International Court say that he can understand why men would rape after three months in the bush. This was in response to hearing about fifteen men raping a pregnant woman in Africa and ripping out and mutilating the fetus. Unbelievable. Men would be found guilty of having knocked a woman unconscious and raping her in Bosnia–Herzegovina and judges would talk about "mitigating circumstances," including the fact that the perpetrator "was a father." For 3–4 years, I would listen to these stories every day. I met a woman from Germany while I was in Bosnia–Herzegovina who came to help women there and when I met her again 2–3 years later, she was emotionally destroyed. (S. Sharratt, personal communication, July 10, 2015)

She goes on to illuminate how hearing these stories changed her. She says,

> They changed me profoundly and not at all. In a real way, I inherited this legacy and could not refuse it when my time came. It's a question of evil. People can commit atrocities. We are all capable of atrocities. It is the nature of humanity, just as much as is kindness. It is not that simple as a few evildoers. Still today, some places are better than others for women to live. Traditional culture is a euphemism for patriarchy. Cultural relativism is a con. We have to be alert to how they lie to us and how women can be unconscious about how their own culture manifests misogyny. The Congo is the rape capital of the world. The U.S. is better, but the conviction rate for rape worldwide is low; 7% in England. The burden of proof is still high. Women are still not believed. There's plenty of political correctness, but in practice, I'm not too trusting. (S. Sharratt, personal communication, July 10, 2015)

Because of all she has learned as a witness to this barbarism, she reveals that she has become a more private person. She doesn't want to get into too much intimate communication with others. She doesn't want to say a lot about herself. "Many of us who do this work don't talk much about our lives" (S. Sharratt, personal communication, July 10, 2015).

One of the few exceptions to this rule was when she was able to find feminists who were helpful to work with while she was at the courts. Some of them were even judges and prosecutors. When she started at the courts, there was no one supporting the rights and experiences of women, even the women of the court. She says of the experience, "We were very, very alone. It's important to find support." These early experiences taught her about the dangers of loneliness and isolation. They taught her, despite her fears, "about the importance of friends and colleagues who think the way you think" (S. Sharratt, personal communication, July 10, 2015).

Dr. Sharratt also went to the "killing fields" in Cambodia in the 1980s where there had been a genocide, decimating close to one third of the population. She describes,

When [I] go to these places it draws [me] back to the same feeling I have when I go to a museum and view a painting. I love art. It reconnects you to yourself in depth. I connect to the love and respect for all the people who died or endured. Women are so strong. I have a tremendous amount of respect and compassion and empathy for the human being who has suffered. I experience absolute silence in these places. Healing must be shared with the person who endured the suffering.

It's strange to go to a place where everybody over 20 years old has been impacted by war. [I] move through the place in a different way—tenderly, which allows [me] to connect in a loving, tender way. You learn to pay close attention and treat them with respect and kindness because you know what they've been through. These places are not hostile. It's the energy; it's different, and you're different. You get in touch with deep compassion and humanity. (S. Sharratt, personal communication, July 10, 2015)

Despite the years of frustratingly slow progress, Sharratt still feels that activism is vitally important. She says,

The practice of staying in your office means we've gone backward. We worked hard to get away from this. Feminist psychology must help the cause of women in the world. Otherwise, I don't get it. I don't think one-on-one work is powerful enough to make significant changes. (S. Sharratt, personal communication, July 10, 2015)

She notes that despite its importance, most psychology programs still don't offer training in activism or community organizing. She notes the danger of psychologists or legal professionals being seen as "activist." If you are perceived this way, you run the risk of not being seen as a serious therapist or judge. Judges hate when you accuse them of making "political decisions" because they want to be seen as "objective."

The notion of true objectivity in psychotherapy and in law, especially, strike discordant notes for Sharratt. She says,

It turns out that there is no such creature as objective. We each see the world from our own perspective. It is built in to us as a species. Therapists can't be apolitical. It's impossible. We should be aware of our own decisions and ideas, but not necessarily impose them on clients. I don't hide my ideas. (S. Sharratt, personal communication, July 10, 2015)

Sharratt goes on to describe how her personality and therapeutic and teaching styles have been affected by all that she has witnessed. She says, at times, that she is more "herself" in these places and situations and that she "can recognize [her]self more clearly." She also found that to be true when she was working as a therapist. She elaborates,

Of course, when you talk to women who have been abused, there's a tremendous sense of compassion and respect, but you have to also confront women. You also need to be tough. I am not one to sugarcoat things. I'm driven by my own sense of integrity. I'm congruent in what I say and what I practice. My feelings are aligned with my behaviors. With me, what you see is what you get. I think students appreciate it a lot. I wanted to be a role model. I was a little bit rude and vulgar at times, but I was open and very valuable for them, I think it never occurred to me to do something different. It's about morality and justice. (S. Sharratt, personal communication, July 10, 2015)

When asked what advice she would give to young activists who are doing this work, she suggests,

Take a break! Do something else for a while. Get out of the traumatic situations. Do research, plan conferences, and offer solutions to peacekeeping workers. And support each other. It is too easy for a context so painful to cause the very workers to turn against each other. Try to live an ordinary life sometimes. Remember that progress is not linear. Continue struggling. Become activists and knowledgeable about the world. Believe in yourself and your own perspectives and feelings. And do not bleed to death. (S. Sharratt, personal communication, July 10, 2015)

Looking Back

As Sharratt looks back on her history as a feminist, therapist, and activist, she reveals, "You need to be transparent. This is what I believe. Be respectful. I once had a class with one woman student who was from the highest caste in Nepal and another woman who was from the lowest caste in Nepal. They had to learn how to talk to each other and respect each other. Learn acceptance of different visions" (S. Sharratt, personal communication, July 10, 2015).

Sara is very proud of having been a co-founder of two feminist psychotherapy clinics, which offered sliding fee scales, enabling women from all economic backgrounds to afford professional mental health services. She notes that with progress also come some losses.

We're going backwards in some ways. Gender issues can get grouped with others, while I believe that they are central and underlie any real change. We have to push back and acknowledge gender injustices and address them as their own issues. If there's no gender equality, there's no justice or freedom, and no democracy. Feminism always made sense. What was hard was having been blinded by trying unsuccessfully to belong. (S. Sharratt, personal communication, November 17, 2015)

Over time Sharratt's sense of being an outsider in the field of traditional psychology with its lack of attention to the social, political, and cultural contexts of one's life forced her to forge a new path, one paved with the stories of women who were also made to feel that they didn't belong. At long last, a field of study was born that acknowledged women's lived experiences and the strengths, determination, and profound wisdom that lies within.

References

Cox, S. (1976). *Female psychology: The emerging self.* Chicago, IL: Science Research Associates.

Sharratt, S., & Kaschak, E. (Eds.). (1999). *Assault on the soul: Women in the former Yugoslavia.* New York: The Haworth Press, Inc.

Sharratt, S. (2011). *Gender, shame and violence: The voices of witnesses and court members at war crime tribunals.* Farnham, Surrey, UK: Ashgate Publishing Group.

Feminist Psychology and Psychotherapy: A Personal Journey

Reiko Homma-True

ABSTRACT

While growing up in a traditional, patriarchal family in Japan, I struggled between my wish to pursue my own dreams and the prevalent expectations for women to be subservient to men. The opportunity to come to the United States through marriage and to study at the University of California, Berkeley, was a catalyst for me to make major personal changes. I was also strongly influenced by the Civil Rights Movement that erupted around me, opening my eyes to the racism and sexism prevalent in the country. Learning from African American and Latino activists, I became an activist, first focusing on Asians in general. I then recognized that Asian American women were struggling under the double oppression of racism and sexism within their own community and in the majority world outside. I first did not think feminist psychology or feminist psychotherapy could be helpful for Asian American women as it appeared primarily designed for the middle class, White women. However, I was inspired by the minority feminist psychologist leaders to develop the feminist treatment approach that addresses the cultural diversity issues unique to Asian American women.

I am grateful to the editors of this special issue for encouraging me to reflect on my life and share with other women how I started out as a naive, insecure young woman and became empowered over many years to become a strong leader and a feminist. It was a long, circuitous road, starting out with haphazard attempts at finding my way in the world, trying to escape painful memories of domestic violence in the past. Throughout my journey, I received tremendous support from many mentors, mostly women, but some men as well. I first did not think feminist psychology or psychotherapy could be incorporated into my work with Asian American women as I felt it was designed primarily to meet the needs of middle class, White women. However, my ideas were radically changed after meeting and learning from powerful minority feminist psychologists who recognized what changes were needed for women of color to benefit from the approach. I was inspired by them to develop my own approach for working with Asian and Asian

American women who were struggling under the double oppression of racism and sexism within their own community and in the majority world outside.

Growing Up in Japan

I was born in 1933 and grew up during the turbulent years of World War II, which started with the Japanese attack at Pearl Harbor on December 7, 1941, and ended on August 15, 1945, soon after atomic bombs were dropped on Hiroshima and Nagasaki. It was a few days before my twelfth birthday. The tragic consequences of the war made a deep impact on me so that I became a pacifist and developed firm opposition to military aggression. I grew up in a traditional, conservative city called Niigata, which is located by the Japan Sea, facing China, Korea, and Russia. The city is the capital of the prefecture famous as a rice and sake-producing region and for its port, which was a gateway to China and Korea. It was rumored that the city was the next target for the atomic bomb attack after Hiroshima and Nagasaki because of the importance of its port. Fortunately, we were spared. My father was a high school teacher of Japanese and Chinese literature. He later tried other ventures, including being a travel agent and working in relatives' businesses. His family ran a prosperous restaurant business for two generations before, but lost the business during the Depression era. However, they managed to send two of their daughters to colleges, one to a pharmacy school and the other to a medical school. Both of them never married. My youngest aunt, Mutsu, became a pioneering female physician and later the first female public health director in the country. She was a brilliant physician who also earned a doctorate for her research on tuberculosis treatment, which was prevalent in Japan at the time. People respected her for her medical expertise, but treated her as an eccentric as she dressed in men's clothing and behaved like a man, drinking and smoking. She was most likely a lesbian, but never acknowledged it. She was estranged from my father and was held up by my family as a negative role model, with a warning such as "Don't be like your aunt, don't get too educated. If you do, no one will marry you." I later realized how wrong they were and that she was a great positive role model for me. I was fortunate to get to know her better later and was close to her before she passed away in 2012 at the age of 97.

My mother's father was a prefecture official in charge of building and road construction and was fairly affluent. My mother had four older brothers, and as the youngest and the only daughter, she was loved and pampered. In order to protect her from potential hardship of marrying into another family, her parents were planning to adopt a groom for her so he would marry into her family. This was a practice often adopted in order to maintain the family line when there were only daughters or when the family was wealthy enough to set aside sufficient assets to establish a new household for a treasured daughter. The male candidates, who were willing to renounce their own family names and take on the wife's family name, were the second and third sons who had no prospect of inheriting his family's asset under the law of primogeniture. The women in such arranged household had greater rights and status than women who marry into another family. However, her idyllic life was turned upside down when her mother died suddenly, probably from a heart attack, when she was 15 years old. Her older brothers had all left home by then, and she was all alone. It must have been a traumatic experience for her, but she found refuge in the Methodist Christian Church, which was started not too long before that time with the help of American missionaries and was attracting young people. Within a few years, her father decided to take a second wife, and two younger step-sisters arrived in quick succession. There was no longer any chance of my mother establishing her own household under the Uesugi family name. By the time her father and the stepmother arranged for my mother to marry my father, she was 21 years old. My mother used to confide in me that she felt her parents did not do a careful background check on my father as it would have revealed that he was a womanizer and his first marriage ended in divorce after 5 years.

My father's family was a traditional patriarchal family in which the members were expected to obey the dictates of the male head of the household, and all the males in the household commanded greater privilege than females. Even a simple family routine such as serving meals or taking a bath illustrated this dynamic. During mealtime, my mother would serve my father first, then my grandfather, younger brother, and finally my grandmother, me, and my mother last. I used to beg my mother to serve me ahead of my brother once in awhile as I was older than him. However, I would be always reminded that I was a girl and boys needed to be served ahead of girls. This patriarchal pattern was further reinforced outside of our home by the militarist, nationalist government policy that demanded the subservience of women to men's dictates. We, girls, were constantly reminded to take to our hearts the Confucian dictates of the three Obediences: (1) when you are a child, obey the father; (2) when married, obey the husband; and (3) when old, obey the son. In school, we were taught our ideal model for womanhood was to be a good wife and a wise mother, setting aside our own personal needs and aspirations in order to serve our men. When I started to question the dictates in my later years, I learned that women in other Asian countries, especially China and Korea, were also subjected to the same Confucian dictates about the subordinate place of women, and it continued to have powerful influence over Asian American women in United States as well (Shon & Ja, 1982).

While the world outside of my family was engaged in a disastrous war, the scenes within my family were also turbulent with frequent scenes of domestic violence. My father, who was a spoiled first son and had big dreams of recovering the family fortune with various ventures, was constantly in debt and often left my mother to scramble for money to feed the family. She often received financial help from her brothers. My parents would often fight about money or my father's womanizing, which often ended up with my father beating my mother up. When I became older, perhaps by 13, I used to try to stop my father by stepping between my parents, and he would stop, as he did not wish to hurt me. Inevitably, the frequent domestic violence resulted in a fatal accident one day when my mother fell on the sharp edge of a desk. She had severe headaches, but did not think it was serious. However, she apparently suffered an internal brain hemorrhage and suddenly suffered severe convulsions that night. By the time we took her to a hospital, she was pronounced dead. It was in June of 1949. I was not quite 17 at the time, my brother was 15, and my youngest sister was only 4 years old. I had often thought and told her that she should give up on my father and divorce him. However, what prevented her from taking this action was the fact that a divorce for women at that time was very difficult, and it also meant she had to leave us children with my father as she had no custody rights under the civil code at that time. Trapped in the miserable marriage, she found relief in the church and belief in God again as she had done earlier when she lost her mother. Although I was not able to think clearly at that time, this whole tragedy was a catalyst for me to eventually be committed to fight against injustices and to try to help the oppressed and the abused. No criminal charge was filed against my father, and he remarried within 6 months after my mother's death. My stepmother was a much more subservient woman who would not challenge my father, and there were no more incidences of domestic violence in the home. Although I was troubled by his re-marriage, it was a relief for me as well as I was getting exhausted taking care of my sister, cooking, and doing the household chores, while trying to go to school at the same time.

Although I was skeptical earlier of the benefit of God and the church for my mother, I sought relief from the church after my mother's death and found spiritual peace there and my belief in God just as my mother did when she lost her mother. I became an active member of the church and participated in volunteer work at orphanages and childcare programs during high school and my college years. We moved from Niigata to Yokohama before my mother's death, and I attended a high school in Yokohama, which stressed academic excellence and encouraged students to seek higher education. This was a major shift at that time from the war time policy of encouraging girls to get married early and discouraging any aspirations for higher education. Most of my classmates were planning to go to colleges and were applying for stiff college entrance exams. As I was a good student, my teachers also encouraged me to apply. Although my family's financial status was precarious, I wanted badly to try as I thought of getting a college education as a way out of dependence from my father. Thanks to the new constitution enacted in 1947, the education system was opening up for women in ways we could not dream before. It was a time for radical social and political changes. Although non-Japanese knew about Japan's new constitution for its renunciation of war and for making the Emperor as the symbol of the country only, other provisions changed the status of women dramatically. The new constitution was largely drafted by General MacArthur's staff, which declared in Article 14 that there should be no discrimination in political, economic, or social relations because of race, creed, sex, social status, or family origin. The Constitution also declared that matters related to marriage and family were to be based on the essential equality of the sexes. Based on the Constitution, the public education system became co-educational, opening up previously male exclusive universities to women. Although entrance exams were very competitive, I applied and was accepted as an English major at a university known for quality language education. Although I was not sure if my father would approve of me going to college or supporting me financially, he was able to pay for the first semester of my tuition, making it clear that I had to finance my education after the first semester. As I also did not want to depend on my father, I obtained a student loan and a part-time job tutoring high school students.

It was only the third year after the university was liberated for women. There were three women in our class of 80 students, two women in the year ahead, and only one woman 2 years before us. It was awkward for all of us at first. None of us had experience studying with the opposite sex after elementary school. Professors were all males, but they all tried to be accepting of the presence of women students. Eventually, we all became adjusted to the situation and enjoyed being friends. I learned a great deal and enjoyed being a student. However, I was not prepared at the end of the 4 years when I could not find an employer willing to even interview me. My vague hope was to work for a company that dealt with international businesses. Although my male classmates were going for job interviews, these companies made it clear they were not accepting women graduates. My two female classmates were better prepared and secured nice jobs through their family connections. I learned later that companies did not wish to hire women graduates with 4 years of education and preferred to hire junior college graduates as they considered them easier to mold in the way they wanted to use women employees. One of my professors was kind enough to arrange an editorial staff job for me at a small publishing firm. On the first day at the job, the president called me into his office and informed me that this was the first time he hired a woman as a professional staff. He made it clear he did not want his women clerical workers to feel he was giving me special treatment and ordered me to accept the tea serving duty along with other female staff. It meant taking turns serving tea to all the male staff and the female staff, as well as to visitors who came into the company. As my editorial staff job often required me to go out of the office and work late into the evenings, I started to owe tea serving duties to other clerical staff. I was exhausted and felt defeated. After 6 months of working there with mounting debt of tea serving duties, I resigned and accepted a proposal from an American man who kept pursuing me to marry him.

Marriage and Life in the United States

I met my ex-husband at a Lutheran Christian church in Yokohama where I was an active member. He was working as a civilian for the U.S. Army in Yokohama. He was a graduate of a Baptist college and wanted to proselytize in Japan. My minister thought I would be a good candidate to be an interpreter, and I worked with him for about a year when he decided he wanted to marry me. At first, I did not take this seriously, thinking there were too many complications in an inter-racial marriage. However, after feeling rejected by the Japanese sexism and unconfident about the prospect of finding a non-violent Japanese husband, I decided a Christian man, even though he was not Japanese, was probably not going to be abusive and could be a good husband. It was a very immature way of choosing a marriage partner, but I had no older person to confide in and give me guidance about choosing a marriage partner. It was a shock to my school friends as inter-racial marriages were frowned upon in Japan at that time. My family, including my grand-mothers, accepted my decision as they probably thought I was a poor candidate to be a wife to a Japanese man anyway. During the first few years, my husband was kind and helpful. I became pregnant right away, and my son was born in July, 1957. He was a healthy, sweet boy, and I was quite happy being a full-time mother and a wife.

When my son was 8 months old, my husband decided it was time to return to United States, and we arrived in San Francisco in the spring of 1958. My husband found another position with the Army base in Oakland, California, and we lived with his mother in South San Francisco. I thought I should help contribute to the family finances and found a job as a secretary with a Japanese American organization. After a year there, I accepted a clerical job with a state agency, which monitored labor conditions and statistics. During my work there, I was encouraged by my supervisor not to be content as a clerk and to try to seek graduate training to improve my career possibilities. Through frequent discussions with my supervisor, I decided to apply for the Social Work graduate program at UC Berkeley. By that time, my second child, a daughter, a beautiful, sweet baby, was born. It was a difficult time for me as I was driven by the urge to study and I could not give the undivided attention to my daughter during her early years. It was also very difficult for me as my English was still limited to perform at the graduate school level. I managed to survive the first year by taking 2 years to complete the require-ments. For my second year of internship, my professor encouraged me to choose the mental health placement, which was just starting to grow right after the passage of President Kennedy's Community Mental Health Act in 1963. I was placed at a traditional psychoanalytically oriented clinic in San Francisco. It was a tremendous learning opportunity, although I kept thinking it would be difficult for Japanese or Asian clients to be treated by this approach. In fact, there were no Japanese or Asian patients at the clinic. After graduating from UC Berkeley in 1964, I started working at an outpatient psychiatric clinic in Oakland and was fortunate to meet a supervisor named Mary Edwards. She was a wonderful mentor throughout my career, and we became lifelong friends. She is better known by her second married name as Mary Goulding. She and her husband, Bob Goulding, were known as the founders of Redecision Therapy (Goulding & Goulding, 1979), which combined behavioral, cognitive, and affective work, integrating the Gestalt work of Fritz Perls and Eric Berne's Transactional Analysis approach.

The Civil Rights Movement and Activism

Soon after I started working, the Free Speech Movement erupted at the UC Berkeley campus and anti-Vietnam War protests rocked the communities around the San Francisco Bay Area. Mary was an activist, and she urged me to join her in the protest marches. We marched down the famed Telegraph Avenue with my son in tow and my daughter in a stroller. This was the time of my political and social awakening, turning me into an activist. However, my relationship with my husband was deteriorating steadily. Although he grew up in a Southern Baptist family, he became increasingly eccentric, rejecting the Baptist church as too compromised from the true teaching of Christ. He aligned himself with a Pentecostal group and wanted us to join him in the services and talked of moving away to a rural area to get away from the evils of the cities. I had little knowledge of the complexities of the various Protestant Christian groups and was appalled in having to participate in prayer sessions where people would speak in tongues and speak of seeing visions of Christ and God. No doubt, it did not help our relationship as I started to change from a compliant, sweet woman to a woman who started to express her own opinions and began challenging his dictates. Although there was no violence, we had frequent arguments. Finally, it was my husband who decided he had enough and walked out of the house, declaring he was through with our marriage. Although he changed his mind later, I also realized our marriage was over. We had been married for 10 years at that time, and our children were 9 and 6 years old. I must confess I felt anxious and insecure at that time about being a single mother in a foreign country and exposing my children to possible bullying as children of a broken marriage. My co-workers, including Mary, were great support for me, and a competent attorney helped negotiate a reasonable divorce agreement. It was a difficult adjustment for our children, but they managed to cope and eventually thrive much better than growing up in a household with parents fighting constantly.

After the divorce, I was less constrained by my ex-husband about my involvement in activist causes. Within a few years, I met a partner, also a White American, with whom I had fun, shared similar values, and was able to develop a mutually supportive partnership. I was deeply concerned that there were so many unmet needs in our Asian communities. I learned to form alliances with other concerned Asian and minority activists to press for funding for needed services. I first worked with others to create a support program for Japanese newcomer women who were mostly married to American service men and were called "war brides." They were often isolated and had trouble adjusting to the new country. Some of them were abused, abandoned by their husbands, or rejected by their families. The Japanese American community was also not sympathetic to them, as they considered the women no better than prostitutes. With a small grant, we were able to hire a part-time Japanese social worker to help them cope with problems with cultural adjustment with the hope of eventually creating a self-help support group among them so that they could help each other. We named the group *Himawari* (sunflower) to symbolize our hardiness, thriving in foreign soil, and to make a clear distinction from the stereotypical image of Japanese women as "fragile like cherry blossom." After the grant funding ended, the group was able to continue through small fundraisers and now boasts 43 years of not only supporting each other, but helping various Japanese American community groups. Although I did not realize it then, this was the start of the empowering actions encouraged by feminist psychologists.

After the successful launching of the *Himawari* group, I worked with other activists to advocate for and create various health, mental health, and social service agencies for Asian American communities. As I started to get acquainted with Asian American communities, I was appalled with the extent of the unmet needs and indifference of the establishment organizations for them. Although I worked for a large Alameda County mental health system, I rarely saw any Japanese or Asian individuals as patients there. The director and the managers' attitude at the time was that Asian Americans did not need the services as they thought that they were either mentally healthy, or if sick, the Asian tradition was for families to take care of them, avoiding the established services in the majority community. If a few very sick people were brought in for services, often against their will, their treatment was grossly inappropriate. There were no bilingual services for non-English speakers, and no effort was made to arrange for interpreters. If they were very sick, they were sent away to a state hospital where they were warehoused, but not treated. I was personally involved in trying to bring back a Japanese woman who had been hospitalized for many years in Napa State Hospital for problems that could have been treated much more effectively by a bilingual provider within the community. What we needed badly were services within our communities with easy access, providing bilingual services, which were culturally appropriate. However, the policy makers and establishment organizations ignored the needs and maintained the status quo, citing lack of data to substantiate the needs. This fueled our activism to work harder, learning how to create political alliances. It helped that our timing coincided with the launching of the War on Poverty, and we were eventually able to obtain funding to create many services in our community. All of these services proved there were plenty of Asian people in need. What was needed was the right kind of services within our own community. Most of the agencies we created have survived through the financial crisis in California during the 1980s and are thriving, proving people will accept the services if they are provided in ways acceptable to their communities.

Graduate School and Psychology

After working for several years, I became increasingly aware of the limitations of my knowledge of mental health and clinical skills. As my children were growing up and I had some money saved up, I decided to return to graduate school and chose to go to California School of Professional Psychology (CSPP) in 1972. I chose CSPP for its emphasis on clinical practice instead of returning to social work program at UC Berkeley, which emphasized academic teaching and research. Although I had enough savings to last for a year, I was fortunate to receive funding from NIMH, which provided funding support for an additional 2 years of study with the condition to work for them for 1 year. It was a great opportunity for me. For the first time, I did not have to worry about finances and was able to immerse myself in the study of psychology, with a focus on minority mental health issues. At the same time, I also began learning about the discrimination and difficulties faced by American women in receiving gender appropriate care (Chesler, 1972; Miller, 1976). As I learned about the struggles of American women, I started recognizing that Asian American women were subjected to even greater challenges and oppression, compounded by the racist discrimination against Asians in the majority community. I began meeting with several like-minded Asian American women in consciousness raising discussions about our own personal struggles within our own families, our own community, and in the majority community as well. We talked about the existing, demeaning stereotypes of Asian American women, portraying us as sex objects, subservient hand maidens, or if too assertive, as a dragon lady (True, 1981). We also began studying the history of women's lives in our own Asian countries of origin to understand the context under which our lives were defined. I found an exhaustive study on the history of women in Japan by Takamine (1972), which provided eye-opening research on how the Japanese social system was originally matrilineal and matriarchal, but their power and status deteriorated over the centuries as the country became dominated by warrior Samurai clans. I also learned that the creation myth for the island of Japan attributed the work as the collaboration of two gods, one male and one female, and it was the goddess, Amaterasu, who symbolized the Sun, which was in contrast to the Greek myth of male god, Apollo (Earhart, 1974). We also learned that the earliest social system in China was matriarchal and there was a powerful role model for Chinese women in the legend of woman warrior (Chin, 2007), later popularized as Disney's Mulan. Based on what we learned from each other, we decided to teach the Psychology of Asian American Women as an Asian American Studies course at UC Berkeley in 1976. We believe this was one of the earliest classes on Asian American women. Our goal was to raise the consciousness of young Asian American women students about the sexism and racism around them, help them redefine their own identity, and empower them to overcome the challenges they faced around them.

After completing my graduate studies, I joined the Region IX office of NIMH in San Francisco to fulfill my work obligation. It was a major shift in my career from being a community activist to joining the establishment organization. I was assigned to work with the state of Nevada and then Arizona, helping community groups and local governments develop community mental health center programs. It was an eye opening experience, learning how to help local groups develop program ideas, submit grant proposals, participate in the grant review process, and provide support and monitoring to the funded groups. I had some concerns about the potential conflict of being a government bureaucrat, which might severely constrain my community activism. Although there were limitations, I learned that I could be effective from inside the establishment to advocate for our community's needs and to persuade some hardheaded scientist-bureaucrats who had trouble accepting there were needs in underserved communities without statistics and data to back up the needs. I worked there for 5 years until I realized I preferred working more directly with local community programs and accepted a position with San Francisco Community Mental Health Services as its Deputy Director. It was a time of tremendous growth in the city's mental health and substance abuse treatment system. I was able to help develop many creative community programs for minority and women's groups, including such programs as a rape treatment center, services for child victims of child and sexual abuse, and halfway house programs for mothers with children who were recovering from psychiatric or substance abuse problems.

My career up to this point had been smooth and successful, receiving recognition for helping to develop innovative programs for culturally diverse groups and for dealing effectively with a series of frequent crisis. For this reason, I was not prepared for the treatment I received in 1984 when the public health administration decided to eliminate my position, along with the other Deputy Director, who happened to be an African American psychologist as a cost cutting measure. I was stunned and did not know what I could do. It was when my network of Asian American women went into action for me by organizing a petition campaign and stood with me on the streets of Japan Town to publicize my plight. The husband of one of them was Harry Bridges, who was a legendary ILWU (International Labor and Warehouse Union) leader, famous for the bloody general strike of San Francisco in 1934. Although he was retired and in poor health by then, he led a delegation to the Mayor's office to protest the decision. It also helped that a key member of the Board of Supervisors believed in me and was instrumental in convincing the department to find the funds to restore the positions for myself and the other director. The next shock was when I was ranked as the top candidate for the Director of Community Mental Health Services position when the position became vacant in 1985. This was the first time a woman and a person of color was a strong candidate for the position. Although I was not surprised by the outcome of the exam, as I felt I had solid knowledge and experience, allegations were expressed in the media that there was an element of reverse racism because the interview panel was biased against White candidates and it should be invalidated. I was dismayed, but felt heartened when many Asian American civic groups and other key people in the city came to my defense. Despite the opposition, I was appointed to the position in 1985. I can take satisfaction in the fact that while the previous directors kept running a large deficit every year, I was able to stop the deficit from the first year of my appointment and was successful in bringing in new funding for innovative programs. I retired from the Public Health Department in 1996 and was involved in training master's level psychology students in Japan for 9 years. I now maintain a part-time private practice near Japan Town, with a priority to serve Asian American women.

Feminist Psychology and Practice

My first encounter with a feminist psychologist was with Nancy Felipe-Russo at a White House reception in 1978 after the completion of the President's Commission on Mental Health during the Carter administration. Nancy was the director of APA's Women's Program and worked on women's needs. I was there for my work with Asian Americans. Although I told her that I was critical of APA's poor record of serving the needs of the minority population, she encouraged me to become more involved with APA so that I could help make the changes within the organization. Later, I was invited to serve on the Committee on Women in Psychology (CWP) where I had the opportunity to meet many dynamic, feminist leaders, both White and non-White, including

Florence Denmark, Carolyn Payton, Laura Brown, Ellyn Kaschak, and Lillian Comas-Diaz. I was encouraged by the committee's effort to address the concerns of women of color, lesbians, as well as women with disabilities. I learned from them how they struggled to reflect the issues of cultural diversity into their conceptual framework, theory, and practice, which had been previously criticized for their focus on middle class, White women (Brown & Root, 1990; Comas-Diaz & Greene 1994; Espin, 1994).

My own approach for working with Asian American women is an integrative approach, described by Comas-Diaz (1994), using a variety of treatment modalities most appropriate for a client's particular needs and difficulties. They include psychodynamic approach, Redecision therapy, CBT, DBT, mindfulness meditation, as well as a variety of somatic therapies such as exercise, yoga, t'ai chi, massage, and relaxation techniques. I try to incorporate feminist values and principles relevant for Asian American women into these modalities, which include consciousness raising about existing sexism and oppression, empowerment activities, and activism as needed. Additional issues that I try to be attentive to are:

- **Diversity among Asian American women:** Although Asian Americans are often perceived as a single category, the term encompasses diverse racial-cultural groups, including Chinese, Korean, Japanese, Indian, Filipino, and Southeast Asian people (Le & Dinh, 2015). When working with clients of Asian descent, I try to learn and understand as much about their specific sociocultural background, including the variables of level of acculturation, recency of immigration, educational background, and parental attitude toward gender roles, and to develop the most effective and meaningful assistance to them.
- **Interdependence vs. Independence**: While individualism and independence is encouraged in the Western culture, greater emphasis is placed on the value of interdependence within the Asian and Asian American culture (Bradshaw, 1990; Markus & Kitayama, 1991). Although the emphasis on interdependence in personal relationships can lead to mutually enriching growth, it was translated among the patriarchal Asian community to expect women to sacrifice her own needs for the benefit of their families, especially for the needs of their men. In a therapeutic relationship, I try to help the client understand the historical context in which the value of family interdependence was developed, but I also emphasize the importance for the woman to recognize her own needs and to find ways to meet them. If the family is too rejecting of her own needs, she can be encouraged to seek the support from outside her immediate families, including friends, teachers, co-workers, and mentors, so that she can continue to embrace the value of interdependence.
- **Egalitarian Relationships**: Although promoting egalitarian relationships is the major foundation of feminist therapy (Brown, 2010), the age of the

therapist could create complications for work with Asian clients whose culture places particular emphasis on respecting the elders. While the client could have difficulties disagreeing or challenging the older therapist, the reverse dynamics could also develop when a therapist is younger than the client. Another aspect of Asian culture is the high status placed on education and professionals with expertise, including teachers and psychologists. In both situations, it is important for the therapist to be sensitive to the dynamics of the therapeutic relationship, not to abuse the power hierarchy for her own personal needs or to be defensive towards critical clients, and to focus on empowering the clients to gain confidence in their own ability to overcome the difficulties.

- **Handling of Anger:** Although anger issues are frequently included as an important element of feminist psychotherapy, it is a challenge for therapists to help women of color validate and manage the anger (Espin, 1994). It is often difficult for Asian woman to recognize it within herself. My approach with Asian-American women is to help them recognize and validate their anger. However, instead of angry confrontations, I help them explore productive ways to express or manage that anger without further inviting rejection or punishment from their families or community.

- **Domestic Violence:** Although domestic violence is present in the Asian American community, it is often hidden or condoned and accepted with a fatalistic attitude (Ho, 1990). It is important for the therapist not only to help the client find ways to deal with the abuse in a therapeutic context, but take greater proactive actions to promote healing and changes within our community. For myself, this includes organizing psycho-educational workshops on the topic and participating in the creation of the Asian women's shelter in San Francisco to meet the needs of abused, non-English speaking, Asian women to escape from potentially lethal situations.

Looking Back and Forward

Throughout my life, I have encountered many crises and managed to overcome and become empowered from these experiences. The support I received from many mentors and friends was critical for my growth. Although I first placed priority on meeting the overwhelming needs of the Asian American community, I began recognizing the pervasive sexism and oppression both within our own community and in the majority community. Without realizing I was adopting strategies developed by the feminist psychologists, I took actions to organize and help Asian American women clients. I was later greatly inspired by pioneer feminist psychologists who tried to respond to the needs of women of color. With their guidance, I was able to improve my understanding of feminist psychology and have tried to develop culturally competent ways of working with Asian American women. My priority at this stage in my career is to mentor Asian American women just as my mentors supported me earlier in my career (Homma-True, 2010). An increasing number of Asian American women are now entering the field of psychological study and practice. I am encouraged by their enthusiasm and look forward to work with them to improve the lives of the Asian American women in our community.

References

Bradshaw, C. (1990). A Japanese view of dependency: What can Amae Psychology contribute to feminist theory and therapy?. In L. S. Brown & M. P. P. Root (Eds.), *Diversity and complexity in feminist therapy* (pp. 67–86). New York: Harrington Park.

Bradshaw, C. (1994). Asian and Asian American women: Historical and political considerations in psychotherapy. In L. Comas-Diaz & B. Greene (Eds.), *Women of color: Integrating ethnic and gender identities in psychotherapy* (pp. 72–113). New York: Guilford Press.

Brown, L. S. (2010). *Feminist therapy*. Washington, DC: American Psychological Association.

Brown, L. S., & Root, M. P. P. (Eds.). (1990). *Diversity and complexity in feminist therapy*. New York: Harrington Park Press.

Chesler, P. (1972). *Women and madness*. Garden City, NY: Doubleday.

Chin, J. L. (2007). Psychotherapy for Asian American woman warriors. In D. M. Kawahara & O. M. Espín (Eds.), *Feminist reflections on growth and transformation: Asian American women in therapy* (pp. 7–16). New York: Haworth.

Comas-Diaz, L. (1994). An integrative approach. In L. Comas-Diaz & B. Greene (Eds.), *Women of color: Integrating ethnic and gender identities in psychotherapy* (pp. 287–318). New York: Guilford Press.

Comas-Diaz, L., & Greene, B. (Eds.). (1994). *Women of color: Integrating ethnic and gender identities in psychotherapy*. New York: Guilford Press.

Earhart, H. B. (1974). *Religion in the Japanese experience: Sources and interpretations*. Encino, CA: Dickenson.

Espín, O. M. (1994). Feminist approaches. In L. Comas-Diaz & B. Greene (Eds.), *Women of color: Integrating ethnic and gender identities in psychotherapy* (pp. 265–286). New York: Guilford.

Goulding, M. C., & Goulding, R. L. (1979). *Changing lives through redecision therapy*. New York: Brunner/Mazel.

Ho, C. K. (1990). An analysis of domestic violence in Asian American communities: A multicultural approach to counseling. In L. S. Brown & M. P. P. Root (Eds.), *Diversity and complexity in feminist therapy* (pp. 129–150). New York: Harrington Park.

Homma-True, R. (1981). The profile of Asian-American women. In S. Cox (Ed.), *Female psychology: The emerging self* (pp. 124–135). New York: St. Martin's.

Homma-True, R. (2010). Mentoring Asian American women. In C. A. Rayburn, F. L. Denmark, M. E. Reuder, & A. M. Austria (Eds.), *A handbook for women mentors: Transcending barriers of stereotype, race, and ethnicity* (pp. 149–160). Santa Barbara, CA: Praeger.

Le, P. L., & Dinh, D. T. (2015). The intersection of gender and ethnicity: Asian-Pacific Islander American women. In C. Z. Enns, J. K. Rice, & R. L. Nutt (Eds.), *Psychological practice with women: Guidelines, diversity, empowerment* (pp. 135–157). Washington, DC: American Psychological Association Press.

Markus, H., & Kitayama, S. (1991). Culture and the self: Implications for cognition, emotion, and motivation. *Psychological Review, 98*, 224–253. doi:10.1037/0033-295x.98.2.224

Miller, J. B. (1976). *Toward a new psychology of women*. Boston, MA: Beacon.

Shon, S. P., & Ja, D. Y. (1982). Asian families. In M. McGoldrick J. K. Pearce & J. Giordano (Eds.), *Ethnicity and family therapy* (pp. 208–229). New York: Guilford.

Takamine, I. (1972). *Joseino Rekishi [History of women]*. Tokyo: Kodansha.

Feminist Pioneer: Lenore E. A. Walker

Giselle Gaviria, Rachel Needle, Rachael Silverman, and Lenore E. A. Walker

ABSTRACT

Dr. Lenore E. A. Walker is one of the early feminist psychotherapists whose career has been described in this article to show the evolution as the values of women's contributions to the world and psychology changed over time. She began as an elementary school teacher for emotionally disturbed children after having strong women mentors. Her feminism was nurtured through contacts with other feminist psychologists as the field developed in the 1970s and 1980s. Involvement in APA politics was another area where mentorship was practiced as policies supporting women and children's rights to live a violence-free life were emphasized. Her research, clinical practice, and teaching all intersected with both science and feminism, sometimes having to make hard choices like in the O. J. Simpson case. Three of her former students, now making names for themselves in feminist psychology, discuss how Walker's mentorship helped them throughout their career development.

Preface (LW)

When I was first asked to contribute this article to the early history of feminist therapy and how it impacted my ability to mentor other psychologists, I discussed it with three of my former students who now have made important contributions to the field of feminist psychology. They were excited to interview me and write the article while offering me the ability to edit and comment. Although this was a little different than what the editors originally suggested, we decided to try it and see what happened, which we all felt was a feminist process.

Introduction (GG, RN, & RS)

As we sit at Dr. Walker's kitchen table, overlooking the ocean, and eating bagels, we began to explore her journey from childhood to internationally renowned feminist pioneer. We all reminisced as we shared our different individual experiences of working, collaborating with, developing friendship, and traveling the world with our friend, colleague, mentor, and "mother away from home." We are excited to tell you about the life of this extraordinary woman!

Growing Up Feminist

Dr. Lenore Elizabeth Auerbach Walker was born in the Bronx, NY, to David Auerbach and Pearl Auerbach on October 3, 1942, which was in the midst of WWII. Her family was considered lower middle class, although her father was a government employee and her mother worked as a part-time receptionist to earn extra money. They were "culturally Jewish" and attended High Holiday services. Dr. Walker's father was drafted in the army in 1942 and subsequently relocated to Texas. While her mother would travel to Texas to visit her father from time and time because "they couldn't stand being apart," Dr. Walker would stay with her Aunt Rose. By the age of one, Dr. Walker and her mother moved outside of the large army base in Tyler, Texas, to be closer to her father. Her father would train the troops who were next to be deployed. Dr. Walker described this time of her life as both "happy" and "stressful" because they did not know if her father would be deployed.

Dr. Walker describes herself as "not an easy child." An example of this was when she went to the PX Army Base store with her mother when the Christmas ornaments caught her attention. She wandered over to them and proceeded to eat one of them. Another woman who was standing there quickly took the pieces of glass out of her mouth before she could swallow them. That afternoon, they went back to the store, and Dr. Walker began wandering on her own again. A security guard approached her mother and said, "You had better watch your daughter as there was a little girl in here earlier who ate a Christmas ornament this morning." This story was retold again and again to her to remind her and others that she would not be deterred from going after what she wanted. As a result of the freedom she was given to explore her environment combined with her curiosity and determination, Dr. Walker was fearless from a young age.

In 1945, when she was 3 years old, Dr. Walker recalls playing in her backyard, which was close to a park. Although her backyard was enclosed by a gate, that didn't stop Dr. Walker from wanting to play in the park. She quickly taught herself how to open the gate and began going to play in the park by herself. "I remember the kids in the neighborhood would pick me up and take me back home on the basket of their bikes … I just never had any danger cues. Mother never saw it as getting into trouble, but just as a child being curious. The family just accepted it as part of my personality." Today, we would call it "free range" parenting. Concerned for his daughter's safety, Dr. Walker's father made her a necklace with her phone number and address on an army tag.

In 1946, the family moved back to the Bronx, NY, and her brother, Joel, was born. "I came home speaking like a Texan. The neighbors would tease and call me a rebel, so I tried hard to rid myself of the accent." During this time, Dr. Walker resided in an apartment near her extended family. "Everyone was in everyone's business. It was a typical Jewish family." Dr. Walker's paternal grandmother bought three bungalows in Rockaway Beach when she was 8 years old so that her eight children and their families could spend summers at the beach. She spent much of her adolescence with her family and extended family in Rockaway Beach. Although she was there with 10 cousins around the same age, she initiated many other friendships and would bring them over to meet her family. During this time, she developed an interest in the Perry Mason and Nancy Drew books and would frequently ride her bike to the library to read more. Reading these detective series was the beginning of her interest in forensics.

Dr. Walker attended public school in New York City and was identified to be a "smart kid" at an early age. New York City's Department of Education just kept skipping the grades of gifted children like Dr. Walker. She described New York City as a wonderful place to grow up and be educated. She felt like you "had the world at your fingertips" and learned to negotiate the subway system at an early age opening up the museums and other cultural events to her. She graduated from high school at the age of 16 in 1959. It was never a question in her family whether she would go to college, but rather, which college. Dr. Walker attended Hunter College, which is part of the City University of New York (CUNY), where her cousin was also a student. Although she was encouraged to become a teacher, like most women of her day, she was more interested in the healthcare field. Her cousin suggested that she major in psychology because education was not considered an academic major at Hunter at that time. She graduated college at the age of 19 in 1962 with a major in psychology and a minor in education. During this time, she met Virginia Staudt-Sexton and Florence Denmark, both faculty there, who became her mentors. Virginia Staudt-Sexton, her undergraduate professor, had a profound influence on Dr. Walker's life. Dr. Walker recalls Virginia Staudt-Sexton refusing to take her husband's last name when she was getting married and stating, "Why do I have to and why should I not be who I am?" Her husband, Richard Sexton, was totally supportive, and they all remained colleagues and friends until Dr. Staudt's death. Dr. Walker resonated to these early feminist attitudes as they reflected her independent yet collegial spirit. Florence Denmark, another early mentor, was also a strong feminist and an internationalist. She has supported more women scholars than anyone else and continues to do so. Under Dr. Denmark's influence, Dr. Walker began attending international conferences and presenting her work on women in psychology. Dr. Walker learned how to mentor other students from Dr. Denmark's example. Dr. Denmark sponsored Dr. Walker's election to the Hunter College Alumni Hall of Fame.

Dr. Walker appreciated the value of money early in life, and she learned that if you wanted something, you had to work for it. At the age of 14, she worked part-time as a sales clerk at Macy's department store until she graduated from high school. While Dr. Walker attended college, she worked part-time as a secretary for a temporary agency that sent her to different offices in New York City. After a few months, she saw that some temporary secretaries got better jobs in nicer offices and figured out what additional skills they had that she didn't have. She learned how to use the executive typewriter on her own and was then hired by different offices on Wall Street and by developers all over New York City, even one in the Empire State Building.

In order to achieve a teaching degree, Dr. Walker worked as a student teacher for children with disabilities (i.e., disability in emotions, mobility, or blindness) in her last year of college. She was then hired as a substitute teacher and managed to get paid for her work as well as credit as a student teacher. Later, after her children were born, she worked with children and their parents in providing preventive mental health services in Coney Island Hospital and local schools. It was here that she learned how much she enjoyed helping people feel more competent in teaching and learning.

Dr. Walker married Peter at the age of 19 and subsequently moved to Brooklyn. She was employed at an elementary school teaching emotionally disturbed children. During this time, she was pregnant with Michael, but knew her marriage was not good. In 1964, when Michael was 2 months old, Dr. Walker decided to leave Peter. However, he promised to try couples' therapy, and when he did, they got back together. Around the time that Michael was 8 months old, Peter informed Dr. Walker that he had changed the family's last name from Wolkowitz to Walker. She was outraged that he was able to do this without her signature and felt like she had lost her identity. She became a strong advocate of women's rights to keep their own last name upon marriage. Today, her students all know they will get the lecture about keeping their own name, although she is tolerant of their making a choice to change it once they have carefully thought about the issue. After all, the feminist way is to think about choices carefully before making them. In 1969, she graduated with her Master's in School Psychology from City College of CUNY and was pregnant with her second child, Karen. She then moved the family to East Brunswick, New Jersey, where she attended Rutgers, the State University, for her doctorate in School Psychology, after learning that she needed it to practice as a school psychologist in New Jersey. Shocked that New Jersey's standards required a higher credential than New York City, she took a few courses as a special student during the year that the Kent State riots occurred against the Vietnam War and was then admitted as a full time doctoral student with an NIMH fellowship.

Feminism, Politics, and Psychology

Her feminist roots began to take a stronger hold during the 1960s with the formation of the National Organization for Women (NOW) and the Women's Equity Action League (WEAL)'s chapter at Rutgers, which fought for equalizing the salaries of men and women, "It was a very exciting time to be a woman!" The mayor of East Brunswick was a woman and supporting her is how Dr. Walker became involved with local feminist politics. At Rutgers, however, she worked with groups of other women in stopping the biases against women students, including asking female applicants questions during the interview, such as, 'are you going to get married and have babies?' In the fight for equal rights and salary, Dr. Walker discussed with Dr. Virginia Bennett that WEAL would add her name to the list given to the administration of those women faculty whose salaries needed to be equalized with male professors, but asked her never to ask those sexist questions again to a female student. Dr. Bennett who was a product of her time "played with the boys," which women felt was the only way to get ahead at this time. Walker described how, "You could not be an uppity women at this time." By 1972, Dr. Phyllis Chesler had written *Women and Madness*. "Uppity women were doing conscious raising and groups at this time. Women were really fighting hard for our rights ... I think I was becoming a feminist all along but this point was a demarcation. I stood up and said 'I am fighting for equality for everyone, even people that were not behaving in a feminist way.'"

Dr. Walker also had male mentors. Perhaps one of the most important ones was Jack Bardon, who was the head of the School Psychology program at Rutgers. Since it was difficult for Dr. Walker to return to graduate school after working for several years, she also worked part-time at a mental health clinic, running groups while in school. Dr. Walker graduated with her doctorate in School Psychology from Rutgers in 1972 after only 3 years. Her earlier work was approved as her internship as APA or APPIC internships were not required at that time to become licensed. Upon receiving her doctorate, she was invited to join the Rutgers Medical School clinical faculty and offered a position as the Director of the Educational Outreach Services. There, she supervised clinicians who identified 'at risk' children for mental health problems in the school systems serviced by the community mental health center. She also was able to use her position to advocate that schools be more supportive of young girls so that they would be encouraged to become leaders and allowed to do a variety of activities. This was considered preventive mental health at the time.

Feminist Professor

During the mid-1970s, while she was working at Rutgers Medical School, there were 35 men and only 5 women on the psychiatry faculty. However, the Chair and most of the staff members were extremely supportive of her feminist identification. At this time, Johnson & Johnson had an initiative to help women students integrate and adjust in medical schools that, up until the early 1970s, were predominately male. She actually identified herself with a feminist orientation when she took the NJ licensing exam in 1974 and later, in 1979, the American Board of Professional Psychology (ABPP) boards in clinical psychology. Violence against women and children became an important topic to be studied. It was at this time that Dr. Walker began working on the early child abuse laws and publishing her work. During her time at Rutgers Medical School (1972–1975), she began to collect stories of battered women with some of them coming from interviews in Miami Beach, Florida, while visiting her parents who had moved to South Florida.

Feminist Researcher

In 1973, her marriage dissolved. Dr. Walker attended a preventive mental health conference in Monterey, California, where she met her second husband, Morton Flax, a psychologist from Denver, Colorado, and in 1975, she moved there with her two children. Mort encouraged her activism in feminist politics, and she was elected as one of the Colorado delegates to the 1977 UN National Conference on Women in Houston where she met many of the early feminists, including Colorado Congresswoman Patricia Schroeder, psychologist and writer and psychologist Phyllis Chesler, and Gloria Steinem, an American feminist, journalist, and social and political activist, among others. These women supported her research on battered women. With her Congresswoman Patricia Schroeder's introduction to the federal research funds through the National Institute of Mental Health (NIMH), she applied for and won a large research grant to study what she then called "Battered Woman Syndrome" or the psychological effects from domestic violence on 400 battered women. "I named my work 'Battered Woman Syndrome' copying the child abuse work called 'Battered Child Syndrome.'" This was the first investigation by a psychologist that was funded by the NIMH from 1978 through 1981, and the results appeared in the psychological literature as well as presentations and conferences (Walker, 1984). As a result, Dr. Walker was invited to speak all over the country and the world to assist in developing policies to remove barriers to help battered women heal. The research is now up to the fourth edition (Walker, 1979, 1984, 2000, 2009, 2016).

In 1978, Mort passed away, and Dr. Walker immersed herself professionally in disseminating the grant results. An opportunity arose when she was asked to evaluate and testify in the case of a Montana battered woman, Miriam Grieg, who killed her husband in what she claimed was self-defense. Working with a seasoned criminal attorney, Charles "Timer" Moses, Dr. Walker learned how to present the data so that the jurors understood why this woman had a reasonable perception that her life was imminently in danger because her partner was going to seriously harm or kill her. Ms. Grieg was found 'not guilty' by a jury of 12 women. Dr. Walker went on to evaluate and testify in the Ibn-Tamas case in Washington, DC, where her testimony was not admitted due to its novel nature. However, after several years of appeals and several other high publicity cases, eventually, the 'battered woman syndrome' became admissible in all states by the 1990s (Walker, 2000). Most recently, in 2013, she was the first psychologist to get her battered woman syndrome testimony in Hong Kong, China, on behalf of a woman who killed her abusive husband in what she claimed was self-defense.

Feminist Forensic Psychologist

In the early 1980s, after the NIMH grant was completed and Colorado Women's College, where she was on the faculty, closed due to financial reasons, Dr. Walker subsequently went into the independent practice of psychology full-time. She continued her work in her private practice, providing feminist psychotherapy, assessment, and expert witness testimony in forensic cases, consultation and presentations around the world, and continued research on gender violence, adding sexual assault, rape, and exploitation to her expertise for the next 25 years. She founded the non-profit International Domestic Violence Institute and opened branches in many countries, working with local psychologists and advocates. Sometimes attorneys on the other side of cases would try to make fun of her feminist philosophy by calling her "Mizzzzzz Walker" instead of Dr. Walker or directly ask her why she hated men, but Dr. Walker says she learned to stay calm and respond as if she was trying to help a not-so-bright student get the message. When they would take quotes out of context from her book, she would often turn to the dedication page, which praised her father and husband, as a retort to their negativism.

During this time (January 1981 to May 1981), Dr. Walker was hired to teach on the Semester at Sea program for the University of Colorado, sailing with her two children on a ship that went around the world. That semester, the University of Pittsburgh received the academic contract with the University of Colorado, and she taught courses on human sexuality and feminist psychology of women. She accepted the job on one condition … contraceptives had to be sold on the ship. After all, these were college-age students, many of whom were sexually active. It was a life changing few months as she and her two children sailed around the world.

APA Governance Policy Challenges and the Feminist Therapy Institute

Having been active in the American Psychological Association's Division 35, The Society for the Study of Women, Dr. Walker met a group of women who were also interested in Feminist Therapy, which began life-long friendships with many of them, including Laura Brown, Hannah Lerman, Natalie Porter, Adrienne Brown, Rachel Siegel, and Lynn Rosewater. Together with others from the Association for Women in Psychology (AWP), they decided to hold their own conference since they were unhappy with the lack of attention their work received in the traditional mainstream conferences. Dr. Walker volunteered to host and organize this conference in Vail, Colorado, in 1981. They invited mental health professionals who identified as feminist therapists throughout the country to join, and over 50 came. The conference was a great success! Initially, they discussed topics such as gender, lesbian, and heterosexual women's relationships and multicultural issues. Then the discussions morphed, and they began developing Feminist Therapy theory and subsequently developing the first such treatment model. The Feminist Therapy Institute was born, and they decided to have yearly meetings and ultimately edited several important books (Rosewater & Walker, 1985).

She also continued her political activism in APA becoming President of several divisions, including Division 35, Women in Psychology; Division 46, Media Psychology; and Division 42, Independent Practice. She began governance service as an elected member of the Council of Representatives, serving six 3-year terms and a year on the Board of Directors over the past 30 years. In fact, she was just re-elected to her second 3-year term by the members of Division 42. She served as Chair of the Committee on International Relations in Psychology and was a member of the Public Interest Committee, the Child Abuse Policy Committee, and chaired the Presidential Task Force on Violence and the Family. As she continued her role in APA governance, she worked with others to introduce feminist principles into psychotherapy at all levels, including participating in a national conference on feminist psychotherapy that resulted in a book edited by Norine Johnson and Judith Worell (Worell & Johnson, 1997).

The O. J. Simpson Case

Then came the infamous O. J. case. This case led to the feminists dividing. Most went after Dr. Walker for agreeing to testify on O. J.'s behalf. They claimed that by accepting the case, she was betraying them and all battered women. Dr. Walker took a psychological stand to say that just because O. J. was a batterer, it didn't mean he was a killer. Rather, other evidence would be needed to prove that he committed homicide against his ex-wife,

Nicole Brown. After analyzing huge amounts of evidence, Dr. Walker believed O. J. abused Nicole, but couldn't say he killed her based on what she had learned, both from her evaluation of him and from interviewing others, reviewing thousands of pages of documents, and listening to various parts of the trial testimony. It was difficult for the media, the general public, and many feminists to understand or accept. Although most women are killed by men who have previously abused them, most men who abuse women do not kill them. Despite many feminists pleading with Dr. Walker not to go forward with the case, Dr. Walker felt a professional obligation to present the accurate data. Fortunately, she never had to testify in the criminal trial, but did give a deposition in the civil trial. Neither side wanted her to testify in the end as her data could not prove whether O. J. was guilty or not guilty. Interestingly enough, while it took her many years to be trusted again by some of the battered women advocates, her work with the O. J. case helped her psychology colleagues respect her advocacy for science rather than doing what would have been politically advantageous.

During this period, Dr. Walker testified in 36 states in an attempt to get the testimony admitted for battered women who killed their abusers in self-defense and she testified numerous times to Congress to help set national policy. In the 1990s, she began to travel part-time to Fort Lauderdale, Florida, when the Public Defender's Office hired her for 1 week a month to train lawyers to use psychological testimony in their difficult cases where mental health issues were being raised. There, she met President Ray Ferarro from Nova Southeastern University and learned that one of her colleagues, Dr. Ron Levant, was being appointed as the new Dean of the Center for Psychological Studies. A new mental health court was being developed with Judge Ginger Lerner-Wren, and it seemed like a natural place for students to be trained in forensic psychology while providing desperately needed services for defendants. Dr. Levant asked Dr. Walker to meet with some faculty members who were interested in developing a forensic concentration in the clinical psychology doctoral program. Although she did not plan to return to academia at that time, she was persuaded by Dr. Levant to come on the faculty part-time to start the program. The program was very successful, requiring the Dean to hire another forensic psychologist. Since Dr. Walker and Dr. David Shapiro, who was teaching at John Jay College of CUNY, were dating at the time, she suggested he be considered. After a 1-year guest appointment, he joined the faculty where he remains as a professor and her current husband.

Professor at Nova Southeastern University

Eventually, in the 2000s, Dr. Walker moved to Florida full-time. She remembers it being difficult to be a feminist back at that time because feminist thinking was not mainstream given the large number of immigrants from Latin America where feminism was not well supported by their culture. Nonetheless, the issues around gender violence were important, and Dr. Walker was able to continue her research, along with her teaching and supervisory responsibilities. She continued her independent practice with an emphasis on forensic psychology and remained at the Public Defender's Office until 2006 when she became a full-time faculty member at Nova Southeastern University's (NSU) Center for Psychological Studies. Many of the graduate students worked together with her in the research program and in providing forensic services. Today, Dr. Walker remains an active member of the NSU College of Psychology faculty and continues to work on some forensic cases from time to time (Douglas & Walker, 1988).

Mentorship

While Dr. Walker's life is interesting and impressive, what is most extraordinary about Dr. Walker is how she exemplifies both a mentor and a feminist. Dr. Walker has touched the lives of so many around the world in a powerfully personal way. The authors of this article would not be where they are in their professional lives today had it not been for Dr. Walker's guidance and support. Dr. Walker doesn't just mentor. She ensures that those working with her are afforded the best opportunities to succeed in the field. For example, Dr. Walker is the type of mentor who plans a trip to Peru to present at a conference and includes 10 students on the panels and then extends the trip by 10 days so that the students have the opportunity to experience the country, its culture, and the people, too. Dr. Walker creates opportunities for her students and guides them on a path to learning and understanding the field and ultimately finding success.

On a personal note, Dr. Walker is fun to be around and witty. She is also nurturing and loving. In a field where many professors and advisors can be difficult to connect with, Dr. Walker makes sure we all start on equal ground and are awarded the same experience and opportunities.

Yes, Dr. Walker gets to know her students on a personal level, but she also cares about getting to know our families as well. She supports our ideas and desire to explore the field and does so in such a self-sacrificing way.

RN stated,

> I connected with Dr. Walker immediately with our shared passion for women's reproductive rights. Dr. Walker cares about women having safe and affordable access to reproductive health care. After having an in depth discussion, literally the first time I met Dr. Walker in my first year of graduate school, we decided we would write a book together! We discussed the lack of knowledge that therapists have regarding reproductive laws, rights, and the truth about women's experiences when faced with an unplanned pregnancy. We quickly

wrote up a proposal and gauged interest from publishers. We published our book titled *Abortion Counseling: A Clinician's Guide to Psychology, Legislation, Politics, and Competency* in 2006. When the publisher sent us the first draft of the cover, I saw that my name was printed first. Dr. Walker is the type of mentor that allows students the opportunity to be first author on publications and even insists on it at times (Walker, Duros, Aleah, Gill, & Needle, 2009; Walker, Needle, et al., 2009; Walker, Needle, Duros, & Nathan, 2009). She is selfless, giving, loving, and cares about her students and their futures. I consider Dr. Walker a mentor, a colleague, and a great friend. I feel beyond lucky to have Dr. Walker in my life. Her support and passion for feminism have helped shape the person and therapist that I am today.

RS stated,

While attending a Florida Psychological Association Convention in 2007, I was introduced to Dr. Lenore Walker. I was immediately moved by her enthusiasm and passion for psychology as a whole and, in particular, her strong connection to feminism. She took me under her wing and taught me about female empowerment. She encouraged me to be confident in myself and to go out into the psychological community standing up for what I believe in because that's what she did. Dr. Walker taught me how to be a female leader and rally other strong women in psychology. Today, I was just elected as President of the Palm Beach Chapter of the Florida Psychological Association and have been the co-editor of the newsletter and on the board of the American Academy of Couples and Family Psychology.

While I was a graduate student, I witnessed firsthand her impact on other students. Her open door policy was evident as she was always teaching students in her office and in the classroom. When a student had an idea for research, she would find a way to make it happen, even if she had to create the opportunity herself. Through her warmth and generosity of spirit, she has the ability to make others feel at home, safe.

Dr. Walker's energy and confidence are contagious. She guides her students through challenges, always looking out for them and their long-term success. Students and professionals are naturally drawn to her strength and compassion. Dr. Walker inspires those around her through her support, guidance, empowerment, and most of all her leadership.

GG stated,

Dr. Walker continues to inspire me with her work in Feminist Therapy and forensic psychology. I first met Dr. Walker when I was an undergraduate student and president of the Psi Chi Honor Society at Nova Southeastern University. I was holding brown bag lunch lectures, and she attended as a speaker. From that day on, she became my mentor and "my mom away from home." She has encouraged me and shown me that there are no limits to what we can do in the field of psychology and in life as women. Dr. Walker has taught me to be strong and resilient in the face of adversity and to continue to go after my dreams. She has incited and supported my interests in Feminist Therapy, multiculturalism, immigration, and sex trafficking. Dr. Walker and I are co-editing a book on *Sex trafficking: Feminist and Transnational Perspectives* (Walker, Gaviria, & Gopal, 2017). We have presented together at several conferences nationally and internationally on various topics (Gaviria, Sarachago-Barato, Mahler, & Walker, 2015; Lopez, Gaviria, Benjamin, Shapiro, & Badaan, 2013; Walker, Gaviria, Mahler, Sarachaga-Barato, & Jackson, 2015; Walker et al., 2014).

Internationalist or Transnational Feminist

Dr. Walker is not only a feminist pioneer, but also an internationalist or what today is called a transnational feminist. She has traveled around the world teaching and giving lectures on topics, including gender violence, domestic violence, child abuse, trauma, sexual exploitation, sex trafficking, and the defense of women's rights. Dr. Walker has published her book *Terrifying Love* (Walker, 1989) in many languages, such as Spanish and Greek. *The Handbook of Feminist Therapy* (Rosewater & Walker, 1985), written by Dr. Walker and co-edited with Lynn Rosewater, was also translated and published in Japanese. She has published several articles in Latin American, Europe, Asia, and Africa, the most recent one on the history of the psychological research and practice with battered women in French (Walker, 2015). Most importantly, she has broadened the original definitions of feminist psychology to include the transnational intersectionality with culture, poverty, and other forms of discrimination that impact women's lives.

Feminist Therapy

Many current therapists now use techniques developed from early tenets and principles of what was then considered Feminist Therapy, such as egalitarianism and how you negotiate with your clients for goals for treatment. Both the client and the therapist communicate in one language. The therapist is not the authoritative figure. Clients have the best knowledge about themselves, and the therapist is the expert on how to treat them. The goal is to work together. Empowerment is an important part of Feminist Therapy. All relationships have power issues that are important to understand and acknowledge, both by role and personality. Once you think about power, it goes beyond gender and intersects with multiculturalism, white privilege, poverty, and LBGTQ issues. Today, Feminist Therapy is moving one step further into intersectionality as is evidenced by the International Summit on Transnational Feminism, sponsored by Division 35 at the 2015 APA pre-conference workshop. Dr. Walker and one of the authors (GG) co-led a group on sex-trafficking issues (Walker, Gaviria, & Sidun, 2015). During the development of Feminist Therapy, many women were researching and practicing in different areas of interest. From the start, Dr. Walker chose to work in various areas of gender violence and focused her attention on violence against women and domestic violence. Later, she combined her earlier interest in child abuse together with domestic violence, sexual assaults, and exploitation, which remains as her focus today. This is just a short summary of all the accomplishments and barriers she has broken to enable women to succeed.

What About Feminist Therapy is Still Important Today

The editors of this special issue asked the following question: "Because this issue is so important for those who may not know the beginnings of feminist psychotherapy, what would Lenore Walker want to tell or let those who were not alive during those beginnings know or learn from her?"

Dr. Walker believes that one of the important things to remember about Feminist Therapy is that much of what it is today seems like it is natural to a good therapist. Yet, many of the tenets and values of feminist therapy were not considered important by other psychotherapies in the 1970s when all the feminist criticisms were leveled at how psychotherapy was being used to oppress women in society. The changes in the way we think about these values make a lot of what we did in these days less difficult than they were. It was extremely difficult to help women think for themselves rather than taking everyone in their family's viewpoints. Learning to nurture oneself was an important principle. Many of the "shoulds" that were part of the prescribed female sex role socialization taught to women were re-examined in Feminist Therapy so that women could be supported in non-traditional as well as traditional roles.

It was also difficult to move away from diagnosis and considering women that were different and following a different pathway as having some kind of mental disorder. Today, we usually don't think about it in those terms anymore so it is harder to understand why it was so necessary to remove the mental illness stigma from normal behaviors. Nonetheless, we still have to be vigilant about gender differences and similarities. We have not yet reach equality between women and men. We still have a 'glass ceiling' and all the other kinds of societal issues. For Dr. Walker, one of the major areas Feminist Therapy helped was to provide a way to separate out an individual woman's problem from internal issues that she brought into the situation from the environmental factors that made it difficult for her to function. For example, a woman may not be able to complete her education in the way she wants to because she may have intellectual difficulties, or she may not be able to financially afford the cost of her education, or both. We are trying to separate those issues out for women and find ways to overcome barriers in each of those areas.

Finally, I believe it is important to understand that the word *feminist* does not mean a man hater, which is what we were called in the early days. We are not bitches and maybe we are pushy and stand up for our rights, but in the end, we are trying to make a better world for men and women, boys and girls. My good friend and feminist therapist colleague, Hannah Lerman, once said, "we have two eyes; one to look backward to see how far we have come and the other to look forward to see how far we still have to go." I believe that is true today.

References

Douglas, M. A., & Walker, L. E. (Eds.). (1988). *Feminist psychotherapies: Integration of therapeutic and feminist systems*. New York: Ablex Publishing Co.

Gaviria, G., Sarachaga-Barato, N., Mahler, C., & Walker, L. E. (2015, August). *Understanding survival sex within LGBTQ youth & its links to sex trafficking*. Poster session presented at the annual convention of the American Psychological Association, Toronto, Canada.

Lopez, V., Gaviria, G., Benjamin, A. H., Shapiro, D. L., & Badaan, B. H. (2013). Our broken family courts – Lack of protection for trauma-exposed. Paper presented at the Annual Convention of the American Psychological Association, Honolulu, HI, August 1–4.

Needle, R. B., & Walker, L. E. (2007). *Abortion counseling: A Clinician's Guide to psychology, legislation, politics, and competency*. New York, NY: Springer.

Rosewater, L. B., & Walker, L. E. (Eds.). (1985). *Handbook of feminist therapy: Women's issues in psychotherapy*. New York: Springer.

Walker, L. E. A. (1979). *The battered woman*. New York, NY: Harper & Row.

Walker, L. E. A. (1984). *The battered woman syndrome*. New York, NY: Springer.

Walker, L. E. A. (1989). *Terrifying love: Why women kill and how society responds*. New York, NY: Harper Collins.

Walker, L. E. A. (2000). *The battered woman syndrome* (2nd ed.). New York, NY: Springer.

Walker, L. E. A. (2009). *The battered woman syndrome* (3rd ed.). New York, NY: Springer.

Walker, L. E. A. (2015). Looking back and looking forward: Psychological and Legal interventions for domestic violence. *Ethics, Medicine, and Public Health, 1*, 19–32. doi:10.1016/j.jemep.2015.02.002

Walker, L. E. A. (2016). *The battered woman syndrome* (4th ed.). New York, NY: Springer.

Walker, L. E. A., Duros, R., Aleah, N., Gill, K., & Needle, R. (2009). Body image and health concerns. In L. E. A. Walker (Ed.), *The battered woman syndrome* (3rd ed., pp. 145–165). New York, NY: Springer.

Walker, L. E. A., Gaviria, G., & Gopal, K. (2017). *Sex trafficking: Feminist and transnational perspectives*. New York, NY: Springer. Manuscript in preparation.

Walker, L. E. A., Gaviria, G., Mahler, C., Sarachaga-Barato, N., & Jackson, M. (2015). Sex trafficking – A new look at an old problem. In L. E. Walker (Chair), *The parallels of gang affiliation and sex-trafficking*. Paper presented at the Annual Convention of the American Psychological Association, Toronto, Canada, August.

Walker, L. E. A., Gaviria, G., Mahler, C., Sarachaga-Barato, N., McCue, M., & Rosenblatt, K. (2014, October). Raising the bar: Taking group-based interventions to the next level. In L. E. Walker (Chair), *Special issues with ethnic minorities*. Chicago, IL: Panel conducted at SAFE CHR Coalition for Human Rights.

Walker, L. E. A., Gaviria, G., & Sidun, N. M. (2015). *Working group: Psychotherapy issues with trauma survivors of sex trafficking, Risk factors for the trafficking of women and girls*. Work group conducted at the meeting of the International Summit-APA Division 35 Society for the Psychology of Women, Toronto, Canada, August.

Walker, L. E. A., Needle, R., et al. (2009). Cross-cultural and cross-national issues in domestic violence. In L. E. Walker (Ed.), *The battered woman syndrome* (3rd ed., pp. 275–310). New York, NY: Springer.

Walker, L. E. A., Needle, R., Duros, R., & Nathan, A. (2009). Sexuality issues. In L. E. A. Walker (Ed.), *The battered woman syndrome* (3rd ed., pp. 167–198). New York, NY: Springer.

Walker, L. E. A., Richmond, K., House, T., Needle, R., & Smalley, K. B. (2009). History. In L. E. Walker (Ed.), *The battered woman syndrome* (3rd ed., pp. 21–39). New York, NY: Springer.

Worell, J., Johnson, N., (Eds.). (1997). *Shaping the future of feminist psychology: Education, research, and practice*. Washington, DC: American Psychologist Association.

Index

A Mote in Freud's Eye 140, 142
Abnormal Psychology 162
abortion 2, 40, 63, 160
Abortion Coalition 122
About Men 42
academic pursuits: Annette Brodsky 25–6
"acid heads" 139
activism 124–5, 160–61, 172–4, 182–4
advice for future feminist therapists 69–70
advocacy 30–34, 125–6
AFTA *see* American Family Therapy Academy
Against Our Will 41, 85
Ahrons, Connie 102
Ain Harod 38
American Academy of Psychotherapists 97
American Board of Professional Psychology 196
American Family Therapy Academy 101–2
American Orthopsychiatry Association 16, 18–19
American Psychological Association 12, 31–3, 40, 53, 85–8, 95–103, 115, 126, 130, 137, 186–7, 198; finding feminists in 97–8; governance 97–9, 198; policy changes 198; Task Force on Clinical Training and Practice 99–100
American Psychologist 100, 105
AMPP *see* American Board of Professional Psychology
An American Bride in Kabul 38
Anderson, Carol 102
anger management 188
Angle of Repose 122
anti-feminism 124–5, 141
anti-psychiatry 157–8
anti-racism 125
anti-Semitism 37, 42, 45–6, 84, 117–19, 168
Anti-war Movement 108
APA *see* American Psychological Association
Appeal to Color Citizen of the World Movement 54
Asian American women 88, 187
Assault on the Soul 171

Association for Women in Psychology 28, 40, 52, 56, 130, 142–3, 198
attachment theory 150
Ault-Riché, Marianne 152
awards/recognitions: Annette Brodsky 34; Ellyn Kaschak 130
awareness-raising 13
AWP *see* Association for Women in Psychology

Baby M 44–5
Banks, Amy 16
"Battered Woman Syndrome" 46, 196–7
Bateson, Gregory 11, 121–2
battered women 39, 87, 160, 196–9, 202; *see also* domestic violence
Beigel, Astrid 141
Benito, Odio 125–6
Bennett, Virginia 195
Berman, Ellen 97
Bernardez, Teresa 148
Bernays, Ann 13–14
Berne, Eric 182
best of times... 95–106; *see also* Hare-Mustin, Rachel T.
bigotry 54
biography of a feminist: Judith Herman 110–111; Phyllis Chesler 40–42; Sara Sharratt 170–71
Bittner, Egon 60
Black Liberation Movement 53, 159–60
Block Lewis, Helen 107
blowing in the wind 155–66; *see also* Marecek, Jeanne
body memory 163
Boethals, George 61
Bolgar, Hedda 141
Bonhime, Walter 12
borderline personality disorder 88
Boston Feminist Therapy Collective 76
Boston Globe 19
Boston Psychoanalytic Society 62
Boston Women's Health Collective 16

INDEX

Bowen Family System theory 152
Boxer, Barbara 44
Braverman, Lois 102
Bread and Roses 85
breaking the silence 75–6
Bridges, Harry 186
Broderick, Patrick 101
Brodsky, Annette 24–36, 98, 100; early academic pursuits 25–6; empowerment/advocacy 30–34; family response to work 28; forces in becoming a feminist 26–7; hopes for future 34–5; mentorship 27–8; recognitions 34; scholarship 28–30; start of her journey 24–5
Broner, Esther 43
Brown, Adrienne 198
Brown, Laura 187, 198
Brownmiller, Susan 41, 85
Buddhism 130–31
building Feminist Therapy on activism 160–61
Burnett, Carol 147
burqas 48

California School of Professional Psychology 74, 79, 125, 141–2, 184
Call Off Your Tired Ethics group 54
Cambridge Health Alliance 58
Cameron, Norman 156
Cancer Journals 150
cancer support 125–6
Cantor Zuckoff, Aviva 42
Caplan, Paula 44
Carter, Betty 152
Carter, Jimmy 186
Cassidy, Harold 44
Change 101, 163
changing the world 83–94; *see also* Greenspan, Miriam
Chesler, Phyllis 37–49, 85, 96, 121, 195; Aileen Wuornos 46; burqas 48; contribution 49; early feminism 39–40; early life 38–9; education 39; feminism—looking ahead, back 46–7; feminist biography 40–42; feminist Passover seder 42–3; honor related violence 47–8; Judaism/Israel/anti-Semitism 42, 45–6; women/children/custody 44–5; World Conference of UN Decade for Women 43–4
Childs, E. Kitch 50–56; selected bibliography 56
Chodorow, Nancy Julia 57–71; conclusion 69–70; contributions/legacy 61–6; history/background 59–61; retrospective narratives 67–9
chronic disconnection 15, 21
Chrysalis 170
circumstantial feminist journey 74–5
civil disobedience 159–60
Civil Rights Movement 39, 53, 108, 122, 149, 159–60, 182–4
classism 128

CLGBT *see* Committee on LGPT Concerns (APA)
Cohen, Bill 3
Cole, Ellen 46
collaborative feminist theory building 17–20
collegial support 104–6
Comas-Diaz, Lillian 187
Combrinck-Graham, Lee 102
coming out 75–6
Committee on LGPT Concerns (APA) 126–30; *Engendered Lives* 128; Mattering Map 128–9; scholarship 127–8; *Sight Unseen* 129–30
Committee on Women in Psychology 126, 186–7
Communist Party of the United States 107; *see also* red-diaper baby
community mentorship 27–8
concern about ethics 96–7
confusion 76–7
Connell, Noreen 41
consciousness-raising groups 13, 18, 32, 42, 54, 84, 110–111, 121, 140, 158–61
Contextual Psychology 115–32; *see also* Kaschak, Ellyn
contraception 160, 197
Contratto, Susan 62
contributions: Annette Brodsky 28–34; Harriet Lerner 150; Nancy Julia Chodorow 61–6; Phyllis Chesler 48
Conversations with History 108
Costa Rica 125–6
Counseling for Battered Women Project 39
Council for Racial Equality 12
COYOTE *see* Call Off Your Tired Ethics group
CPUSA *see* Communist Party of the United States
CR *see* consciousness-raising groups
Critical Psychology 104
cross-cultural individuality 60–61
CSPP *see* California School of Professional Psychology
cultural revolution 86
cultural sexism 5
Cummings, Nicholas 99, 141
curiosity 79–80
Cushman, Philip 163
custody 43–5; *Mothers on Trial* 43–4; *Sacred Bond* 44–5
CWP *see* Committee on Women in Psychology

Dalai Lama 21
Daly, Mary 158
Dammann, Carroll 102
Dance of Anger 148, 150–51
Dance of Deception 150
de Beauvoir, Simone 135
Death of Feminism 47
Denmark, Florence 187, 193–4
depression 136

208

INDEX

Dialectic of Sex 96
Dickerson, Victoria 102
dis-ease with psychotherapy 157–8
dis-illusioning psychology 115–32; *see also*
    Kaschak, Ellyn
discourse analysis 103
discrimination 168, 184
disrespect 123–4
dissociative amnesia 112
Distinguished Publications Award 130
distribution of power 14–15
diversity 16, 160, 187
domestic violence 5, 39, 46, 110–111, 160, 188,
    196–9
Dual Relationships in Psychotherapy 93
DuBois, W. E. B. 61
Durkheim, Émile 61
Dworkin, Andrea 44, 85

early feminism 39–40
early years: Annette Brodsky 24–5; Ellyn
    Kaschak 117–19; Jean Baker Miller 10; Judith
    Herman 108–9; Nancy Julia Chodorow
    59–61; Oliva Espín 72–4; Phyllis Chesler
    38–9; Sara Sharratt 167–9
ecocide 92
education: Annette Brodsky 24–6; E. Kitch
    Childs 52–3; Ellyn Kaschak 119–22; Hannah
    Lerman 134–6; Jean Baker Miller 10–12;
    Jeanne Marecek 156–7; Leonore E. A. Walker
    193–4; Oliva Espín 72–4; Phyllis Chesler 39;
    Reiko Homma-True 184–6; Sara Sharratt
    168–70
egalitarianism 187–8
ego integrity 67
Einstein, Albert 21
Elkin Waskow, Irene 100
Ellman, Mary 85
empathy 19, 21, 90
empowerment 30–34, 202–3; consciousness-
    raising groups 32; seeking the Holy Grail
    30–31; sexual misconduct in therapy 33–4
Engendered Lives 115, 128
engendering San Francisco's early Feminist
    Therapy Collective 122–3
enhanced interrogation techniques 104
Enloe, Cynthia 100
Envy and Devaluation of Women 148
epistemology 115–32
Equal Rights Amendment 1, 101
ERA *see* Equal Rights Amendment
Erikson, Erik 32, 67
Erturk, Yakin 111
Espín, Oliva 72–82; background 72–4;
    Boston Feminist Therapy Collective 76;
    circumstantial feminist journey 74–5; coming
    out 75–6; conclusion 82; confusing, conflicted
    road 76–7; from Boston to San Diego 78–9;
    importance of spirituality 80; intersections

77–8; living in contradictions 80–82; selected
    bibliography 82; writing from experience
    79–80
ethics 54, 96–7
Ethics Committee of APA 96–7
ethnomethodology 60
exploitation 33

false memory syndrome 112
Family Process 101, 103, 105
family response to work 28
Family Therapy 100–102; paradigm change in
    100–102
FBI *see* Federal Bureau of Investigation
Federal Bureau of Investigation 85
Felipe-Russo, Nancy 186
Female Eunuch 85, 157
female impersonation 146
female offenders 28–9
female slavery 92
female solidarity 161
Feminine Mystique 13, 102, 157
feminism 131
feminist biography 40–42, 110–111, 170–71;
    About Men 42; *Women and Madness* 41;
    Women, Money, and Power 41–2
feminist dis-ease with psychotherapy 157–8
Feminist Foremothers in Women's Studies... 46
feminist journey 133–44; *see also* Lerman,
    Hannah
feminist mentors 152–3
feminist Passover seder 40, 42–3; *With Child* 43
feminist politics 195–7
feminist practice 112–13, 149–50, 186–8
Feminist Psychological Association 140–41
feminist psychotherapy 176–90
feminist research 196–7
Feminist Therapy 160–61, 202–3; through
    activism 160–61
Feminist Therapy Collective, San Francisco
    122–3
Feminist Therapy Institute 56, 127, 142–3, 198
feminist understanding 148–9
feminist voice from wheat fields 145–54; *see also*
    Lerner, Harriet
Ferarro, Ray 199
Fields, Karen 61
Fields, Rona 141
5th Amendment 108
finding feminists in APA 97–8
Firestone, Shulamith 96
Fisch, Charles 121
Fisch, R. 101
forces behind becoming a feminist 26–7
forensic psychology 39, 197
Foucault, Michel 79
Fowler, Ray 31
fragmentation 76–7
framing life 59–61

INDEX

"free range" parenting 192
Free Speech Movement 182
Freedom Summer 110
Freeman, Jo 99
Freud, Anna 156
Freud, Sigmund 13, 32, 86–7, 100–101, 137, 144, 157
Freud's Seduction Theory 100
Friar Williams, Elizabeth 88–9
Friedan, Betty 13, 102
from Boston to San Diego 78–9
Fromm-Reichmann, Frieda 156
FTI *see* Feminist Therapy Institute
future feminist therapists 69–70

Garfinkel, Harold 60
Gay Liberation Movement 52
Geis, Lindy 105
gender equality 52–3
Gender Play 63
gender prism 65
gender roles 99–100, 145–6
Gender, Shame and Sexual Violence 171
gendered stereotyping 26, 31–4, 101
gendered subordination 162
Gestalt 182
Gilford, Peter 163
Gilligan, Carol 16, 101
glass ceiling 203
global feminist pioneering 167–75; *see also* Sharratt, Sara
Gold nautilus award 92
Goodman, Emily Jane 41–2
Gornick, Vivian 40, 46
Goulding, Mary 182
governance 98–9, 198
Grand, S. 107
grassroots feminist organizations 87–8, 159–60
Great Depression 10, 177
Great Society initiative 161–2
Greaves, Sarah 17–18
Greenspan, Miriam 83–94, 152
Greer, Germaine 85
Grieg, Miriam 196–7
growing up feminist 192–4
growing up in Japan 177–81
Guidelines for Therapy with Women 142
gulags 84

Halas, Celia 97
Haley, Jay 121–2
half-known life 97
Handbook of Feminist Therapy 142, 202
Hanisch, Carol 158–9, 164
Hare-Mustin, Rachel T. 33, 95–106; APA governance 98–9; concern about ethics 96–7; conclusion 104–6; Critical Psychology 104; discourse analysis 103; finding feminists in

APA 97–8; making a difference 102–3; paradigm change in Family Therapy 100–102; Task Force on Clinical Training and Practice 99–100; *Voices* 97
Harvard Medical School 12, 19, 58
Hashomer Hatzair 38
Haut, Rivla 45
Hawking, Stephen 21
Healing through the Dark Emotions 91–3
Help Your Husband Stay Alive 146
Herman, Ellen 158
Herman, Judith 16–17, 97, 107–114; early years 108–9; feminist biography 110–111; feminist practice 112–13; feminist scholarship 111–12; looking back 113–14; training 109–110
Himawari 183
Hirschman, Lisa 109–110
history, 1970–1975 5–8
Holocaust 83
Holroyd, Jean 33
Holy Grail 30–31
Homma-True, Reiko 176–90; Civil Rights Movement 182–4; feminist practice 186–8; graduate school 184–6; growing up in Japan 177–81; looking back, forward 188–9; marriage/life in US 181–2
homophobia 119–22, 128
homosexuality 51–4
"honor" killings 47–8
honor related violence 47–8
hopes for the future 34–5
Horney, Karen 13, 156
Horney, Karl 140
hyper-individualism 20

ILWU *see* International Labor and Warehouse Union
impact of interpersonal violence 113–14
imperialism 86
importance of spirituality 80
In a Different Voice 16–17
in the institution 163–4
incest 5, 37, 44, 87, 109–110, 149–50
increasing feminist awareness 13
independence 187
institutional sexism 5
interdependence 187
International Committee for Women of the Wall 45
International Domestic Violence Institute 197
International Labor and Warehouse Union 186
International Women's Day 85
internationalist feminism 202
interpersonal violence 113–14
intersectionality 77–8, 80–82
involvement in community 27–8
Islam 37, 45, 47–8
isolation 84
Israel 37, 42, 45–6

210

INDEX

"It's the only thing you can think" 57–71; *see also* Chodorow, Nancy Julia

Jack D. Krasner Memorial Award 34
Jackson, Don 121
Japan 177–81
Jean Baker Miller Training Institute 21–2
Jessie Bernard Award 57
Jewish Women in America 38
Joans, Barbara. 40
Joffe, Carole 63
Johnson & Johnson 196
Johnson, Noreen 198
Jordon, Judith 17–18, 20, 89, 152
Journal of Social Policy 13
Judaism 42, 45–6, 134; 1970s 42; 1980s on 45–6

kaleidoscope metaphor 81
Kaplan, Alexandra 18, 20, 997
Kaplan, J. 107
Kaschak, Ellyn 1–4, 51–4, 115–32, 170–71, 187; APA Committee on LGBT Concerns 127–30; becoming 119–23; life as a feminist therapist 123–7; more manna 130–31; recognition 130
Kates Schulman, Alix 46
Kawahara, Debra M. 3
Keith-Spiegel, Patti 96
Kell, Bill 136–7
Kennedy, Florynce 54
Kennedy, John F. 161–2, 182
Kent, Kay 152
Kenworthy, Joy 98
"killing fields" (Cambodia) 73
"Kinder, Küche, Kirche" 121
Klein, Melanie 156
Koocher, Gerald P. 34
Kotler, Jeffrey 152
Kovacs, Arthur 141
Kramer, Peter 97
Kravetz, Diane 160–61, 163
Kreisler, Harry 107, 111
kvell 114
kvetching 146

Laing, R. D. 161
Lash, Mary Ann 14
Latin American Sex Role Inventory 124
Latinas 77–8
legacy: Ellyn Kaschak 124–5; Jean Baker Miller 16–17; Nancy Julia Chodorow 61–6
Lerman, Hannah 96, 133–44, 198, 204
Lerner, Harriet 145–54; being a feminist therapist 151–2; contribution 150; *Dance of Anger* 150–51; feminist understanding 148–9; feminists, other mentors 152–3; gender roles 145–6; selected bibliography 153; therapy practice 149–50; Women's Movement 146–8
lesbianism 51–2, 75–6, 79–81

Levant, Ron 199
Lewis, R. 72
LGBT advocacy 125
life as a feminist professor 123–7, 195–6; Committee on Women in Psychology 126; Costa Rica 125–6; Family Therapy Institute 127; legacy 124–5; national arenas 126; teaching 125
life in US 181–2
life on women's behalf 37–49; *see also* Chesler, Phyllis
Liss Resnick, Jacquelyn 97
living an ordinary life 117–23; early years 117–19; engendering San Francisco's early feminist therapy collective 122–3; university life in 1970s 119–22
living in contradiction 80–82
Lodz 83
looking ahead, looking back 46–7; Judith Herman 113–14; Phyllis Chesler 46 7; Reiko Homma-True 188–9; Sara Sharratt 174
Lorde, Audre 53, 150
Lott, Bernice 103
LSD 139

McCarthy Committee 108
McCarthy, Mary 119
McGoldrick, Monica 102, 152
Making a Difference 102–3
male sex drive discourse 103
male–male relationships 42
Managed Heart 63
Mander, A. V. 88–9
Marecek, Jeanne 97, 102–5, 155–66; in the Academy 156–7; building therapy on activism 160–61; feminist tidal wave 157–60; mental health establishment 161–4; w(h)ither feminist therapy? 164
marriage in US 181–2
Masson, Jeffrey 100
Maternal Thinking 62
matriarchy 185
Mattering Map 124–5, 128–9
Mead, Margaret 11
medicalization 162
Menninger Foundation 112, 138–9, 146–8, 152
Menninger, Karl 147–8
mental health establishment 161–4; psychotherapeutic culture 163–4
mentorship 27–8, 124–5, 152–3, 200–202
meritocracy 15
Merrill Lynd, Helen 11
microaggressions 29
Middle East Quarterly 47–8
Middletown 11
migration 77–8
Miller, Jean Baker 9–23, 87, 89, 148; collaborative feminist theory building 17–20; early years 10; education 10–12; impact 16–17;

INDEX

increasing feminist awareness 13; Jean Baker Miller Training Institute 21–2; neuroscience 20–21; Relational-Cultural Theory 20; *Toward a New Psychology of Women* 13–16
Miller, Mike 12
Millett, Kate 44, 46, 85
mindfulness 187
Mink, Patsy 105
Minnich 151
misogyny 87–8, 92
Mitchell, Juliet 85
Moch, Cheryl 42
models of Feminist Therapy 30
Monster 46
Morawski, Jill 103
more manna 130–31; on feminism 131; obituary 131; they keep stealing our stuff 130–31
Morgan, Robin 43, 85, 88
Morse, Josephine 136
Moses, Charles 197
motherhood studies 62
Mothers on Trial 43–4
movement activism 160–61
Ms. Magazine 42–3, 102
multiculturalism 77–8
multiple identities 80–82
Murphy, Gardner 138
myth of motherhood 101

Narrative Therapy 101–2, 131
national arenas 126
National Institutes of Mental Health 33, 100, 162, 182, 184–5, 194, 196
National Organization for Women 157, 195
Nazism 84
neuroscience 20–21
neurosis 88
New Anti-Semitism 45
New Approach to Women & Therapy 86, 89–93
New York Times 41–2, 46
New Yorker 119
NIMH *see* National Institutes of Mental Health 9/11 103
non-mutual relationships 19
nonsexist therapy 33
Notes of a Feminist Therapist 88–9
Notman, Malkah 61
Nova Southeastern University 199–202; mentorship 200–202
NOW *see* National Organization for Women

O. J. Simpson Case 198–9
obituary: Ellyn Kaschak 131
objectivity 89–90
Oedipus fantasy 87
Of Women Born 150
on being feminist therapist 76, 151–512
On Love and Violence 91

oppression 8, 108–9, 179, 188
Our Bodies Our Selves 16
outsiders on inside 161–4

Papp, Peggy 152
paradigm change in Family Therapy 100–102
parliamentary procedures 98–9
patriarchy 37–8, 50, 54, 84–5, 87–8, 92–3, 108
paving the way 24–36; *see also* Brodsky, Annette
Payton, Carolyn 187
Perkins Gilman, Charlotte 100
Perls, Fritz 182
"personal is political" 32, 158–9
personal journey 176–90; *see also* Homma-True, Reiko
Philadelphia Child Guidance Clinic 95–8, 100–101, 161
Pigeonholing Women's Misery 143
Pipher, Mary 152
Planned Parenthood 63
Pleasure and Danger 77
pogroms 117
politics 195–7; feminist forensic psychologist 197; feminist professor 195–6; feminist researcher 196–7
Pope, Ken 999
pornography 37
Porter, Natalie 198
posttraumatic stress disorder 163
poverty 117
practice; Harriet Lerner 149–50; Judith Herman 112–13
pro-choice rallies 157
productivity 107–114
prostitution 46, 54
Psychiatric Times 97
Psychoanalysis and Women 13
Psychoanalytic Psychotherapy 107
Psychoanalytic Theory 100–101, 156–7
Psychology Constructs the Female 157
psychotherapeutic culture 163–4
Psychotherapy 96, 158
PTSD *see* posttraumatic stress disorder

Quaker ideals 95
questions for millennial therapists 155–66; *see also* Marecek, Jeanne

racial segregation 110
racism 37, 54, 86–8, 118–22, 128, 184–5
Radcliffe News 100
Radical Therapy 157–8
radicalization 122
rape 2, 37, 41, 87, 92, 95, 157
RCT *see* Relational-Cultural Theory
Reagan, Ronald 162
real world existence 157–60
recession 51
recidivism 29

212

INDEX

red-diaper baby 107–114; *see also* Herman, Judith
Redecision Therapy 182, 187
relational individualism 64
Relational-Cultural Theory 15, 17–22; *see also* Miller, Jean Baker
relevance of Feminist Therapy today 203–4
religious Apartheid 37
religious fanaticism 92
repressed memory 112
Reproduction of Mothering 57–8, 62, 68, 644
resistance 118
Resnick, Jaquie 98
retrospective narratives 67–9
revolution 46–7; *woman's Inhumanity to Woman* 46–7
Rhude, Beth 97
Rice Dewey, Cindy 97
Rich, Adrienne 41, 150
Riesman, David 12
Robb, Chris 17, 19
Robbins, Bernard 11
Robbins, Rosemary 97
Roe v. Wade 63, 157
Rollins, Judith 61
Rosewater, Lynn 198, 202
Rothblum, Esther D. 46
Rowbotham, Sheila 85
Rowling, J. K. 21
Ruddick, S. 62
Rush, A. K. 88–9
Rush, Florence 41
Russell Hochschild, Arlie 63

Sacred Bond—The Legacy of Baby M 44–5
Salberg, J. 107
Sarachild, Kathie 110–111
Satir, Virginia 121
scholarship 28–30, 111–12; Ellyn Kaschak 124–5, 127–8; female offenders 28–9; Judith Herman 111–12; Sara Sharratt 171–4; therapy with women 29–30; women in academia 29
Schroeder, Patricia 1996
Schumer, Chuck 44
Science 39
Second Sex 135
second wave feminism 5, 51, 67–8, 146
Secrets, and Silence 150
Seduction Theory (Freud) 100
seeking the Holy Grail 30–31
Seidler-Feller, Doreen 97
self-confidence 17
self-defeat 143
self-defense 37
self-disclosure 90
self-evaluation 128
self-help 92, 161, 183
self-interest 20
sex trafficking 92

sex-fair therapy 99–100
Sexes Today: With the Past Recast 140
sexism 5, 32, 50, 86–8, 119–22, 128, 171–4, 178–80, 185, 188
Sexton, Anne 97
sexual abuse 44, 87–8, 100, 109–113, 142–3, 149–50, 179, 196–9, 202–3
sexual harassment 87–8, 119–21
sexual misconduct in therapy 33–4, 96–7
Sexual Orientation and Gender Diversity Award 115, 117
Sexual Politics 85
sexuality 77–8
Shapiro, David 199
Shapiro, L. 107
Sharratt, Sara 124, 167–75; early years 167–9; education 169–70; feminist biography 170–71; feminist scholarship 171–4; looking back 174
Sheehy, Gail 42
shtetls 83
Siegel, Rachel 198
Sight Unseen 115, 129–30
Signs 41
Silverstein, Olga 152
Simon, Bennett 61
Sisterhood is Global 43, 85
Six Culture: Studies of Child Rearing 60
Skinner, Eric 120
Snitow, Ann 46
social justice 50–56
social locations 80–82
Somerville Women's Mental Health Collective 87
"Somewhere Else" 118–19
spirituality 37, 80
Spock, Benjamin 145
St. James, Margaret 54
Stegman, Wallace 122
Steinem, Gloria 43, 102, 146, 150
Stiver, Irene 17–18, 20, 89
Stone Center for Developmental Services and Studies 16–19
Strategies in Psychotherapy 122
su ku sessions 159
subservience 178, 182
supportive data 20–21
Surrey, Janet 17–18, 20, 89
surrogacy 37, 44–5
Swerdlow, Amy 40

Takamine, I. 184–5
Talking Straight and Fighting Fair 152
Talmud 93–4
Task Force on Clinical Training and Practice 99–100
Task Force on Sex Bias 33, 142
teaching: Ellyn Kaschak 125–6
Tennov, Dorothy 158

INDEX

Terrifying Love 202
Theory of Empathy 19
therapy with women 29–30
"they keep stealing our stuff" 130–31
Thinking About Women 85
This Changes Everything 17, 19
Thompson, Clara 13, 156
Thorne, B. 63
tidal wave of feminism 157–60; consciousness-raising 158–9; feminist dis-ease with psychotherapy 157–68; grassroots feminist organizations 159–60
Tikkun Olam 109
Toward a New Psychology of Women 9–11, 13–17, 22, 87, 89, 148
training: Hannah Lerman 138–40; Harriet Lerner 150; Jeanne Marecek 156–7; Judith Herman 109–110; Leonore E. A. Walker 193–4; Nancy Julia Chodorow 60–61; Phyllis Chesler 39; Reiko Homma-True 184–6; Sara Sharratt 171–4
Training Woman to Know Her Place 157
Transactional Analysis 182
transference 88
transnationalist feminism 202
transparency 101
trauma 16–17, 107–8, 111–14, 131, 163, 171–4
Trauma and Recovery 7, 107, 111, 113–14
Treblinka 83
12-step programs 1
Tyler, Leona 142
tyranny of structurelessness 99

UN Decade for Women 43–4, 126
Un-American Activities Committee 12
Unger, Rhoda 103
Unhappy Divorce of Sociology and Psychoanalysis 66
university life in 1970s 119–22
University for Peace 125–6, 167, 170
U.S. Senate Permanent Subcommittee on Investigations 108

Vietnam War 95–6, 137, 156, 182
visionary pragmatism 9–23
voice for the silenced 28–9
Voices 97

WAE *see* Women for Academic Equality
Walker, Leonore E. A. 46, 142–3, 191–205; APA governance 198; feminist, politics, psychology 195–7; Feminist Therapy 202–3; growing up feminist 192–4; inter-/transnational feminism 202; introduction 191–2; O. J. Simpson Case 198–9; professor at Nova Southeastern 199–202; why Feminist Therapy is still important 203–4

Walker, Maureen 16
Walsh, Froma 102
Walter Reed Army Hospital, Bethesda 26–7
Walters, Marianne 152
warrior of resistance 53, 118
Watzlawick, Paul 101, 121
Weakland, J. H. 101
WEAL *see* Women's Equity Action League
Weisstein, Naomi 121
Wells, Theodora 140
"What Happens in Feminist Therapy" 141
Whitehead, Mary Beth 44–5
Whitehead, Michael 102
w(h)ither Feminist Therapy? 164
Whiting, B. B. 60
Willis, Ellen 46
Wilson, Cassandra 41
With Child: A Dairy of Motherhood 43
Woman Hating 85
Woman—Which Includes Man, Of Course 140
Woman's Estate 85
Woman's Inhumanity to Woman 46–7
Women & Therapy 1–4, 91, 125, 127–8; editorial 1–4
women in academia 29
Women for Academic Equality 27
women and children 44–5
Women in Context 152
Women Crossing Boundaries 79–80
Women and Madness 37, 39, 41, 85, 89, 121, 157, 195
Women, Money, and Power 41–2
Women and Psychotherapy 33–4
Women in Therapy 148
Women of the Wall 45
Women's Consciousness 85
Women's Equity Action League 157, 195
Women's Growth in Connection 18
Women's International League for Peace and Freedom 12
Women's Liberation Movement 50–51, 84, 155–6, 158–60, 164
Women's Movement 7, 32, 34–5, 50–51, 108–110, 146–9
Women's Project in Family Therapy 152
women's psyche 64, 68
Women's Ways of Knowing 16–17
Worell, Judith 198
World Conference of UN Decade for Women 43–4; *Mothers on Trial* 43–4
World War II 135, 137, 177, 192
Worley, Jo-Lynne 152
Wounds of History 107
writing from experience 79–80
Wuornos, Aileen 46

Zionism 38